W9-BHS-854

Urban

Politics

MURRAY S. STEDMAN, JR.   *Temple University*

Winthrop Publishers, Inc.

Cambridge, Massachusetts

Cover and design by Joe Guertin

To

EVE

Contents

Preface

Urban America is changing rapidly, and so is its politics. The Old Style of urban politics—with its emphasis on the brokerage function—is on the way out. It is being replaced by a New Style which has distinctive features of its own.

As the system has changed, the assumptions underlying the Old Style politics have become outmoded. The timeworn pluralistic model no longer offers an adequate key for the comprehension of contemporary politics. To understand the New Style politics a different model is necessary.

The main purpose of this book is to describe this great transformation in urban politics and, so far as possible, to explain it. Where it has seemed appropriate, I have offered my own evaluation of developments. Some speculations are indulged in with respect to urban political patterns of the future. From time to time I have deliberately dangled some hypotheses, in the hope that some adventurous readers may feel challenged to pursue them.

It is a pleasure to express my indebtedness to the authors whose works are cited in the text. From them I have drawn both information and insight. Equally important is my debt to those hundreds of former students who, over the years, have joined with me in exploring the intricacies and wonders of urban politics. From their probing questions and lively curiosity, I have gained both humility and knowledge.

I would like to express my particular gratitude to three former students of mine at Temple University: John H. Fuhs, Jr., James M. Tobin, and William C. Crooks, who helped in the preparation of Part Three. I also want to express my appreciation to Charles D. Engle, of the National Institute for the Administration of Justice, for his bibliography on the police which was essential to Chapter 11; and to Samuel Hendel and Clyde D. McKee, Jr., both of the Department of Political Science of Trinity College, Hartford, for their helpful observations on problems considered in Chapter 12. I want to thank also Robert H. Binstock, Brandeis University, and Michael Danielson, Princeton University, for their many helpful criticisms of the manuscript.

My colleagues in urban affairs at Temple University have also, directly or indirectly, contributed to this enterprise. My thanks are due especially to Peter Bachrach, Harry A. Bailey, Jr., Earl M. Baker, Daniel J. Elazar, Mark H. Haller, Robert N. Spadaro, E. S. Whitney Thompson, Conrad J. Weiler, Jr., and Marshall H. Whithed.

Temple University gave me a Summer Research Grant for 1970, which enabled me to pursue my writing over that summer without interruption. Linda Scherr and Harriet Schulman did a masterful job of typing and of proofreading.

Lastly, I want to acknowledge my continuing gratitude to Eve Stedman, my wife. Not the least of her many contributions was the preparation of the Index.

Murray S. Stedman, Jr.
Temple University
Philadelphia, Pennsylvania

1

The

Urban

Situation

People have been living in cities for a very long time; probably, in fact, since 7–6,000 B.C. Although it was thought until recently that the earliest cities were founded about five millenia ago in the great valleys of the Tigris and Euphrates, new archaeological evidence indicates otherwise. In the summer of 1961, a British archaeologist, James Mellaart, discovered the remains of Çatal Hüyük on the Anatolian plain of Turkey. The city spanned the period 7,000–6,000 B.C., and its population must have run into the thousands.[1] One problem in reconstructing the histories of ancient cities, however, is the fact that they were prehistoric. By the time there is anything resembling a permanent record, the city has already developed into a mature form.[2] As a result, the earliest urban developments must be reconstructed from artifacts and from what seem to be a logical series of transitions.

On this basis the usually accepted evolution is from hunting camp to agricultural village to the beginnings of a primitive urban settlement. However, not all experts agree on this sequence: Jane Jacobs, for instance, thinks that the jump from hunting camp to urban settlement was the more likely development. In her reconstruction, early agriculture took place within the city's walls. Yet the dominant viewpoint, expressed by Lewis Mumford and others, is that the city at a very early date evolved from the village, which contained in primitive form many urban structures and symbols.[3] By 2,500 B.C., Mumford declares, the essential features of the city had taken form.[4] They had done so as the result of an area-wide implosion—a movement of various elements toward one central area. Formerly, isolated groups came together and settled permanently in one place.

1

In telescopic form, the general history of cities in the west is well-known. The Golden Age of the ancient Greek cities, especially Athens, occurred during the period between 500 and 400 B.C. When the center of world power shifted to Rome, the emphasis was placed quite properly on the ability of the Romans to manage their own city and to create other cities wherever the Roman legions went.

With the collapse of the Roman Empire, the urban civilization which Rome had created rapidly eroded. During the so-called Dark Ages, the urban arts were neglected, abandoned, and forgotten. Fortunately, urban culture eventually revived, coming to a peak of achievement in the twelfth century. During this remarkably creative medieval period, new towns and cities were established, the arts were reborn, and the self-governing city came into its own. At the end of a long evolutionary process the remarkable civilizations of the city-states of Venice, Genoa, and Florence arose. In the politics of these Renaissance cities, one finds a good deal of the flavor if not necessarily the same tactics as in a modern urban area. For instance, the Florentine attitude toward politics was that it was a highly important and intriguing "game." For such reasons Machiavelli's *The Prince* continues to be a readable and instructive text in how to operate in a vigorous, political world.

CITIES IN AMERICA

The first permanent English settlement in America was Jamestown, Virginia, founded in May, 1607. Although more a beachhead in the wilderness than a city, Jamestown was followed by the establishment of towns up and down the Atlantic coast, the majority of which failed to develop into anything resembling urban centers. The exceptions were Boston, Newport, New York, Philadelphia, and Charleston, S.C.—all splendid ports—which rapidly outgrew their village status and became sites of significant commercial activity.

Precisely when these localities became cities depends on the criteria one employs. One authority, William O. Winter, has ingeniously suggested that the litmus test is whether the place in question has developed a genuine art life of its own. On this basis, he judges that Boston attained city status in 1757 when a Handel oratorio was first performed.[5] He concludes that, on this basis, by 1770 a real urban life had come into being in America, as a whole.

America was primarily an agricultural nation; at the time of the American Revolution, some 95 percent of the American people were engaged in agriculture. But the westward expansion of the early years of the Republic brought with it a notable increase in the number of nascent cities, such as those which now abound in the old Northwest Territory. Yet it was the Civil War which was one of the most profound influences on the development of American urban life. The cities of the south were decimated by the war, which, on the other hand, stimulated manufacturing and commerce in the cities of the north and west. The demographic expansion of these cities was often staggering; for example, the population of Brooklyn jumped from 202,000 in 1854 to about 302,000 in 1865. By 1900, Brooklyn had more than one million people.

With this rapid urban growth came new problems of urban government. The age was the heyday of boss rule based on large blocs of immigrant voters. It was also the age of the sweat shop, of child labor, and of the "robber baron." Mark Twain referred to it scathingly as the "Gilded Age." The unplanned, uncontrolled expansion of cities during the nineteenth century left a legacy of problems which still remain to be dealt with, not only in America but in the rest of the western world as well.

URBAN COMMUNITIES

Since every city is in a county, the question may arise as to why the county—as a subdivision of a state—cannot itself exercise the functions normally associated with a city. Why, in short, is it necessary to have municipal corporations? Or are they, in fact, superfluous? Why can't county governments do what city governments do?

The answers to these questions are deeply rooted in American history. To begin with, it must be noted that the county was originally conceived as a unit of rural government. As such, its powers were those which befitted the conditions of the time and of the area. This is perfectly understandable when one recalls that only about three percent of the American people lived in cities at the time the Constitution was written in 1787. Residents of urban areas were obviously the exception rather than the rule, in 1787.

But persons who did live in urban areas had special needs and requirements which rural counties were not equipped to handle. For example, in the Colonial era cities required, as they do now, special arrangements for public safety, economic regulation, and certain minimal public services. Since such services could be provided for neither by the existing county nor through an unincorporated (i.e., legally powerless) settled area—it was necessary to seek a special legal status for sizeable settlements. The device which was used was the municipal charter, given by the Colonial Legislature, which created a municipal corporation and allocated the necessary governmental authority to meet the felt needs of the area. There was nothing at all new about this practice, for English cities had been created for hundreds of years at first through royal charters and later through acts of Parliament.

In short, special conditions required a special governmental form —the municipal corporation, on both sides of the Atlantic. In the United States, the function of incorporation is no longer carried out by a special act of a state legislature. The common practice is to provide by statute that urban areas which meet certain specifications regarding population will automatically be incorporated.

WHY THE URBAN SITUATION IS WORTHY OF STUDY

One of the most compelling reasons for studying urban affairs is the deeply-felt conviction that knowledge has, or at least ought to have, some potential relationship to power. To know something about a social situation is to create the possibility of taking some reasoned action related to it. Knowledge as to how social processes operate brings with it the chance of controlling the end-products of such processes. Even in the absence of positive controls over the outcome, knowledge results in an understanding which might otherwise be impossible to achieve.

Such beliefs underlie the modern study of urban affairs; one which is multi-disciplinary. It includes not only all of the social sciences, but history, architecture, engineering, law, and city planning as well. As its multi-disciplinary nature would suggest, the study of urban affairs has a complex background. The concentration on urban matters as a specialized area dates from the relatively recent realization of the impact cities have upon human life in general. To put the matter differently, the growth of cities and the spread of their influence over whole national and international societies is now thought to be the major social transformation of modern times. And industrialization has been credited as the key factor in this vast and continuing change.

When studying urban history, modern historians consider the relative importance of such factors as population, technology, environment, and the socio-political organization.[6] Not surprisingly, social scientists, employing a somewhat different vocabulary, ferret out the same key factors. These may be defined as the demographic aspects (population size, composition, and distribution); ecological aspects (the spatial and temporal dimensions of community life); structural aspects (the organization of communities and their parts); and behavioral aspects (socio-psychological facts of the community, including group membership, attitudes, and values).[7]

To the political scientist concerned with urban affairs, both the perspective of the historians and the precision employed by sociologists are of great value. Nonetheless, the emphasis of political scientists is somewhat different from that of their colleagues. For political scientists in general and urban political scientists in particular, the focus is on power. They are interested in such questions as—Who holds power? By what means? What are the rewards for persons who go along with the in-power group? What are the sanctions to be used against those who defy the in-group? How are political wars fought? What are the relationships between principal political organizations and leading interest groups? What are the relationships among interest groups? How does the public perceive the political activity in the community? There are additional questions of structure, finance, and administration that political scientists are also interested in, but the above illustrations are probably sufficient to indicate the general orientation of urban political scientists.

The Present Urban Situation

Americans are much less confident today about the future of their cities than they were sixty or a hundred years ago. Despite the excesses, the vulgarities, and the injustices of Twain's Gilded Age, the feeling persisted that in the long run the country, and its urban areas, would improve. Indeed, the belief that progress was almost automatic was deeply embedded in American culture. Recent developments such as race riots, deteriorating housing, and lowering of educational achievements have done much to undermine this perennial optimism.

The situation was summarized by the unofficial spokesman for America's big-city mayors—Mayor John V. Lindsay of New York City—in an address before an international audience delivered on May 27, 1971, at Indianapolis.[8] After reminding his listeners of the historic ambivalence of Americans toward urban life, Lindsay listed some of the problems facing modern American cities. The two most important, he said, were race and poverty. "Together," he added, "they have brought frustration and despair, polarization and fear, and finally violence and disorder."

How had the central cities become "the repository" of these problems? This had occurred, the mayor asserted, because of the vast population shifts which had taken place during the last 20 years. For instance, in New York City, a million poor Blacks and Puerto Ricans had migrated into the city, while a million whites had opted to live in the suburbs.

The mayor saw no prospect at all that his city could meet its social problems without federal help. He ridiculed state aid as too little and too restricted. He suggested that machinery be established so that the 25 American cities with a population of more than 500,000 be classified as "national cities" and deal directly with Washington. In short, he called for giving these cities about the same powers which the states now possess.

Not all of the delegates to the Indianapolis conference agreed with Lindsay's prescription, but there was general concurrence with his diagnosis. Many of the mayors were quick to point out, however, that the situation in their own cities was by no means so grim as that in New York. Even so, there was a general feeling that the urban condition had deteriorated in cities large and small and in all sections of the country. The optimistic mayors were those who thought that the decline had been—in their own cities—arrested.

Why are the Urban Areas in Bad Shape?

In one way, it is strange that there is so much talk of "an urban crisis." There is a great deal of solid evidence which points toward a continuing improvement in certain aspects of over-all urban life. By any measurements, there is less poverty in the cities today than there was fifty years ago; housing is improved; more people go to school, and stay there longer; and the treatment of racial and ethnic groups is far superior to what it was in the 1920's, when discrimination against minorities was overt and was sanctioned by most Americans. Why then, on the part of the mayors and of nearly every one else, is there so much unhappiness with the present situation?

The most immediate explanation is that the improvements have not kept up with rising expectations. As Edward C. Banfield has put it: ". . . although things have been getting better absolutely, they have been getting worse relative to what we think they should be."[9] The result, of course, has been fairly massive discontent on the part of substantial segments of the urban population, especially slum-dwelling Blacks and Puerto Ricans.

But it is useful to go beyond this attitudinal explanation to one based on historic economic development. In this view, the cities have failed to create a humane environment because the city planning was left to the private sector, not to governmental officials. Sam Bass Warner, Jr. in his historical study of Philadelphia, puts it this way: "Cities have failed. Why? Under the American tradition, the first purpose of the citizen is the private search for wealth; the goal of a city is to be a community of private money makers."[10] Warner dates the basic problems of the cities from about the middle of the nineteenth century. Since that time, their "successes and failures" have depended upon the unplanned outcomes of the private sector. "What the private market could do well American cities have done well; what the private market did badly, or neglected, our cities have been unable to overcome."[11]

This tradition of "privatism," which Warner found in Philadelphia, he also believed had been repeated in other cities, including Cincinnati, St. Louis, Chicago, Detroit, Los Angeles, and Houston. As a result, these cities lacked the desire, power, wealth, and talent necessary to create a "humane environment" for all of their citizens.

Why Have the Problems not been Solved?

Several general explanations may be given in order to account for the failure to solve urban problems. One is that constitutional and other restrictions tie the hands of the municipalities. A second is that private enterprise alone cannot create a decent environment for the totality of the citizenry. A third is that we continue to create new problems (and expectations) while solving the old ones—with the result that we are never satisfied. Yet overshadowing all of these explanations of urban problems is the general trend toward social change, and its continuing impact on the political institutions of the country, including the urban political institutions.

Consider some of the key indices of social change in the U.S. during the last 20 or 25 years. From 1940 to 1967, the population increased from 131,700,000 to 200,000,000; a growth of 50 percent. The migration from rural to urban areas has resulted in a vast decrease in the farm population—from 30 percent in 1920 to 6 percent in 1966. The 1970 Census revealed that a majority of the people now living in metropolitan areas live outside the central cities. Or, to take some economic indices, the gross national product rose from $212 billion in 1945 to more than $1 trillion in 1971, and the public debt rose from $215.8 billion in 1940 to $1,450.7 billion in 1965. Other indices—from automotive transportation, from education, from mass communications—reveal similar staggering increases in growth.

These indices of rapid social change in the U.S. have generated demands which have subjected the existing social and political institutions to tremendous stress. These demands range from specific ones, such as better police protection, to general objectives, such as equality of opportunity and an improved physical environment. Under the circumstances, it is understandable—if not entirely forgiveable—that America's urban political institutions have found it difficult to cope with new problems and situations. In later chapters, this situation will be examined in more detail, but for the moment it may be helpful to explain the process of "urbanization" more thoroughly.

Urbanization

Urban politics takes place within an environment of its own; one which is distinct, although not isolated from the national or international political setting. Even though the cities have their own political environment, this environment does not insulate them from national trends and tides. The "urban crisis" of our time is in large measure part of the larger crisis which has been affecting American life. For example, while the cities have become—to repeat Mayor Lindsay's remark— the "repositories" of the problems of race and poverty, it is not the cities which created the problems in the first place. These problems may largely be attributed to the failure of the national government to develop and to sustain consistent and humane policies in the economic and social spheres. Nor are the cities even remotely capable of solving such problems by themselves.

Yet the cities do have problems and conditions which are unique and with which they must deal as best they can. By any standards, there has been an urban explosion, and this has in fact brought about a genuine social revolution in big and small cities and in their suburbs. Though there is a good deal of evidence which could be cited to illustrate urban growth, the most spectacular figures relate to population. A few statistics suggest the magnitude of the transformation: the population of the country doubled in number from 1870 to 1900, and redoubled by 1950; it is expected to reach the

300,000,000 mark before the end of the century. The 1970 Census revealed a total population of 204,765,770. The proportion of rural population to this total population has fallen for 200 years: from 54.3 percent in 1910, it dropped to about 25 percent in 1970. Since 1950 the decline has been absolute as well as relative. Consequently, since 1910 there has been a steady increase in the percentage of the population living in urban areas, with the exception of the 1930–40 decade, when increases were about equal. The 1920 Census was the first to report an urban majority, when the percentage of urbanites stood at 51.2.

However, urban growth during the last few decades has been uneven. In the northeast, the urban population has increased at a slightly faster rate than in the rural areas, but the greatest increases in urban areas have taken place in the west and in the south. Population growth has also affected other aspects of American life, for example, the problems of air and of water pollution are clearly related to population expansion. But there is some evidence that this population growth is currently slowing down, and there is even a long-range possibility that the American population will become stabilized in several decades. In the meantime, the total population is expected to increase substantially. As projected at present, this increase will occur primarily in urban areas. The prospect is that our urban majority—which has existed for many years —will continue to grow both in terms of numbers and as a proportion of the total population.

Obviously, what happens—or does not happen—in urban America is of cardinal importance to the well-being of the country. Since this process of *urbanization* has been such an important development in America, we shall examine the process and its political consequences in more detail.

Urbanization has proved to be a key concept in American political development. During the early years of the nation, when the economy was primarily agrarian, it was reasonable to assume that the great crop regions would constitute sectional units. From this perspective, political conflict was viewed as a series of contests among wheat areas, cotton regions, and so on.

But the diversification of economic interest diluted the theory of sectionalism, especially following the Civil War period. The weakening of sectional blocs came from the multiplication of economic interest within the regions. These alterations in the previous economy were related in one way or another to increasing urbanization, as finance, manufacturing, and distribution tended to be centered in the cities.

The erosion of sectionalism is especially visible in the south, where rapid urbanization has resulted in changes that occurred decades earlier in the northern cities. Whole new business classes were created which had more in common with their northern counterparts than with southern sectional interests. This attitude was particularly evident in such burgeoning industrial and regional centers as Atlanta and Houston. Southerners began to act, politically, more like people in other sections of the country, with profound political consequences. Not only has the structure of historic agrarianism been undermined in the south and elsewhere, but the class basis of politics has been changed. The influence of labor unions in politics, for instance, has been directly related to urbanization.

All aspects of the governmental process are affected by urbanization. New problems are created, which in turn require the creation of new governmental agencies. The national party system was affected as the Democratic Party became more and more dependent on urban support. In national Democratic affairs, party leaders in New York, Boston, Chicago, and other large cities assumed more prominent roles, and the metropolitan vote became increasingly pivotal in presidential elections.

Urbanization developed a politics based on class. As the principal voting behavior studies have shown, there is today a close correlation between class and party preference. In the metropolitan areas, party cleavages tend to follow class lines. In so far as the recent in-migration to the cities consists of low-income Blacks and Puerto Ricans, the net effect should be to reinforce and perhaps to strengthen the Democratic Party organizations.

From this discussion, it is evident that urbanization and population changes must be given a high priority in any general analysis of urban politics. They are also factors which political scientists make use of in studying the political behavior of a particular city, or in comparing the behavior of one city with that of another. The following paragraphs show the kinds of variables which are employed in such studies.

One set of variables relates to population characteristics. Using this approach, an investigator would classify a population in terms of age, family status, education, occupation, income, race, and religion. Of particular importance is social class. If a community consists primarily of unskilled laborers, factory workers, and adults with no more than an eighth-grade level of education, its politics will reflect this demographic condition. On the other hand, if the community is dominated by skilled workers who have finished high school, business executives, and professionals, then it is reasonable to assume that its political ambiance will be different from that of the lower-class community. There is empirical support for the proposition that social rank and political outlook are closely correlated.

It is also useful to compare city populations on the basis of their relative degrees of "urbanization." Under this approach the key factors are the ratio of children under five years of age to women of child-bearing age, the proportion of women with jobs outside the home, and the proportion of detached, single-family residences to all dwelling units. From these components a scale is developed. High rank on the urbanization index would refer to those persons who lived in apartment houses or rooming houses, single men and women, and childless couples with both spouses working outside the home. Low rank implies the other end of the spectrum—families living in single-family houses, couples with children, and wives who stay at home rather than work.

And lastly, there is an index which measures ethnicity in a community. Here the purpose is to identify and to locate concentrations of minority groups. The idea is to determine the relative proportions of such groups to the total community population, and then to make comparisons among different communities.

Which index an investigator employs depends on the particular situations to be examined. The primary source of data is, of course, the official Census and its derivative publications.[12]

SOME NEW PERSPECTIVES
ON URBAN POLITICS

The current dominant school of U.S. historians has pictured American history as the continuing creation of a "consensus" among hitherto dissimilar groups of people. The motto—"From many, one"—has been taken almost as an historically accurate prophecy. Ever higher unities have emerged from lesser diversities.

From the consensus historians, the great majority of political scientists have taken their lead in the interpretation of American political developments. Political struggle has generally been viewed not as an end in itself but as a necessary means for establishing a new level of agreement. In every case, the emphasis was on the achievement of a compromise solution following intensive bargaining. In terms of political philosophy, this view is called "pluralism," and in terms of party competition, it may be characterized as "brokerage politics."

In recent years, a small minority of historians has come to question the tenets of the consensus school. Some political scientists have also come to be skeptical of the consensus interpretation of political conflict. As they assess the evidence, the importance of consensus in contemporary politics has been exaggerated. By the same token, they conclude that the prevailing orthodox interpretation downgrades fairly severely the part played by conflict in modern American politics.

The view taken in this book is that the key to understanding contemporary urban politics is an appreciation of the role of conflict. The older interpretation, based on a theory of consensus, is held to be no longer adequate in explaining present-day phenomena. This newer interpretation of urban politics—which stresses the importance of conflict—has, no doubt, ancient origins. It may owe something to Thrasymachus, who has the losing side of the argument with Socrates in Plato's *Republic*. In emphasizing class struggles, it may also owe something to Marxism. But mostly the new political interpretation is derived from American urban political experience of the last twenty years.

What, it may legitimately be asked, is "new" about this newer interpretation of politics? The answer is twofold; the first works toward a definition, and the second concerns its characteristics.

A definition of the new politics is one of conflict as opposed to accommodation arrived at through brokerage activities. There is an emphasis on the elements of militancy and of no-compromise. Indeed, there is often a positive glorification of these factors and of the inability to arrive at a negotiated (as against a forced) decision. The new politics operates on the assumption that decisions may quite properly be dictated by those who wield the greatest power. Minority rights—so valued in traditional pluralist theory—are often overriden or ignored. Conflict politicians have little use for what to them appear to be mere philosophical niceties.

The net effect of these five principal characteristics of the new politics has been to politicize a great many areas of American life which were formerly outside the realm of politics. The characteristics are as follows:

1. The area or arena of political conflict is enlarged. Certain areas of life which were formerly considered outside the political arena are increasingly being placed within that arena.

2. There is an increasing intensity to the political struggle. Matters which at one time attracted little political attention are becoming salient political concerns.

3. More actors—individuals and groups—are participating in the political conflict. Formerly excluded groups are now playing an ever more active role.

4. The increase in the number of actors has resulted in an increase in participation in political affairs. The new politics places a tremendous emphasis on participation both for practical results and as a value in itself.

5. Governmental actions are increasingly questioned on the grounds of "legitimacy." Laws and ordinances which at one time would have instantly been obeyed must now be demonstrated to be legitimate before they are complied with.

At present, the theory of conflict politics finds its most extreme manifestation in Northern Ireland. In that rigidly divided province, the opposition parties regularly boycott the regional legislature— the Stormont Parliament. They thereby render a politics of consensus completely out of the question.

No major urban complex in the United States has thus far approached Northern Ireland in its practice of the tenets of conflict politics. But the trends toward increased militancy (by teachers' unions, by the police, by the unemployed) and no-compromise (by community-control adherents, by certain ethnic groupings) are quite apparent for all who will see them. The evidence from current urban politics is presented in subsequent chapters.

THE BASIC QUESTION

Observers of urban government are quite rightly concerned with a multitude of important questions; some highly practical in nature; for example, should a city set up a wage tax and, if so, at what rates? Others are more abstract; for instance, how can American individualism be best adapted to an increasingly collectivist-inclined society? But from the perspective of political science, probably the most basic question is this: Can urban political institutions cope with—or be adapted to cope with—the new and pressing demands of social change? At present, no one really knows.

DEFINITIONS OF KEY TERMS

In the interest of clarity, it is appropriate to give some indication as to what is meant by certain key words and expressions. These terms will be used throughout the text, and it is important that their scope and their limitations should be appreciated. One caveat is in order: The vocabulary of political science is less standardized than would ideally be desirable. But the following definitions have a fairly wide general acceptance among urban political scientists.

"Political science" in its broadest sense is the study of how power is distributed and exercised throughout society. In this definition, it would be perfectly proper to study conflicts inside labor unions or professional associations as political phenomena. Obviously, the definition also includes struggles within established political and governmental institutions, such as political parties or municipalities.

"Political conflict" arises when the distribution of power is being contested, which is most of the time. Politics is thus very much concerned with conflict. This can run the gamut from actual violence to a debate over the distribution of funds. There are therefore many different forms of political conflict.

"Legitimacy" in its historic sense merely means "in compliance with the law." But as used today by urban political scientists the term pertains to the degree of moral authority which a government or one of its actions possesses. An action which is perfectly legal may be perceived by some persons as lacking in legitimacy.

"Urban area" has the broadest meaning of any of the general geographical terms. It refers to an area where there is a high density of persons, and where there is a high-level system of social and economic interaction. In most cases an urban area will have more than one government. The area may encompass territory in more than one state.

"City" is a term with two meanings. In the very extensive meaning, it is roughly used to coincide with "urban area." But in more precise legal usage, a city is a municipal corporation that has been created by a state and given certain prescribed governmental powers. When used in this sense, a city is often placed in contrast to suburbs which surround it.

"Metropolitan area" is both a general term and a technical census definition. (We shall examine its technical definition in a later chapter.) Usually, "metropolitan area" and "urban area" have the same meaning, although some urban areas—small cities—do not qualify as metropolitan areas for census purposes.

"Urban politics" is the political struggle over the distribution of power which occurs in urban areas. This is the basic term employed in this book. Some writers use "metropolitan politics" as synonymous with "urban politics." But strictly speaking, "metropolitan politics" occurs only in those few areas where there is genuine metropolitan government, such as Dade County, Florida (Greater Miami), and Nashville, Tennessee. For that reason "urban politics" is the more accurate term.

CHAPTER
NOTES

1. Noted in Jane Jacobs, *The Economy of Cities* (London: Jonathan Cape, 1970).
2. See Lewis Mumford, *The City in History* (London: Penguin Books, 1966), p. 11.
3. *Ibid.,* p. 23.
4. *Ibid.,* p. 109.
5. William O. Winter, *The Urban Polity* (New York: Dodd, Mead, 1969), p. 58.
6. H. J. Dyos, "Agenda for Historians," in H. J. Dyos, ed., *The Study of Urban History* (London: Edward Arnold, 1968), pp. 1–46. Dyos would also add "cultural setting" as a fifth factor.
7. See Leo F. Schnore, "Problems in the Quantitative Study of Urban History," in H. J. Dyos, ed., *op. cit.,* pp. 189–208.
8. Press release, Office of the Mayor, New York City, dated May 27, 1971.
9. Edward C. Banfield, *The Unheavenly City: The Nature and Future of Our Urban Crisis* (Boston: Little, Brown, 1970), p. 19.
10. Sam Bass Warner, Jr., *The Private City: Philadelphia in Three Periods of Its Growth* (Philadelphia, Pa.: University of Pennsylvania Press, 1968), p. x. The three periods are 1770–1780, 1830–1860, and 1920–1930.
11. *Ibid.,* p. x.
12. For a detailed discussion of these methods, see Joseph A. Kahl and James H. Davis, "A Comparison of Indexes of Socioeconomic Status," Vol. 20, *American Sociological Review* (June 1955), pp. 317–325.

part one

THE URBAN

POLITICAL

ENVIRONMENT

2

The

Urban

Setting

SOME CHARACTERISTICS OF URBAN LIFE

On the basis of observation, common sense, folklore, or merely watching TV westerns, most of us would undoubtedly subscribe to the proposition that rural and urban life styles are different. Beyond that point—unless we were cultural anthropologists or urban sociologists—we might find it difficult to become precise. Fortunately, the findings of two groups of social scientists on this subject are readily available.[1] What follows is a summary of generally-accepted views on the subject.

In a typical rural folk society a strong sense of group solidarity exists. The basic action group is the family, and action is more traditional than personal. Behavioral norms are set by the culture— the conventions which control the ways of living. Incidentally, there is no formal government which passes legislation and enforces statutes.

In contrast, in an urban society, the bonds of kinship and friendship are likely to be very weak, and more formal mechanisms of control must be used to hold the society together. The emphasis is on secondary rather than on primary contacts; even face-to-face contacts tend to be impersonal and superficial. In such a society, a person gains a certain type of personal freedom which does not exist in a traditional folk society, a freedom which may bring concomitant alienation unknown to the more integrated rural folk society.

What these observations point up is the impersonalization of social relations in an urban society. Typically, the working husband leaves his home in the morning, drives or takes public transportation to his place of work, and returns in time for supper. He has been almost totally oblivious of the thousands of other people he has seen during his travel. Even at work, he is unlikely to know any one well outside his immediate peer group, and it may be quite impossible for members of the same work group to meet outside the office or the factory. Indeed, men and women who work together in the central areas of such widely spread urban complexes as New York or Los Angeles are likely to find themselves a hundred miles apart during non-work hours.

This separation of residence from place of work is more typical of American than of European cities, where it is often still possible to live and work in the same quarter. In America superb freeways and fast automobiles have combined to discourage the proximity of residence and place of employment, often with a resultant geographical and psychological fragmentation and isolation.

The American housewife is also likely to meet very few people whom she knows or cares about in the course of a day. At the supermarket, she probably does not know the name of a single employee, nor is she apt to run into many friends. She is lucky if she knows the names—let alone faces—of her children's homeroom teachers. Practically speaking, her contacts are confined to the family.

Another characteristic of modern urban life is the sheer mobility of its citizenry. It is said that, on the average, one out of every five Americans moves during the course of a year. Even if some people move more frequently than others—and thus sustain the averages —the total number of persons involved in the annual movings is tremendous.

The presumption is that such vast population shifts create personal and social problems, for not only are physical roots destroyed, but human relationships are shattered. At the governmental level, the effects of a high level of mobility are also serious, for example, a large percentage of the students in any particular school will be newcomers to that school. As any one who has ever moved from one school district to another will appreciate, the adjustment can be difficult.

What is the political significance of the social characteristics which distinguish the urban from the rural styles of life? The truth is that it is not possible to give any precise answer to this question; further research is needed. The chances are, however, that

such differences have contributed to differing kinds of political out-
looks and behaviors.

THE AMBIVALENCE OF AMERICAN ATTITUDES TOWARD CITIES

As we have noted in the preceding
chapter, the feeling of Americans about their cities has always been
ambivalent. Of all the pronouncements on the subject, undoubtedly
the most famous is that of Thomas Jefferson in a letter written to
James Madison in 1787. "Our governments," he asserted, "will
remain virtuous for centuries as long as they are chiefly agricultural
. . . When they get piled upon one another in large cities, as in
Europe, they will become corrupt as in Europe." De Tocqueville,
the famous French analyst of American society, shared some of
Jefferson's beliefs. "I look upon the size of certain American cities,"
he wrote in *Democracy in America*, "and especially on the nature
of their population, as a real danger which threatens the future
security of the new world."

Despite the fact that the country has become predominantly
urban in the years since Jefferson and de Tocqueville made their
observations, the persistence of the anti-city attitude remains widespread. In commenting on this phenomenon, Scott Greer, a distinguished urbanologist, has noted:

Though Americans have, willy nilly, become a preponderantly urban
people, they have refused to accept an image of the megalopolis as their
true home. Instead, they have endeavored to transform the conditions
of the great city into "garden towns"—and have, in the suburbs, come
close to achieving their aims.[2]

At the same time, some Americans continue to have a positive
attitude toward city life. Proponents of this view often stress the
alleged cultural, artistic, and educational advantages of city living.
Others claim that they enjoy more personal freedom in a large city
than would ordinarily be the case in a suburb or in a small town.
Still others like the established ethnic neighborhoods in which they
were raised and are content to stay where they are. Such questions
as where people live and work, and why, is usually considered a
part of the city's "ecology," a term which we shall now examine
in more detail.

URBAN ECOLOGY

"Ecology" is defined in the *American Heritage Dictionary* as "the science of the relationships between organisms and their environments." For some years students of urban affairs have found it useful to use the expression "urban ecology" in connection with such problems as the patterns of spatial distribution in a city or the dynamics of urban growth. The implication is that human behavior is very closely related to the conditions under which people live and work. Clearly, considerations of this sort are of prime importance to experts engaged in city planning. But it is also true that patterns of growth and of distribution demand the careful attention of analysts of urban politics.

In a general way, we are all amateur urban ecologists when we travel about a city with our eyes open. For example, a ride by car or bus from a residential area to the downtown shopping district will usually reveal a very definite pattern of so-called concentric rings. Typically, the ride may start in a residential neighborhood of shaded streets and one-family houses. When the side street joins the main artery, the physical landscape begins to change. Suddenly, there are stores and some professional offices, and there is a good deal more activity in evidence. The traffic builds up as one proceeds to the core city area, and after some distance, the character of the buildings changes. Multi-family dwellings now dominate the scene. From the signs on the storefronts or the faces of the people, one may conclude that we are passing through a section composed of ethnic or racial groups which differ from those living in the more expensive residential areas. On the periphery of the core city, the entire neighborhood rapidly deteriorates as we enter the so-called blighted area. It is something of a no-man's land, populated apparently by the elderly, the infirm, and the poor. At the end of this run-down and semi-deserted area we come, almost magically, to the downtown section of tall buildings, well tended stores, banks and theaters, with its well-dressed, middle-aged, and busy people.

For those concerned with politics, the type of information illustrated in this typical and commonplace ride is invaluable. In a very real sense, where you live in a city tells any one who is informed about the community what your general income level is and who your neighbors are. This information is also likely to cast a good deal of light upon your political and social outlook.

The ride also illustrates the conception of a city as a series of concentric rings, with significant differences among people living in different rings. The variations in life style are likely to vary greatly from ring to ring, or area to area. In these variations we find important clues concerning variations in behavior, including political behavior.

In the illustration just cited, the model in the background is technically called the concentric zone theory. The idea is that city development took place in a series of rings around a central core. There are, of course, numerous cities where this pattern has actually occurred, for instance, in Youngstown and several other Ohio cities.

But there are two other models which are appropriate for certain other cities. One of these is the sector theory. According to this scheme, urban growth follows the main transportation routes. Hence the key to city development is found in the rail, highway, or water transportation axes of the area.

A specific type of land use begins with the particular transportation axis in the center of the city, and expansion along that line creates a sector of identical land use. The Main Line in metropolitan Philadelphia, for example, grew up in the land area bordering on the main tracks of the Pennsylvania Railroad leading out of central Philadelphia toward Paoli. Similarly, the die was cast early that the Delaware River as it passes Philadelphia should be devoted to shipping and industry, not to residential housing and parks.

Finally, there is a third model, one which rejects the idea that cities grow out of a central core. Called the multi-nuclei theory, this model assumes that large urban areas are organized around several central places or nuclei. The assumption is that certain types of activity are clustered because it is to their advantage to be together. There are both new and old illustrations of this theory. In large cities, the tendency is for the jewelers to be concentrated in one area, the bankers in another, the wholesale food dealers in another, and so on. Newer illustrations of the model may be found in the large shopping centers which have entered into severe competition with the downtown stores. The immense shopping center at Paramus, New Jersey, is an outstanding example of the multi-nuclei theory.[3]

Besides giving careful attention to the growth patterns of particular cities, urban political scientists also concentrate on the dynamic elements of growth. They want to know about significant changes which are taking place inside individual zones, and, even more about interzonal changes. This interest stems from the knowledge that change in the form and land-use patterns of cities is one of the primary sources of urban political conflict. Not only are individuals pitted against each other, but whole ethnic, racial, or economic groups may be involved. At almost every stage of the struggle one and probably several governmental agencies will find themselves inside the arena.

METROPOLITAN AREAS

A chief—and probably the chief —characteristic of modern urban America is its very high degree of metropolitanization—the centering of the urban population in metropolitan areas. The term "metropolitan area" is a loose one, which is used to refer to any large concentration of urban dwellers who evidence a high degree of economic interdependence and social interaction. This particular use of the expression disregards government boundaries and emphasizes instead the common social and economic interests of the population.

As a moment's reflection will indicate these common social and economic interests are very basic. The welfare of the Detroit metropolitan area is intimately related to the state of the automobile industry. The welfare of Seattle is closely related to the state of the airplane manufacturing industry, and so on. In these and other areas, the primary economic interests are supported by a complex transportation infrastructure. Indeed, the historic relationship between metropolitan areas and transportation is very close. Normally, the great urban centers have sprung up where there were potentially good seaports, or at strategic points along great rivers, or at junctions of rail lines and highways.

There is also a psychological dimension to the concept of the metropolis. If queried aboard a transcontinental plane, a person might say he came from Waltham, Massachusetts, but he would be more likely simply to answer "Boston." Similarly, while the same person might follow the fortunes of the local Waltham softball team, he is much more likely to associate his deepest baseball interest with the Boston Red Sox.

Standard Metropolitan
Statistical Areas (SMSAs)

While "metropolitan area" is a useful term in ordinary conversation, it is not especially helpful in scientific studies of urban phenomena. For purposes of comparative research, a standard definition of exactly what constitutes a metropolitan area is necessary. Such a definition has been created by the U.S. Bureau of the Budget and has been used extensively by the U.S. Census Bureau. The present term—"standard metropolitan statistical area"—was adopted for use in the 1960 Census. The concept was originally developed, according to the official government statement on the subject, " . . . to meet the need for the presentation of general-purpose statistics by agencies of the Federal Government, in accordance with specific criteria for defining such areas."[4] Based on these criteria, geographical boundaries have been established by the Bureau of the Budget with the advice of an interagency federal Committee on Standard Metropolitan Areas.

The principal objective in setting up standard definitions was, of course, to ". . . make it possible for all Federal statistical agencies to utilize the same boundaries in publishing statistical data useful for analyzing metropolitan problems."[5] In explaining the basic idea, the Bureau stated: "The general concept of a metropolitan area is one of an integrated economic and social unit with a recognized large population nucleus."[6]

Each standard metropolitan statistical area must meet certain tests. Because of its importance, the Bureau's definition warrants quoting:

The definition of an individual standard metropolitan statistical area involves two considerations; first, a city or cities of specified population to constitute the central city and to identify the county in which it is located as the central county, and, second, economic and social relationships with contiguous counties which are metropolitan in character, so that the periphery of the specific metropolitan area may be determined. Standard metropolitan statistical areas may cross State lines, if this is necessary in order to include qualified contiguous counties.[7]

To determine whether a particular area should be included within the meaning of the definition, it is necessary to apply specific criteria relating to population, metropolitan character, and integration. The key consideration regarding population is a total of 50,000 or more inhabitants. They may be in one city, or in twin cities. If two or more adjacent counties each have a city of 50,000 or more inhabitants, and the cities are within 20 miles of each other, the population criterion is also met.[8]

There are various criteria to determine metropolitan character. Primarily these are intended to establish that the county is a place of work or a home for a concentration of non-agricultural workers.

For example, at least 75 percent of the labor force of the county must be in the non-agricultural force.[9]

The third set of criteria relate primarily to the extent of economic and social communication between the outlying counties and the central county.[10] What is sought is to determine that the area is in fact an integrated unit, not an unrelated collection of communities.

Distribution of SMSAs

Because of population growth, the number of SMSAs constantly increases. As of May 1, 1967, there were 231 such areas in the United States.[11] In addition, there were two entries under the further classification, "Standard Consolidated Area." They were New York—Northeastern New Jersey, with 14.7 million persons, and Chicago, Illinois—Northwestern Indiana, with 6.79. The SMSAs are shown in Figure 2.1.

Three states—Alaska, Vermont, and Wyoming—have no SMSAs. Some 11 states have only one, 5 have two, and 10 states have three. Texas leads the list with 23 SMSAs, followed by Ohio and California with 14 each. Pennsylvania is fourth with 12.

FIGURE 2.1

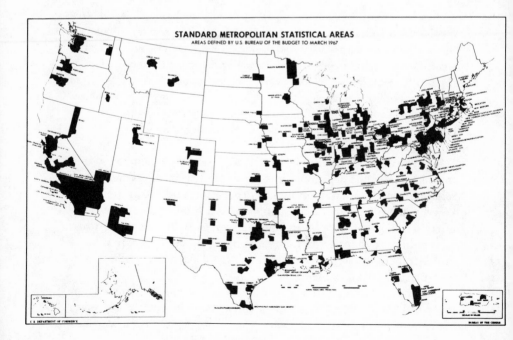

Population

A very large percentage of the population of the country resides in the SMSAs. In 1960, some 63 percent of the people lived in these areas, and the 1970 Census data are expected to reveal an even higher figure. Movement inside the SMSAs has been extensive for several decades, with the central cities outside the south and west showing declining populations. In contrast, the percentages of SMSA residents who live in the suburbs of the largest cities have been increasing rapidly since 1950.

Racial polarization

It was common knowledge during the 1960's that the exodus of white residents to the suburbs, coupled with the in-flow of Black migrants to the central cities, was drastically affecting the racial composition and distribution in the largest metropolitan areas. A census report of February 10, 1971, showed that this belief was essentially correct.[12] In the 66 largest metropolitan areas accounting for half the population of the United States, the white population in the central cities declined 5 percent while the Black population went up 30 percent. Table 2.1 summarizes the findings.

The net result of these migrations is that the nation's big cities are becoming increasingly Black in population, while the suburbs remain overwhelmingly white. Of the nation's 50 largest cities, three—Washington, Newark, and Atlanta—were reported to be more than half Black. Another major city—Gary, Indiana—also

TABLE 2.1
Changes in Racial Composition of 66 Largest Metropolitan Areas. 1960–1970

Central Cities		Suburbs	
White Population	Negro Population	White Population	Negro Population
1960 35.7 million	1960 8.0 million	1960 41.6 million	1960 1.8 million
1970 33.8 million	1970 10.8 million	1970 54.1 million	1970 2.6 million
Down 1.9 million, or 5 percent	*Up* 2.8 million, or 35 percent	*Up* 12.5 million, or 30 percent	*Up* 800,000 or 44 percent

SOURCE: *U.S. News & World Report*, March 1, 1971, p. 24.

had a Black majority. In percentages, the Black population accounted for 71.1 percent of the population of Washington; 54.2
percent of Newark; 52.8 percent of Gary; and 51.3 percent of
Atlanta. Of the twelve largest cities, the only one to gain in white
population was Los Angeles, where the whites increased by 5.3
percent to 2.17 million. During the 1960–70 decade, the largest
loss of white residents took place in Chicago. This came to 505,000
persons, a drop of 18.6 percent from the total population in 1960.

Demographic Trends

The National Commission on
Urban Problems gave considerable attention in its 1968 Report to
current and projected population trends within metropolitan areas.
The Commission was especially troubled by the increasing concentration of Blacks in the central cities. "Negro isolation," it declared,
"could become even more serious than it is today." Projections
based on recent experience show that, between 1960 and 1985,
central cities could lose 2.4 million or 5 percent of their whites, but
gain 10 million nonwhites, a 94 percent increase. This means that
nonwhites would move up from 18 to 31 percent of the population
of the nation's central cities."[13] The projection of the Commission
is shown graphically in Figure 2.2.

In its report, the Commission also examined population data for
metropolitan areas as well as for the central cities. After noting that
the 1920 Census was the first to record that a majority of Americans lived in urban areas, the Commission pointed out that current

TABLE 2.2
*Percent of Growth Within Metro-
politan Areas, 1900–1960*

	Metropolitan total	Central city*	Suburban ring
1900–1910	32.0	37.1	23.6
1910–20	25.0	27.7	20.0
1920–30	27.1	24.3	32.3
1930–40	8.8	5.6	14.6
1940–50	22.6	14.7	35.9
1950–60	26.3	10.7	48.5

* The projections for central cities are within fixed geographic boundaries of
1960, making no allowance for annexations or city-county consolidations
between 1960–1985.
Source: *Building the American City*, p. 42.

growth inside metropolitan areas is in the suburbs. "If present trends are projected," the Report asserted, "central cities will grow in population by only about 13 percent by 1985, but the suburban rings will grow by 106 percent. Put another way, 89 percent of all metropolitan growth will be in the suburbs."[14] Table 2.2 illustrates

FIGURE 2.2
THE PROSPECT OF FURTHER RACIAL SEPARATION
Showing Growth of Nonwhite Proportion in Central Cities and of Whites in Suburbs

Metropolitan Population by Color—Central City and Suburban Ring

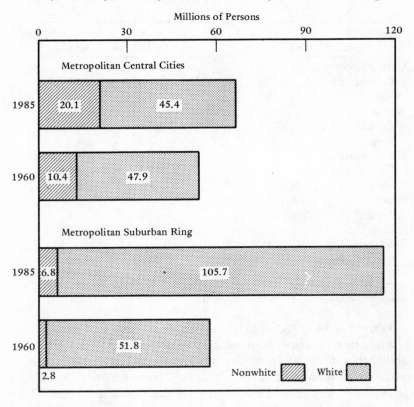

the historical relationship between the central cities and their suburban rings and also shows the Commission's projections.

As the metropolitan areas continue to grow in population, it is
expected that separation on the basis of race will become more
marked. If present trends persist, the percentage of nonwhites in
the central cities will double between 1960 and 1985 but will rise
only slightly in the suburbs. The Commission's projections are
summarized in Table 2.3 below.

Table 2.3

*Percent of U.S. Population That Is
Nonwhite, in Central City and Sub-
urban Ring, By Region, 1960 and
Projected 1985*

Region and residence	Percent non-white, 1960	Percent non-white, 1985
United States:		
Central city	17.8	30.7
Ring	5.2	6.1
Northeast:		
Central city	13.8	26.4
Ring	3.1	3.7
North central:		
Central city	17.1	32.0
Ring	2.8	2.2
South:		
Central city	26.0	38.8
Ring	11.7	13.2
West:		
Central city	13.0	23.3
Ring	4.9	5.3

Source: *Building the American City*, p. 43.

What may be expected to be the impact of these vast population
changes in the metropolitan areas? One obvious result is the probability that there will be Black majorities in the big cities. The con-
tinuation of present trends will produce Negro majorities by 1985
in New Orleans, Richmond, Chicago, Philadelphia, St. Louis, Detroit, Cleveland, Baltimore, and Oakland. Newark, Gary, and Washington, D.C., were more than half Black at the end of the 1960's.[15]
There is no reason at present to anticipate a major shift in non-

white population from the central cities to the suburbs, although there are indications that more middle-class Blacks are moving to the suburbs.

These population changes will also have an impact on the poor, who are now, and will be, distributed unevenly. Inside the metropolitan areas, the poor are concentrated in the central cities. On this point, the Commission declared: "The high percentage of metropolitan poor in central cities is due to the fact that the great majority of nonwhite poor live in these central cities. Almost half of the white poor live in the suburbs."[16] The location of the poor by race is shown in Table 2.4 below.

TABLE 2.4
Location of the Metropolitan Poor
By Color, 1966
(Numbers in millions)

	Total		White poor		Nonwhite poor	
	Number	Percent	Number	Percent	Number	Percent
Central city	9.5	63	5.3	53	4.2	82
Suburban ring	5.7	37	4.8	47	.9	18
	15.2	100	10.1	100	5.1	100

SOURCE: *Building the American City,* p. 50.

From nearly every point of view, the suburbs hold an advantage over the central cities of the metropolitan areas. This advantage will increase unless present governmental population and housing policies are changed. The relationship between good housing and suburbia is explained by the Commission in these words:

The suburban ring has a majority of the residents of the metropolitan area. It also has less than its proportionate share of the poor, and only 5 percent of American nonwhites. Part of the reason that this considerable section manages to retain its present character is that little low-cost housing is being built there; indeed, little low-cost housing is built anywhere, but the central city, so far, has the only substantial stock of housing depreciated far enough to provide a supply of housing, however unsatisfactory, for low-income whites and nonwhites. The suburbs, however, contain nearly half the *white* metropolitan poor—a figure which suggests that the suburbs discriminate more on the basis of race than on the basis of economic status."[17]

Governmental Organization
in Metropolitan Areas

It is important to bear in mind
that most metropolitan areas do not have a single governmental
organization which functions for the entire area. On the contrary,
metropolitan areas abound with units of local governments. A
census report for 1967, for example, revealed that the 24 SMSAs
with populations of more than a million persons had a total of
20,703 units of local government. Even at the bottom of the list,
the figure was impressive, for the 27 SMSAs in the 50,000–100,000
population range managed to produce 682 local units.[18]

In the case of very small SMSAs a single county government
may have jurisdiction over the entire area. But the authority of the
county government is strictly limited. The power to govern will be
exercised by a multitude of municipal corporations and special districts as well as by the county itself. Further complicating the governmental pattern is the fact that many SMSAs cross county and
state lines. For example, of the 212 SMSAs in 1960, some 79 embraced more than one county. At the same time some 24 SMSAs
included territory in more than one state, and to this figure could
be added the "Standard Consolidated Areas" of New York and of
Chicago.

SOCIO-ECONOMIC COMPARISONS
BETWEEN CITIES AND SUBURBS

Big-city politicians, reform-ori-
ented journalists, and debunking novelists have over the last two
decades launched countless attacks upon the suburbs and the
suburban "way of life." In the view of these commentators, the
population of the suburbs of this country is almost entirely upper
class, white, and Protestant. The adult males, for the most part,
manage huge corporations or control banks. When not engaged in
these activities, they meet at the nearest country club to plot the
downfall of their class enemies. How accurate is this concept of
social geography?

At the start, it must be stressed that, in the aggregate, there
are certain significant differences between central cities and their
urban fringes. A 1964 census study examined the socio-economic
status for urbanized areas based on measures of occupation, education, and income.[19]

Using a four-range scale, the researchers found that proportionately more persons of high status scores were found in the suburbs.

Some 23 percent of the urban fringe residents were placed in the highest status category, while less than 4 percent were in the lowest. In the central cities only about 14 percent of the population achieved highest status rank, and some 9 percent fell into the lowest classification.

Yet when the investigators focused their attention on the intermediary as against the extreme classifications, they found that the supposed urban/suburban wall between haves and have-nots does not really exist; instead of a wall, there is a substantial overlap. One-fourth of the suburban residents were discovered to be in the lowest two of the four categories, while more than one-half of the central city population were in the two highest categories. Besides this census study, there is other evidence which indicates that the class composition of suburbs is decidedly mixed. For example, it has been ascertained that about half of AFL-CIO members live in the suburbs, and for those under 40 years of age the figure mounts to three-quarters. In short, the suburbs are not the locale of only the rich and the well-born, but they contain in fact a broad middle range of American society.

An analysis of the St. Louis metropolitan area also pointed up the fallacies of the common city-suburban stereotype. Employing the methods of social area analysis, the study confirmed the general realization that the central city contained more neighborhoods of low social rank, high urbanization, and high segregation than its suburbs. But it was also learned that the governmental boundary between the city and the suburbs was not a social boundary separating the poor from the rich. There were prosperous and poor neighborhoods on both sides of the city line.[20]

In view of such findings, how is one to account for the vast amount of misinformation concerning suburban-urban disparities? Sociologist Leo F. Schnore has come up with a reasonable explanation.[21] He studied 200 SMSAs in order to compare core cities and their urbanized rings on the basis of income, education, and occupation. His findings indicated that the popular view of city and suburban disparities in social status comes primarily from the experience of the larger metropolitan areas. For example, with reference to the three variables (median family income, percent completing high school, and percent white collar), Schnore's data showed that no city of more than 500,000 population exceeded its suburbs on two of the three variables, and only a handful on the third. But as one moved down the population scale, a definite reversal took place. The smallest urbanized areas which were studied contained from 50,000 to 100,000 persons. In these 53 areas, 23

central cities had a larger median family income than their suburban rings; 27 had a higher ratio of persons who had completed
high school; and 37 had a higher percentage of people employed
in white-collar jobs.

Another important determinant in city-suburban differentials
was found to be the age of the city. The general belief that high
status people tend to live in the suburbs was found to be true of
those areas with very old core cities. But this was progressively less
true in the newer urban complexes. In trying to account for the
importance of age as a determinant, Schnore suggested two factors.
First, he thought that the decay of housing structures in very old
core city areas had driven out home owners and replaced them
with new migrants. Secondly, he reasoned that less intense pressure on land use in the newer cities may have set up different de-
velopmental patterns. For instance, industrial expansion that in the
past has grown from the core outward may now be leapfrogging
residential areas and creating industrial and commercial zones at
the outer periphery of the area. The net effect of this theory could
be that central residential areas retain much of their historic attractiveness and livability.[22]

Employment indices furnish another perspective on the central cities–suburbs controversy. The 1970 Census data indicate
that a shift of major proportions regarding place of employment
has been taking place. The trend in the Philadelphia region is typical of the largest metropolitan areas. As of 1970, it was found that
a majority of jobs in the eight-county metropolitan area were still
inside the city of Philadelphia, but only barely so. The exact figure
was 51 percent. At the same time, it was noted that about 60 percent of the people in the area lived outside the city limits.

Some specific statistics point up the significance of the trend.
Between 1960 and 1970, the number of private (non-governmental)
jobs increased nearly 25 percent in the Philadelphia metropolitan
area, but only 5.5 percent in the city. There were 12.1 percent
fewer factory jobs—some 35,000—in the city in 1970 than a decade
earlier. By 1970, only 44 percent of all factory jobs were inside
the city. As of 1970, the area outside the city contained more jobs
in both manufacturing and trade than did the city. The city held
a slight edge in the categories of "services" and of "government."
Its margin was large only in the categories of "transportation
utilities" and of "financial."[23]

If this trend continues—and the expectation is that it will—very
shortly a majority of persons employed in the Philadelphia metro-

politan area will be working outside the city limits. The importance of the Philadelphia story lies in the fact that it is, of course, being repeated in other large metropolitan areas.

PROBLEMS IN METROPOLITICS

Frequently one encounters the expression "the metropolitan problem." In reality—like "the drug problem" or "the international situation"—the metropolitan problem is a complex of interrelated issues. Not all of these issues are directly related to the political process. For example, any program to elevate the moral "tone" of a particular metropolitan area would fall largely within the non-political sphere. Similarly, many economic problems—even very serious ones—fall within the general jurisdiction of the private economic sector. Government officials may exhort or cajole, but the real decision-making power will rest in the hands of corporate officials responsible to their own private constituencies. In short, some metropolitan problems are social; others are largely economic; others are political. The focus in these pages is on the last category, that is, on those problems for which the solutions are usually sought through the political process.

In formulating an overview of these problems, there is a choice to be had among different methods of classification. One might, for instance, concentrate upon questions of communication and circulation. Or, alternatively, the emphasis might be placed upon a battery of social issues such as housing and race relations. More generally useful—and it is the plan followed here—is the classification devised by Carl A. McCandless in his discussion of this subject.[24]

Metropolitan Services

A common and entirely reasonable view is that local governments exist primarily to provide services which are unlikely to be obtained in any other way. From this perspective, the local governments are basically service institutions. They perform those functions which law, convention, and popular preference indicate are in their proper domain, such as education, utilities, highways, public welfare, hospitals and health, sanitation, police protection, housing and urban renewal, fire protection, parks and recreation, and all others.[25]

If the performance of these functions involved merely agreed-on measures of public administration, there would be little political conflict. But, as any observer appreciates, there is constant group conflict over how each of these functions should be performed. Furthermore, conflict arises among interest groups involved within some of the functions, for example, to what extent would "private" hospitals receive governmental aid? On this issue administrators of public and of privately operated hospitals are in continual disagreement.

But an additional series of problems arises when the question is raised as to which governmental units inside a metropolis should perform which functions. Should there, for example, be an area-wide police force (as in Greater London) or should the police function be placed in the hands of a large number of municipal corporations within the area (as in American cities)? What about health? About the water supply? About transportation?

Unfortunately, there is no ready rule-of-thumb by which it can be decided once and for all which functions to assign to which units of the metropolitan area. But scales have, of course, been developed which suggest a graduation from functions which are mostly local in character to those which are mostly area-wide. It is generally felt, for example, that fire protection, public education, refuse collection and disposal, libraries, and police are locally-oriented functions. At the other end of the scale would fall public welfare, hospitals, transportation, planning, water supply, and air pollution control. These are considered to be the most area-wide functions. In an intermediary category come such services as health, urban renewal, housing, and parks and recreation.[26]

Whether such a distribution of functions will in fact take place depends on many factors—constitutional, legal, and conventional, as well as political. Underlying all of them is the value the community places on a high level of performance of particular functions and on competent community planning.

Metropolitan Finances

Not only is there political conflict as to the performance and assignment of governmental services in a metropolitan area, there is also conflict over who should pay for the services. In America, the practice is to tie the taxing arrangements to the specific political divisions within the metropolitan area, not to the area as an entity. Thus, one subdivision, because its people and property are richer than another subdivision, will be able to raise more taxes—especially on property—than a poorer community. Since the tax bases differ, the richer community will even be able to raise more funds at a lower rate than a neighboring poor area. This inequality in revenues causes a concomitant inequality in the performances of services which different local governments in the metropolitan area can render, for example in its schools, public parks, and other highly visible objects. The effects are less obvious, but also true, in such areas as public health activities. Generally, the groups which suffer most from existing tax arrangements are low-income racial and ethnic groups. Unless broader tax bases which include the whole metropolitan area are developed, such groups are likely to continue to receive services inferior to those available in more prosperous areas.

Many plans have been suggested to bring about equalization of revenues among different municipalities inside a metropolitan area. One such approach calls for revenue-sharing on the part of the federal and local governments. The idea here is that the federal government would funnel funds from its Treasury to the receiving localities. These funds would be raised, primarily, from federal income and corporation taxes.

National attention was drawn to the inequalities of local school support when the California Supreme Court on August 30, 1971, held that financing schools by local property taxes was unconstitutional because it penalized children who lived in poorer counties.[27] That court later eased its ruling in an order of October 21, 1971, in which it pointed out that its earlier decision was not a final judgment. The court declared that it had in the August 30 decision only ordered the case returned to a trial court for further proceedings. It had not struck down the current method of school financing in California. The trial court—if it found the existing school financing system to be unconstitutional—was instructed to provide for an "orderly transition" to a new system. Should this eventually happen, the effect will be that the state of California will have to assume most of the financial responsibilities hitherto assigned to local districts. This shifting of school tax responsibilities from the local to the state level could quite conceivably take place in other states.

At the level of political activity, disagreements over the incidence of taxation—which group should pay what—constitute one of the principal sources of continuing conflict.

Governmental Structure

A third way to regard problems of metropolitan politics is from the perspective of governmental structure. While not denying that the difficulties of functional assignment and of finance are very real, this position holds that most of the existing problems could be handled—or at least be made manageable—as a result of restructuring the governmental units, a viewpoint expressed by the Committee for Economic Development in a 1966 study.[28] It is hard to argue with the contention that there are far too many units of local government inside the metropolitan areas of the United States, and that many of them are too small, their jurisdictions overlap, and their performance is inadequate.

There have been numerous studies of this general condition, and a large number of specific proposals for reorganization has been made. These will be considered in some detail in the next chapter. At this point what needs to be emphasized is that a considerable body of expert opinion supports restructuring along the general lines just suggested. But there is lively disagreement not only over the details of restructuring but more importantly over the goals of such a reorganization. If the goal of government were simply "efficiency"—defined in purely economic terms—then some large measure of agreement might be easily reached. But "efficiency" is not what most people are looking for when they think of governmental services. On the contrary, they are more likely to be concerned with such hard-to-define concepts as a better "quality of life" or a "more humane environment." It is probably naive to think that such goals can be achieved merely by low-cost operations, if they can, in fact, be achieved at all.

Decision-Making

Lastly, metropolitics may be viewed as a set of problems in decision-making. Within this framework, such questions arise as: Who makes certain types of decisions within the metropolitan area? What is the claim of the decision-makers to legitimacy? Which group or groups hold power within the area and within the individual communities? How are conflicts among different power groups resolved?

In the growing literature of community studies—which is considered at a later point in this book—the location and the legitimacy of power are the central questions. While there is a good deal of emphasis on fiscal inequalities and some on the assignment of services, very little attention is given to governmental structure. An assumption in many of the community studies is, in fact, that an elite can manipulate any political structure, no matter how complex, to its own purposes. But in another set of studies, the view is taken that governmental structure is important because it defines the arenas of conflict and establishes paths of access to those in influential positions. Yet in the case of both groups—the elitists and the pluralists—the most important question is—Who makes the decision?

Besides these aspects of metropolitics, there is a further consideration that deserves highlighting. This is the frequent shifting of the center for decision-making in metropolitan problems from the metropolitan area to the state capitol. When the governmental units of an area are in disagreement as to how to handle an area-wide issue—and this happens often—the only remaining arena for working out a reasonable solution is that offered by the state government. A very common illustration is public transportation, where state intervention has become almost a necessity for any action at all. Here, as with certain other problems, if the metropolitan area's governments cannot agree on how to resolve a major issue, the state is likely to "impose" its own solution.

CHAPTER
NOTES

1. On aspects of this relationship from the perspective of urban sociology, see Rose Hum Lee, *The City—Urbanism and Urbanization in Major World Regions* (Philadelphia: J. P. Lippincott Co., 1955). On the same question from the point of view or urban geography, see Raymond E. Murphy, *The American City* (New York: McGraw-Hill, 1966). With respect to cultural anthropology, the classical work is Robert Redfield, *Peasant Society and Culture* (Chicago: University of Chicago Press, 1956).

2. Scott Greer, *Metropolitics: A Study of Political Culture* (New York: John Wiley and Sons, 1963), p. 6.

3. For a diagrammatic representation of the three theories, see *Annals of the American Academy of Political and Social Science*, Vol. 242, p. 13.

4. Office of Statistical Standards, Executive Office of the President, Bureau of the Budget, *Standard Metropolitan Statistical Areas* (Washington: U.S. Government Printing Office, 1967), p. vii.

5. *Ibid.*, p. vii.

6. *Ibid.*, p. vii.

7. *Ibid.*, p. 1.

8. *Ibid.*, p. 1.

9. *Ibid.*, p. 2.

10. *Ibid.*, p. 2.

11. *Ibid.*, p. 3.

12. Reported in *U.S. News and World Report*, March 1, 1971, pp. 24–26.

13. National Commission on Urban Problems, *Building The American City* (Washington: U.S. Government Printing Office, no date), p. 5. Published as House Document No. 91–34, 91st Congress, 1st session.

14. *Ibid.*, p. 42.

15. *Ibid.*, p. 43.

16. *Ibid.*, p. 50.

17. *Ibid.*, p. 52.

18. U.S. Bureau of the Census, *Census of Governments: 1967.* Vol. 1, *Governmental Organization* (Washington: U.S. Government Printing Office, 1968), p. 11.

19. Bureau of the Census, *Current Population Reports, Technical Studies,* Series P–23, No. 12, July 31, 1964.

20. See John C. Bollens, ed., *Exploring the Metropolitan Community* (Berkeley and Los Angeles: University of California Press, 1961), pp. 17–18.

21. Leo F. Schnore, "The Socio-Economic Status of Cities and Suburbs," Vol. 28, *American Sociological Review* (February 1963), pp. 76–85.

22. *Ibid.*, p. 81.

23. Philadelphia *Sunday Bulletin,* Oct. 10, 1971, p. 32, summarizing a report by the Bureau of Labor Statistics of the U.S. Department of Labor—"Employment Structure and Trends—Philadelphia."

24. Carl A. McCandless, *Urban Government and Politics* (New York: McGraw-Hill, 1970), p. 127.

25. U.S. Bureau of the Census, *Census of Governments* (Washington: U.S. Government Printing Office, 1962), p. 13.

26. Advisory Commission on Intergovernmental Relations, *Performance of Urban Functions: Local and Areawide* (September 1963), pp. 9–23.

27. *New York Times,* Oct. 22, 1971, p. 15.

28. Committee for Economic Development, *Modernizing Local Governments* (New York: July, 1966), p. 44.

3

Political

Institutions

and Processes

We have seen that urban politics takes place within an environment of its own; one which is distinct from international or national politics. Some familiarity with the principal legal relationships among different governments is also indispensable for a proper understanding of urban politics in general. Local governments function within a legal system; one which both defines the arena of combat and constitutes the rules of the game. The rules of the game are rarely neutral, and whoever masters them has a tremendous advantage over his untutored opponents. Skilled players among city officials employ their knowledge of the rules to further their governmental objectives. For amateur city politicians, the going can be very rough indeed.

THE LEGAL FRAMEWORK

The basic document setting forth the distribution of governmental powers is, of course, the United States Constitution. The 10th Amendment states that all powers not conferred on the federal government are "reserved" to the states. Since cities and other local governments are not mentioned in the Constitution, the assumption is that they fall under the jurisdiction of the state governments. There is therefore no inherent right for a community to exercise local governmental powers unless and until such powers are conferred by the state. All the powers local governments possess they derive from the state. The legal position of municipal corporations received its classic formulation in a statement by Judge John F. Dillon (1831–1914) a famous jurist and legal commentator, in a work first published in 1872. "Dillon's Rule" is as follows:

41

It is a general and undisputed proposition of law that a municipal corporation possesses and can exercise the following powers, and no others: First, those granted in express words; second, those necessarily or fairly implied in or incident to the power expressly granted; third, those essential to the accomplishment of the declared objects and purposes of the corporation,—not simply convenient, but indispensable. Any fair, reasonable, substantial doubt concerning the existence of power is resolved by the courts against the corporation, and the power is denied.[1]

Judge Dillon clearly went far beyond the assertion that municipal corporations possess only those powers which have been delegated by the state, for he declared in addition that these powers ought to be very strictly construed by the courts. What the doctrine means in practice is that cities may be chartered only by state action. Further, the form of government of a city is provided by the state. The limits of a city's powers are also set by state legislation, and the continuance of a city as a municipal corporation is dependent upon the state.

On occasion, a court has challenged Dillon's Rule by suggesting that a city may have certain inherent powers of self-government. But rulings of this sort have not been followed by the vast majority of state courts. On the other hand, the present constitutions of New Jersey and of Michigan are very explicit in declaring that constitutional and statutory provisions concerning local governments should be liberally construed in their favor. On balance, it appears that the traditional rule of strict construction will continue indefinitely, but that it may undergo some erosion in the years ahead through both judicial decisions and constitutional and statutory provisions.[2]

How Cities are Incorporated

In legal theory, the power to grant incorporation to the inhabitants of an urban area is legislative in nature and may not be delegated. But the actual practice today is considerably different.

Originally, a community wishing to incorporate petitioned the state legislature, which could pass a specific statute of incorporation. But as the number of such requests increased, state legislatures assigned part of this job to other agencies—usually the chief legislative and administrative agency of a county. When certain requirements were met on the part of the community, that agency was empowered to proceed with incorporation. The fiction of legislative action was maintained by assuming that the county was merely performing an administrative, not a legislative act.

Today, typically, incorporation proceeds through these major steps: a significant percentage of the residents of an area, through petition or referendum, must indicate that they favor incorporation; this petition must state the precise areas of the proposed corporation. In some states a particular level of population density must exist for further consideration of the petition. If the county agency accepts the petition, that authority appoints a set of temporary officials or provides for the election of regular officials. The incorporation is then made a matter of public record, and is evidenced by the granting of a charter, which becomes the constitution of the municipality.

City Charters

There are several different types of city charters all of which—except in the case of home rule cities —are drafted by state legislatures. Until about the 1850's the usual procedure was for a legislature to incorporate a city by passing a special act. Yet this practice resulted in a twofold problem: the work load on a state legislature became unnecessarily burdensome, and various special acts led to a crazy quilt of differing, even idiosyncratic municipal charters.

To meet this situation, state legislatures began to adopt general laws of incorporation, where uniformity is emphasized. A single charter of incorporation is granted to all communities which successfully apply for a charter—the inadequacies of this procedure are evident.

Today, the usual method is for the state to grant classified charters. Occupying a middle position between special and general charters, classified charters are applicable to all cities within a single class. Commonly, the basis for classification is population, although the assessed value of taxable property is sometimes used as well. What happens to the city's charter when its population growth might seem to entitle it to move from one class to another? The answer is: nothing. The general rule is that a change from one classification to another is not automatic but rather depends on some prescribed formal procedure.

Some states have set up a plan whereby a city may choose among several different types of municipal charter. Frequently, the state legislature drafts three forms of charter and the city may select one of them by popular vote. The three most common plans are those relating to the mayor-council form, the commission form, and the council-manager form.

Home Rule

In the discussion of charters, no mention was made of home rule, because this subject demands particular attention. The term itself has a variety of meanings, both in the technical literature relating to municipal corporations and in court decisions. The basic difference between the charters analyzed so far and home rule charters is this: an ordinary charter may be changed by the state legislature at any time, but a home rule charter, which was drafted originally by the city, grants the municipal corporation a high degree of independence with regard to charter changes and revisions.

It is well to distinguish between two types of home rule charters. When cities are allowed by action of the state legislature to draft their own charters, the consequent type of home rule provided is termed "legislative" home rule. Where this is the practice, the state legislature still retains, of course, the authority to reverse itself and to cancel the existing home rule charters. In practice, however, the independence granted by cities under this type of home rule has proved to be remarkably durable.

Since the second type of home rule charter stems from authority granted in the state constitution, it is called "constitutional" home rule. This means that the legislature has been denied the power to prescribe for the cities the form of government which those cities shall have. Under this plan a city may adopt whatever form it feels best meets its needs, regardless of the sentiments of the legislature. Constitutional home rule first began in 1875 when the Constitution of Missouri was amended to make home rule available for the two largest cities of the state.

Though the appeal of home rule is self-evident, it is well to bear in mind that it is not in itself a panacea for all urban ills. Constitutional home rule does not free the city from the state government. A great deal of the state action continues directly to affect the city, and the general acts of the state legislature remain applicable. Furthermore, the line of demarcation is murky between powers given the state under general laws and powers given the city under home rule charters—it is not even possible to show where the powers of home rule cities begin and where those of state legislatures end.[3]

Annexation and Consolidation

It is relatively simple for a municipal corporation to change from one type of charter to another. For cities under classified charters rather than home rule, the procedure is simple: once the preconditions for possible change have been met, all that is normally involved is a favorable vote on the part of a city's voters.

To change existing boundaries of incorporation is somewhat more involved. The two basic methods are annexation and consolidation. As the term implies, "annexation" means the extension of existing city boundaries in order to bring contiguous unincorporated areas within the city limits. "Consolidation" refers to a procedure whereby two or more existing municipal corporations may be combined into a single city. Both annexation and consolidation must proceed under authorizations contained in state law, and there are wide variations in procedure among the 50 states.

Other Legal Aspects

A municipal corporation, as we have mentioned, has a particular legal status. Like a private corporation, a municipal corporation can sue or be sued. Of particular interest to citizens is the question of the liability of municipal corporations for the acts of its employees. Cities are liable in law for the fulfillment of valid contracts made through their agents. But if the persons who negotiated a contract did so without proper authority, the city is not liable.

To what extent are municipal corporations liable for the torts (civil wrongs other than the failure to live up to the terms of a contract) of their employees? (An example would be the injury to a person or property resulting from the negligence of a city employee.) The general answer under common law rules is this: in the performance of so-called "governmental" functions, the city is not responsible for the negligent acts of its employees. But in the performance of so-called "proprietary" functions, the city must assume the same liability that private corporations have. Governmental functions are those of a public character, such as police, fire, health, and education. Proprietary functions, on the other hand, are those which are essentially private in character, such as supplying gas or water or maintaining a public transit system. In practice, this distinction is not satisfactory, and some state courts have taken steps to broaden the liability of cities.

FORMS OF CITY GOVERNMENT

In the United States there are three principal forms of city government—mayor-council, commission, and council-manager. The mayor-council plan, adapted from the English model, has been the traditional and most common form. Of those cities with a population of more than 5,000, more than half operate under the mayor-council system.

The commission and council-manager forms are of more recent origin, having been developed in this century. Commission government probably began in the Galveston charter of 1901, and the circumstances of its development are interesting. In September of 1900 a disastrous flood engulfed Galveston, Texas. The city government, operating under a mayor-council plan, quickly proved itself totally incompetent to deal with the emergency situation. At the request of a group of imaginative Galveston citizens, the legislature of Texas by a special act granted the commission form of charter. So successful was the new government in Galveston that it was widely imitated. Houston requested and received a similar type of charter in 1905. The peak of popularity for the commission form of government was probably reached about 1917, at which time some 500 cities were operating under the plan. Since that time, the number of adoptions has been small, and there have been frequent abandonments. The plan has always had its greatest appeal in places of less than 50,000 population, probably because its structure is fairly well adapted to the administration of smaller municipalities.

As to the precise origin of the council-manager plan there is some disagreement. But most experts credit Staunton, Virginia, with having had the first city manager. His post was established by an ordinance of the city council in 1908. The first city to operate under a council-manager charter was Sumter, South Carolina, in 1912. The first city to adopt a council-manager plan under home rule was Dayton, Ohio, in 1913. Active interest in the plan, and its widespread adoption, effectively date from the Dayton experience. The manager plan—like the commission form—has enjoyed its greatest popularity among cities of medium or small size. Like the commission plan, the manager plan is easy to understand and adapts well to the administrative requirements of middle-sized localities. The largest city ever to adopt a council-manager form was Cleveland, Ohio, which abandoned the system after seven years. In recent years the biggest cities to use the plan have been Cincinnati, Ohio,

Dallas, Texas, San Antonio, Texas, and San Diego, California. Of all cities in the country with a population of more than 5,000 persons, the council-manager plan is now used in about 40 percent. Some of its popularity is undoubtedly due to the fact that it has been extolled for several decades by the National Municipal League as an efficient and business-like type of government.

Mayor-Council Government

In the mayor-council plan, the main agencies of government are an elected council and an elected mayor. The council is the policy-determining body, while the mayor —at least in theory—is the chief executive. This plan retains the separation of legislative and executive powers which is so characteristic of American national and state government.

Today nearly all city councils are unicameral—that is, one-chamber, but at one time it was quite common—again in imitation of the federal and state models—for many large cities to maintain two-chamber or bicameral councils. The size of councils may vary, usually between five and twenty members.

Members of the council, called aldermen or councilmen, are chosen by popular vote for a term of usually two or four years. Nomination is ordinarily by primary election. Both the primary election and the general election are partisan in some cities, nonpartisan in others.

It is possible to elect all council members from the city at large, but the more common practice is to choose them from a ward or district. This is the prevailing system in the largest cities. Again, the two plans may be combined, with some councilmen chosen at large while others are selected district by district. Sometimes the council president is elected at large, while other councilmen are selected by wards or districts.

In an effort to guarantee representation on the council in proportion to voting strength, some cities have adopted proportional representation (P.R.) in council elections. The practice was inaugurated in Ashtabula, Ohio, in 1915. Cincinnati used P.R. from 1926 to 1958, and Cleveland employed the same system from 1921 to 1931. From 1938 to 1949, New York City used a form of P.R. which was based upon the individual boroughs as the election districts. Party designations of candidates were listed on the ballots. The results are said to have produced a calibre of councilmen higher than that under the district system. The abandonment of P.R. in New York City came about largely because the system elected an occasional councilman—usually a Communist from Brooklyn—whose political affiliation was offensive to the majority of New York's voters.[4]

Councils meet regularly on a weekly or monthly schedule. As is the case with most legislative bodies, a good deal of the work of councils is done through a network of standing committees. In some cities, the mayor is the presiding officer. In yet others that officer—the council president—is chosen either by the council itself or by the city's voters.

So far as their powers are concerned, councils in their legislative capacity give their principal attention to financial and to regulatory matters. The councils regulate such fields as health, traffic, building standards, and zoning. They may let contracts and authorize public improvements. The action of a council ordinarily takes the form either of an ordinance or of a resolution. If it has properly been passed, an ordinance operates within a particular city as the local law. On the other hand, a resolution is usually employed by a council to take an action on some administrative matter.

Under the mayor-council plan, the mayor is, as we have noted, the chief executive officer. Following nomination by primary election or by petition, the mayor is elected usually by a simple plurality vote, although a few cities use a preferential vote system. Ordinarily, the mayor's term is two or four years.

From the point of view of his powers, the mayor's authority falls into two different categories. His executive or administrative powers include appointment and removal (with or without the approval of council, depending on the city), and the authority which derives from these powers. In the legislative area, the mayor's most important powers are the right to cast a veto and the ability to make recommendations to the council. Again, as in the federal and state governments, the mayor's veto may be overriden by the council, usually by a two-thirds vote.

Like other units of government, cities in their public administration follow the usual pattern of departmentalization. There are specific departments charged with specific functions, such as police, fire, public works, public health, and finance. Heading each department is a single officer, often called a commissioner, or in some cases a collective board. In contrast to the old practice, the current practice is for the mayor to appoint department heads. The preferred way of handling these appointments is to vest exclusive appointing power in the mayor, thereby strengthening his role as chief executive of the city.

Typically, a city will have other top administrative officers, including a city clerk (usually chosen by the council, but sometimes elected), a treasurer (chosen by popular election or appointment by the mayor), and a city attorney (often chosen by the mayor in the largest cities, but usually elected or chosen by council in smaller cities).

It is important to distinguish between two types of mayor-council governments—the weak-mayor type and the strong-mayor type. As the term implies, the weak-mayor type is characterized by a mayor whose power in administrative matters is very weak in proportion to the power of the council. Specifically, the mayor's authority may be feeble in the areas of appointment, removal, and budget-making. Under these conditions, the dominant agency in controlling administration is the council, and the mayor is the chief executive in name only. Even today, the weak-mayor form exists in the majority of mayor-council cities, especially the smaller ones. This is largely the result of a distrust of executive authority which goes back to colonial days.

In the strong-mayor plan, the emphasis is reversed. The mayor's administrative powers are very real, and the role of the council in this area is proportionately reduced. The council, in fact, becomes almost entirely a legislative body. Experts in public administration almost unanimously prefer the strong-mayor to the weak-mayor type—they feel that responsibility in municipal government is possible only if administrative power can be centralized in the hands of one agency. Where this power is split between the mayor and the council, it is difficult to determine who is responsible for what. There is also the lesser but convincing—at least in the abstract— argument that efficiency in municipal operations is more likely to occur under the strong-mayor type of organization.

Recently, in very large cities, the tendency has been to increase the capacities of the mayor by appointing under him a professional officer to serve as a second-in-command for city administration. It is contended on behalf of this approach that it releases more time for the mayor to go into policy questions by freeing him from much routine administrative supervision. New York City, Chicago, Philadelphia, San Francisco, and New Orleans, among other cities, now provide for a managerial officer to work directly under the mayor.

But the overwhelming superiority of the mayor-council form over its rivals stems not so much from administrative as from political considerations. An elected mayor has enormous popular advantage over a commission mayor who is simply one of several commissioners, or over an appointed city manager. Psychologically, the elected mayor is viewed as the local counterpart of such towering figures as the governor or the president. He may frequently be

viewed as representing the general interest in contrast to the parochial interests thought to be represented in the council. Like the
president, he performs and is expected to perform noteworthy ceremonial and symbolic as well as administrative functions. An elected
mayor has a constituency to which he is directly responsible, and
which is likely to demand leadership from him. Because the commission and the manager plans have failed to meet the leadership
standards demanded by the electorates of large cities, they have not
generally been successful in such cities.

Commission Government

Though the details of commission
government vary considerably from city to city, the essential features of the plan are the same everywhere. In its simplest form,
the plan provides for a commission of five to seven commissioners,
who are the only elected officers of the city. Usually, they are
chosen at large, and the nonpartisan ballot is normally used in both
the primary and the general election. As a group, they form the
commission, are termed commissioners, and are responsible for both
policy-formulation and legislation in the municipality.

Under this plan, each commissioner serves as the head of one of
the administrative departments. This means that the separation
of powers principle is abandoned, as both administrative and legislative authority are placed in the same officers. There are alternative
ways in which a commissioner may be assigned to a given department. In some cities, commissioners are elected to head specific
departments; in others, the commission itself makes the assignment
by majority vote. In addition to heading one of the administrative
departments, one of the commissioners will be accorded the title of
mayor. Again, there are various routes for arriving at this office:
in some cities, the voters elect the mayor to the post; in others, the
commission by its own vote designates one of its members as
mayor; in still other municipalities, the commissioner who received
the largest number of popular votes in the general election is called
mayor. Yet however the mayor is chosen, he is merely the titular
head of the city. He presides over commission meetings and he
greets visiting dignitaries on behalf of the city. But such duties
aside, he has the same authority as any other commissioner.

What are the advantages of commission government? Basically,
the plan provides for a very short ballot (only a handful of officials
are elected), and the framework of government is simple and understandable. On the other hand, the objections are very serious. In
the first place, city administration is totally under the control of

amateurs and, in the second place, administrative responsibility is highly decentralized, even fragmented.[5] As these deficiencies became more apparent, the attractiveness of the commission form plummeted.

Council-Manager Government

The council-manager form was intended to overcome the principal weaknesses of the commission plan, by providing for a professional city manager who operates directly under the supervision of the council. Typically, the council tends to be smaller than that in a commission city—with nine or more members. It is common for councilmen to be elected at large, but frequently they are chosen by wards or districts. In many, but by no means all, of the council-manager cities the nonpartisan method of election is used.

As in the commission plan, there is no separation of powers in the council-manager plan. But—and this is highly significant—the council-manager form provides for an effective separation of functions. To be sure, the council performs the legislative function, but instead of relying on councilmen to carry on the city's administrative work, the plan calls for the council to appoint a manager. The manager, in turn, chooses the department heads and supervises their activities. The council, therefore, performs two main functions: it acts as the city's legislature, and it appoints the city manager.

Again, as with the commission plan, the council-manager arrangement provides for a mayor whose office is purely titular and ceremonial and he possesses neither appointive nor veto power. He is usually selected by the council from among its own membership, although in one variation of the plan he is popularly elected.

For the council-manager form, the essential relationship is that between the elective council and the appointive manager. It is a difficult relationship to describe, for it is likely to vary among cities and, depending on the particular persons involved, inside particular cities over a period of time. At first glance, it might appear that the line between policy-formulation by the council and policy-execution by the manager is a clear and obvious one. But this has not been found to be the case in actual fact. The most successful managers have always been formulators of policy, but they must exercise this function with great skill and with consummate tact. Some conflict between dynamic managers and councils is very human and quite inevitable. But the manager must always remember that he serves at the pleasure of the council, which can discharge him at any time.

The advantages of the council-manager plan are obvious: it centralizes in a single official the responsibility for total administrative supervision, and it emphasizes the professional aspect in the selection of this top administrator. Criticisms of the plan have been chiefly on two grounds. It has been alleged that the plan is undemocratic, in that the manager is appointed and not elected, although this allegation misses the key democratic criterion that power must be exercised responsibly. The second common objection is that the plan fails to provide for adequate political leadership. There is probably some validity to this line of reasoning, especially in the largest cities where vigorous and visible activity is expected from the mayor. It seems unlikely that New York City, Chicago, Philadelphia, and other large cities would look with favor upon any system which reduced their mayors to merely titular figures.[6] On the contrary, what the electorate seems to prize is a combination of actual power and skilled showmanship as illustrated, for example, by John V. Lindsay of New York.

OTHER URBAN GOVERNMENTAL FORMS

Smaller Municipalities

In common usage, the term "city" is applied to the larger municipalities. But, as we have seen, a very large part of the urban population resides in smaller municipalities within the various standard metropolitan statistical areas. Usually, these smaller units are called villages or towns or sometimes boroughs, depending on the laws of the state. The proliferation of such units within a single county can be staggering. For example, in Delaware County, Pennsylvania, which is adjacent to the city of Philadelphia and included within the Philadelphia SMSA, there are, in addition to the county government, these subdivisions: third class city—one (Chester); boroughs—27; townships—21. Nor can one tell much about the relative populations of the communities by their classification alone. For example, the population of Chester, a city, stood at about 56,000 in 1970, while that of Upper Darby, a township, was about 95,000.

Counties

Whether a person lives in a central city or in a suburb, he will in either case usually come under the jurisdiction of both a municipal and a county government.

There are some exceptions to this general statement, for example, where city-county consolidation has resulted in one combined governmental unit. Other exceptions come from New England, where the basic units of government are the town (which when populous enough evolves into a city) and the state itself. In Connecticut, as an illustration, the county today is little more than a judicial district. A final exception comes from Washington, D.C., which as a federal district is not part of any county.

In the United States in 1967 there were 3,049 counties, a large percentage of which were classified as rural. On the other hand, there exist many urban counties. The Committee for Economic Development, in its 1966 study, found that there were 102 SMSAs which possessed a single county government, that is, one governmental authority which embraced the entire metropolitan area. In addition, of course, there are numerous SMSAs which include two or more counties.

Urban counties have, for the most part, the same governmental structure as their rural counterparts. While the specifics of county organization differ from state to state, it may be noted that all counties have a general governing board, and all have a series of officers, boards, and commissions charged with various tasks.

For the general governing board—officially called the board of commissioners, board of supervisors, or some similar name—the chief duties are to control the fiscal affairs of the county, perform some administrative functions, and exercise some authority over county affairs in general. It is the usual custom to elect members of the county board. The two most common forms of organization are (1) a relatively small board of county commissioners, or (2) a larger county board of supervisors. Of these forms, the more prevalent is the board of commissioners. It is employed nearly everywhere in the south and west, and is common in other sections. It may consist of from three to seven members—on occasion more—and election is by the county's voters at large.

The alternative kind of county board—the board of supervisors—may be quite large, as in New York, Michigan, and Wisconsin. General practice is for each township to elect one supervisor, with the more populous townships being accorded additional supervisors. As a result of this electoral base, nine Illinois counties in 1955 had boards of supervisors which exceeded forty members each. But the record was apparently held by the board of Wayne county (Detroit), Michigan, which in 1952 had some ninety-seven members.[7]

In comparison with the scope of legislative authority conferred by the states on municipalities, the powers of the county board are not impressive. Its principal legislative power relates to county finance. Yet the board usually possesses a good deal of executive and administrative power, and the courts usually regard the board as an administrative body. The administrative powers of the county board would ordinarily include control over county property, the making of contracts on behalf of the county, appointment of certain county officers, and various duties connected with the supervision of elections. The usual practice is for one of the members of the board to serve as chairman.

Counties seem to have made very little progress toward integrating the activities for which they are responsible. In general, county administration may be regarded as a collection of relatively independent agencies, instead of a small number of coordinated departments. Functions that are similar tend to be distributed among different agencies instead of being brought into a single department. The administration of counties, in short, is not one of the crowning glories of American public administration.

Despite this generally bleak picture, there are some reasonably bright spots on the administrative landscape of the counties. The need for a county executive to coordinate the varied activities of county government has been underscored for many years by specialists in public administration. Because of pressure from this and other sources, there has been a tendency—happily, a growing one —for counties to establish an overall executive with power over major administrative functions.

A county executive may be provided by election, or by appointment. The practice of electing a county executive goes back many years, for example, Cook county (Chicago), Illinois, has had an "elective president of the county board" since the 1890's, and since 1900 Hudson and Essex counties in New Jersey have elected executives with the title of county supervisor. However, the modern drive in this direction dates from the 1930's, when Nassau and Westchester counties in New York adopted charters which provided for an elected county executive. In these counties, the executive is in fact the chief administrative officer of the county, and holds powers similar to those of a strong mayor. But one should not exaggerate the strength of the tendency to elect county heads, for it was reported in 1965 that only 12 counties in the entire country did have elective executives with the powers normally possessed by strong mayors.[8]

As an alternative to electing county executives, they may be appointed by the county board itself. More than 20 counties now operate under a county-manager plan. Here, as is the case with city managers, the manager appoints and supervises the heads of the administrative departments. He carries out the general policies of the board, and serves at the board's pleasure. The results to date under the county-manager system appear to be highly satisfactory, but it should be noted that it has been adopted primarily in large urban counties.

A variation of the county-manager system—one that has been termed the "quasi-manager plan"—has been tried in a number of states, including Tennessee, South Carolina, Ohio, and, especially, California. Under this approach, the manager—called "chief administrative officer"—has many but not all of the powers given under the orthodox county-manager arrangement. A count made in 1961 showed that 32 of California's 57 counties had at that time administrators of the quasi-manager type.[9]

Special Districts

A large share of governmental activity in America—including urban America—is carried on by special districts. The magnitude of their operations is suggested by Table 3.1.

In Table 3.1, school districts and special districts are listed separately in order to show the numbers in each classification, but school districts constitute one very common form of special district. Usually, school districts are organized along the same lines as council-manager governments. There is a small elected school board, which appoints a superintendent who in fact runs the school system.

Other types of special district include fire protection, transit, soil conservation, park, mosquito abatement, cemetery, library, irrigation, and drainage districts. Some of these are relatively small; others are gigantic. The revenue of the Chicago Sanitary District exceeded $65 million in a recent year, while the same city's transit authority employed 13,000 people and had an income of $138 million. Of similar Gargantuan proportions is the bi-state New York Port Authority, which at the same time reported 5,708 employees and an annual revenue of around $148 million.[10]

In terms of organization, the structure of special districts other than school districts varies widely. At one end of the spectrum are elective boards which are responsible for the operations of the

Table 3.1
Local Governments in the United
States, 1962 and 1967

Type of Government	1962	1967
All local governments	91,185	81,253
Counties	3,043	3,049
Municipalities	17,997	18,051
Townships	17,144	17,107
School districts	34,678	21,782
Special districts	18,323	21,264

Sources: U.S. Bureau of the Census, Census of Governments: 1962 Vol. 1: Governmental Organization (Washington: Government Printing Office, 1963), p. 1. Data for 1967 from U.S. Bureau of the Census, Governmental Units in 1967 (Washington: Government Printing Office, 1967). Cited in Thomas A. Flinn, Local Government and Politics (Glenview, Ill.: Scott, Foresman and Co., 1970), p. 15.

district. At the other end are appointive boards whose members are selected for long, overlapping terms by one or more local government authorities. In such cases, control over the activities of the special district by elected officials is likely to be virtually non-existent. Practically speaking, such districts are autonomous principalities.

Proposals for
Metropolitan Government

Dissatisfaction over the presence of the very large number of governmental units within a metropolitan area has led to repeated suggestions for the establishment of some kind of metropolitan government. Three different types of proposals have been advanced over the years, and each will be briefly examined.

The first proposal is the cooperative approach. Under this plan, the existing governmental units would be retained, but a large number of cooperative arrangements would be entered into by the governments. It is possible to classify such arrangements along three lines. One of these is a contract for the performance of specific services, for example, a city could make a contract with the county to have the latter body collect its taxes on a fee basis. Or, to take the extreme example, a city could contract with a county for the full range of municipal services, as the city of Lakewood had done with Los Angeles County. A second instance of the cooperative approach is for two or more governmental units to contract to operate jointly some service—a very common practice in library operations in adjoining small cities. Lastly, there may be an agreement that cities will enter into, as it were, a mutual assistance pact to be activated in time of emergency. Agreements to pool fire and police resources furnish ready examples.

There are additional variations in the cooperative approach which do not involve formal and binding contracts. One of the most successful of these is the use of metropolitan councils, a movement which began in the Detroit area in 1954. These councils usually consist of the chief administrative officers of the entire area, and their function is to provide a forum for the airing of common problems. The council in San Francisco, for example, has given a good deal of attention to regional planning.

A second approach calls for the creation of a single municipal-type government for the entire metropolitan area. In abstract terms of financing government operations and of administrative coordination, the idea has an obvious attraction. But because of tremendous popular resistance to the plan, there has been little experience with it in actual operation.

The one-government plan could be put into effect through annexation or consolidation, or through the creation of an urban county government with jurisdiction over the entire metropolitan area. In cities of recent population growth, such as Phoenix, Arizona and Houston, Texas, annexation of unincorporated areas around the city borders has been successfully used. Consolidation usually requires a favorable vote in a referendum in each of the cities considering combination, and therefore encounters obvious political difficulties. On paper, the creation of a single county government in those 102 metropolitan areas that are located in a single county appears to have many advantages. But, again, the political opposition to such a development is evident. There is, of course, no inherent reason why some state legislature could not experiment with this plan—provided it had almost unanimous community support for such an action.

Lastly, there is a third approach toward metropolitan government. Known as the two-level or two-tier scheme, this plan seeks to provide a central government with jurisdiction over the entire standard metropolitan statistical area. At the same time, existing local governments are permitted to exercise local jurisdiction within their own boundaries. Essentially, this is the application of federal principles to metropolitan government. As with federalism generally, the basic problem is the allocation of powers between the two levels of government.

This form of metropolitan government—metropolitan federation —was adopted for Dade County, Florida (greater Miami) as the result of a favorable referendum vote on May 21, 1957. Under a new home rule charter, the county government took over a number of functions formerly performed by the 26 local governments. In the traditional federalist pattern, other functions were reserved to the municipalities. The voters in the Miami area approved of the experiment in metropolitan government by only a bare majority, and the opposition of political officials remains intense. A close observer of the situation, Thomas R. Dye, has warned that "The future of metropolitan Miami is by no means assured."[11]

Experience with metropolitan governmental change indicates that a citizen's grumbling about municipal government does not necessarily imply that the grumbler will support sweeping governmental reorganization. Many problems which trouble journalists, social scientists, and government officials are simply not perceived by many urban residents to be particularly serious—their dissatisfaction remains a question of degree.

INTERGOVERNMENTAL RELATIONS

The Role of the States in Urban Affairs

It has been noted that a state can deal legally with a city any way it wants to, subject, of course, to restrictions in the state's constitution. Practically, of course, the state does not have a free hand, because the play of political forces tends to confine and to limit what the state may actually do.

Since most states now have an urban majority which is concentrated in metropolitan areas, it would be foolhardy for such officers as governor and lieutenant governor to adopt belligerent anti-urban poses. Even where the rivalry between governor and big-city mayor is virtually institutionalized—as is the case of New York State and New York City—the governor always maintains that he acts in the best interests of the city. Whatever his party affiliation, any governor of New York State maintains that he takes a broader, more profound view of urban problems than does the mayor of the state's—and the nation's—largest city.

However, it is in the legislative, rather than in the executive, branch of state government that a continuing anti-urban bias is to be found. Historically, the major reason for this condition was the over-representation of small town and rural areas in the legislatures. Although the country was shown in the 1920 Census to possess an urban majority, this fact was not reflected in the apportionment of state legislative seats. Of course, there was no way in which the state legislature could be forced to reapportion if it did not want to do so. As a result, the inequities in representation often reached startling proportions. Six votes cast in Cook county, Illinois, for example, had about the same electoral weight as one vote cast in certain downstate counties.

It was the U.S. Supreme Court which finally untied this Gordian knot. The breakthrough came with the case of *Baker* v. *Carr* (369 U.S. 186) in 1962, a case involving apportionment in the Tennessee House of Representatives. In the Tennessee legislature, the House had not been reapportioned since 1901. As a result, the areas of the state with the fastest growing populations were grossly under–represented. In appeals to state courts, a group of city officials sought to force the state to reapportion. When these efforts failed, several Knoxville lawyers brought suit in a federal court in an effort to prevent state officials from enforcing the 1901 apportionment act. Among other things, the lawyers contended that citizens living in under–represented areas were being deprived of "equal protection of the law" guaranteed by the 14th Amendment of the United States Constitution. Acting on the basis of established precedent, the federal district court dismissed the suit on the grounds of lack of jurisdiction. This decision was appealed to the Supreme Court, resulting in the opinion of *Baker* v. *Carr*.

In its opinion, the Court did not rule on the validity of the Tennessee act in question. It did however state that federal courts possessed jurisdiction to decide cases involving apportionment in state legislatures. It further held that this kind of action could be brought to the courts under the equal protection clause, that is, a citizen who claimed his rights were deprived could challenge the state apportionment practices in federal court.

As a result of the Court's action, the doors of federal courts were now open to apportionment cases, and aggrieved citizens were quick to respond. On June 15, 1964, the Court rendered decisions in eight state apportionment cases. In one of them—*Reynolds* v. *Sims* (377 U.S. 533)—the Court gave recognition to the importance of the equality criterion by endorsing what came to be called the "one man, one vote" principle. Under prodding from federal courts, the states—with considerable reluctance—embarked on the process of implementing this principle in their own legislatures. Consequently, most state legislatures—on a population basis—are reasonably fairly apportioned.

Because populations grow at differential rates in different areas, reapportionment cannot be a once-and-for-all-time affair. Ideally, the states should reapportion shortly after each decennial census, but legislatures tend to procrastinate. When this happens, appeals must once again be made to the federal courts.

However, the historical anti-urban bias of state legislatures may not necessarily wither away with more equitable apportionment, for there are several forces at work against this tendency. The first is a distrust of politicians from very large cities, one firmly rooted in American political culture. In addition, reapportionment has created some new alliances in state legislatures. For example, in the case of Tennessee, the former alignment of country versus city has been replaced by one in which the rural areas and the suburbs have united on certain important issues to oppose the cities. Rapid growth in the suburban population suggests that this pattern may increase.

What this means is that the urban ranks in Tennessee and in some other states have been split into two separate forces—those of the cities and those of the suburbs. This has been one of the political effects of the dramatic increases in the population of the suburbs and of their corresponding increase in importance generally. Formerly, it was possible to regard the political contests in many states as primarily a contest between rural areas and the cities, with the suburbs playing a minor and insignificant role. Today, the suburbs have grown up and have become a major force in state politics. Beyond any doubt, the role of suburbia in state politics is on the rise almost everywhere in the United States. For this reason, a triadic interpretation of the state legislative struggle has replaced the former dualistic one.

In supervising local government, the state has at its disposal two broad forms of control—judicial and administrative. In judicial control, the constitutional and statutory provisions relating to local government are enforced by the courts in suits brought before them —for example the issuance of a writ of mandamus to direct a public officer to perform a particular duty imposed upon him by law.

Administrative control by the state takes many forms. These include giving advice and assistance, inspection of local government facilities, and regulations prescribed by state agencies. The power to remove certain local administrative officers may be vested in a state agency. It is common to provide that state officials must approve or review certain local administrative activities.

Just as conditional grants-in-aid give the federal government a means of control over the states, so similar grants give the state government some controls over local governments. State grants-in-aid are most frequently found in such areas as education, health, welfare, and highways. In order to receive the grant, the local government must comply with certain conditions set by the state.

Finally, there may be emergency situations where the state temporarily engages in direct administration of what are normally considered to be local functions. Most states for example, provide that state public health officers may move into a community if local health services have broken down. Or, again, the governor may use the National Guard to take control of some emergency situation which is beyond the capacities of the local police to handle.

The Role of the Federal Government in Urban Affairs

Under the American Constitutional pattern, the cities are tied to the states, not to the federal government, and the state-city relationships are the basic ones. But in practice these relationships have often been restrictive and negative, and city officials have found it more rewarding to turn toward Washington for assistance. In fact, the federal government is more urban-oriented than the state governments, and has recognized the special needs of large cities for the last three or four decades. Where the federal government has responded to such needs, the response in recent years has mostly been expressed through grants-in-aid, which is to say, money.

Prior to the 1930's, national-local relations tended to be informal and not extensive. The Great Depression, however, brought about a dramatic change in federal-local relationships. Confronted with heavy relief costs and high unemployment, the cities turned to the states for help. But the states—most of which operate under legal debt limitations—were hard pressed to meet their own obligations. Only the federal government, whose borrowing power is constitutionally unlimited, had the kind of money needed to cope with the crisis.

During the early years of the Depression, Congress authorized funds to be sent to local governmental units for direct relief purposes—a temporary measure. The various federal work-relief programs were of more lasting importance. The best-known of these programs was operated by the Public Works Administration, which made grants and loans to state and local governments for a wide variety of projects, including the building of schools, hospitals, and highways.

Another outstanding aspect of the federal works program was the subsidization of low-cost public housing. Under the United States Housing Act of 1937, substantial funds were channeled to city and county housing authorities for the construction and operation of housing projects. Interrupted by the Second World War, housing and urban-renewal projects were continued after the war on the basis of national-local cooperation.

This direct federal-local relationship which developed during the Depression has expanded tremendously with time. In addition to the vast increase in programs which are federally financed, there has been federal recognition of national responsibilities toward urban areas in another important way, namely, the establishment in 1965 of the Department of Housing and Urban Development at the cabinet level. In creating this new Department, Congress intended that the new agency should perform functions for urban areas somewhat similar to those performed by the Department of Agriculture for rural areas.

In channeling funds to the cities, Congress ordinarily uses the device of federal grants-in-aid, by which it writes into the legislation certain controls, which the appropriate federal agency is empowered to exercise. It is sometimes charged that these controls slow down the flow of funds and tend to create administrative blocks and delays. These inconveniences have not interfered with the determination of big-city mayors to shift as much urban financing as possible to Washington. One way of doing this—and one without strings—would be through the kind of federal-state-city revenue-sharing that President Nixon has proposed. The U.S. Conference of Mayors has vigorously endorsed the principle of revenue-sharing, although its plan would by-pass the states.

The bulk of federal payments in urban areas occurs in the fields of commerce and transportation; housing and community development; health, labor, and welfare; and education. For the fiscal year ending June 30, 1971, federal aid to states and local governments amounted to about $30.3 billion, or approximately one-fifth of all state and local government costs. In 1960, about half of all federal payments went to finance urban programs. By 1970, about two-thirds was flowing into metropolitan complexes.[12]

The legal status of cities and their relationship with the federal government thus no longer corresponds to reality. The cities have emerged as a very powerful third partner in the American political environment. For reasons which we have mentioned, the political reality is that the cities have become increasingly allied with the national government, and increasingly estranged from the states—a significant development which any realistic political analysis must take into account.

The Interdependence of Governments: Pollution Control as an Example

Nowhere is the interdependence of governments better illustrated than their attempts to deal with problems of air and water pollution. These problems are no respecters of political boundaries, and attempts to treat them on a local basis have usually been insufficient. Yet the efforts of local governments to deal with pollution problems go a long way back into American municipal history.

Regarding water pollution, cities were historically concerned with the maintenance of adequate standards for drinking water. Understandably, the responsibility for combating pollution of sources of drinking water was assigned to public health departments—a pattern followed in the state governments.

The federal government began its first stream pollution investigations in 1910. In 1912 the U.S. Public Health Service was authorized by law to conduct investigations into pollution found in navigable waters. Until the landmark legislation of the last few years, the greatest federal effort took place as part of the New Deal public works programs. Millions of dollars were spent in the construction of waste treatment works.

But waste treatment plants deal with only one kind of water pollution—domestic sewage. An even more important source of pollution is industrial waste. There is also a large volume of pollution from agriculture, including animal wastes, farm chemicals, and irrigation drainage, and a problem of natural pollution, principally from sediment and eutrophication. Activities of man have aggravated natural pollution by speeding up the cycles and developments, for example, the dumping of industrial wastes into Lake Erie has speeded up the natural aging process of that lake.

It took many years for the extent and complexity of water pollution to be generally realized. In 1948, an important step was taken when Congress passed the Federal Water Pollution Control Act. This was amended in 1952, 1956, and 1961. This legislation committed the federal government to a permanent program of technical and financial assistance to the states and localities in building sewage treatment facilities.

But it was not until 1966 that the federal government acknowledged that water pollution was more than a health problem and was really a resource problem.[13] In that year the federal Water Pollution Control Administration (originally a branch of the U.S. Public Health Service) was transferred from the Department of Health, Education, and Welfare to the Department of the Interior. It was eventually renamed the federal Water Quality Administration, and was one of the major components taken from several departments in December, 1970, to form the Environmental Protection Agency.

There have been some success stories growing out of the drive to clean up the nation's waters, for example, Lake Washington, at Seattle, which had become a community sewage dump, has been partially restored. But there are numerous examples of continuing extreme pollution, the most notorious of which is perhaps the oily Cuyahoga River in Cleveland—which caught fire in 1969. A report issued by consumer advocate Ralph Nader in April, 1971, indicated that the battle to save the water sources had so far been a losing one. There is no evidence, the report declared, "that the seven laws passed and more than $3 billion spent by the federal government have reduced the level of pollution in any major body of water."[14]

Municipal concern with air pollution also dates back many decades. The first air pollution law in the United States was an 1881 ordinance adopted by the Chicago City Council. In this ordinance, the council declared that "the emission of dense smoke from the smokestack of any boat or locomotive or from any chimney anywhere within the city shall be . . . a public nuisance."[15] There is no indication that this type of ordinance was ever seriously enforced in Chicago or elsewhere.

Prior to World War II, all efforts to control air pollution had been directed at smoke, or what is technically known as "particulate matter." Then Los Angeles, whose public had been annoyed by the odors of a wartime industrial plant, initiated in 1947 the first modern air pollution control program. Nationwide interest in the problem was stimulated a year later as the result of the Donora disaster. In October, 1948, twenty deaths and nearly 6,000 cases of illness were attributed to a prolonged smog which hung over the industrial community of Donora, Pennsylvania.

As interest in combating air pollution spread, the focus of research turned to gases emitted by automobiles. By 1951 the automobile became the major contributor to the Los Angeles air pollution problem. With this discovery began the current effort to control the harmful but invisible substances of carbon monoxide, hydrocarbons, and nitrogen oxides. Together, they are said to account for 70 percent of all air pollution in the United States, as measured by weight.[16]

The federal government was slow to perceive the nature and dimensions of the air pollution problem. It was not until 1955 that the first major federal legislation on the subject was passed—a statute which gave temporary authority for research, demonstration, and training. In 1963—by which time a good deal more was known about the problem—a second major act was enacted. Called the Clean Air Act, it authorized action to abate interstate air pollution and provided assistance to state and local control agencies. Other legislation then followed rapidly: The Motor Vehicle Air Pollution Control Act, in 1965; the Air Quality Act, in 1967; and the Clean Air Act of 1970.

Under the last act, the administrator of the Environmental Protection Agency (E.P.A.) was required to set standards for common pollutants. The statute provided that the states should have until Jan. 1, 1972, to submit plans to achieve these standards. The E.P.A. is empowered to review the plans submitted by the states with power to approve or reject them. If the plan of a state is rejected, E.P.A. is authorized to impose its own plan on that state. The state then has until July 1, 1975, to put the plan into effect.

On April 30, 1971, E.P.A. administrator William D. Ruckelshaus announced standards for six principal pollutants: sulphur oxides, particulates (soot and smoke), carbon monoxide, hydrocarbons, nitrogen oxides, and photochemical oxidants. He conceded that it would be difficult for cities to meet the standards. For example, to bring air pollution down to the announced standards for particulates and for sulphur oxides in New York City would require a massive shift from coal and oil to natural gas in the operation of electric power plants and municipal incinerators. Other cities expected to have difficulty in meeting the 1975 deadline were Chicago, St. Louis, Baltimore, Hartford, Buffalo, and Philadelphia.[17]

Under the same Clean Air Act, automobile manufacturers were also given a 1975 deadline to meet certain standards. They were ordered to produce cars whose emissions of carbon monoxide would be 90 percent below the allowable standards for 1970 models. In order to meet this legal deadline, the E.P.A. administrator asserted that some cities would have to make "drastic changes in their transportation system," for instance by developing rapid transit lines from the suburbs and limiting private cars in the inner cities.

FINANCING URBAN GOVERNMENTS

The financing of urban governments obviously involves substantial economic questions. It also raises serious political conflicts. Of these, the most troublesome problems concern the sources of revenue and the share of the burden which different sections of the population should bear.

In general, public attitudes toward taxes range from mild resignation to open hostility. Why is this so? A plausible explanation is that there is no visible and direct connection between what a person pays in taxes and what he receives in return. When a person purchases a loaf of bread or a car, he has something tangible to show for the transaction. But he has nothing tangible to show as the result of paying a tax on his house. Recognizing this attitude, politicians often find it convenient where possible to relate a particular service to specific charges, for example, by paying off the cost of a bridge through fees collected from motorists, instead of financing the operation through general taxation. Other illustrations would be charges for the use of public facilities, such as swimming pools, zoos, and libraries.

Another element in public thinking is that, roughly, people should pay in accordance with their ability. But the difficulty with this attitude is that those who are most in need of governmental services are likely to be least able to pay for them. Not only do the greatest demands for welfare programs and health services come from the citizens with the lowest incomes, but the poorest sections of cities are in the greatest need of fire and police protection. For this reason it is not possible to use service charges to support such public services.

Even if taxpayers were to make a 180-degree turn and regard taxes more amiably, the fact is that the cities and other municipalities have come very close to the limit they can collect in taxes. Weighing the cities' needs against their expected income for the year 1972, Maxwell S. Stewart projected a "revenue gap" of about

$35.5 billion. The continuing financial crisis, he warned, was a very real one.[18]

In decades past, the cities, when in a financial bind, would with some confidence have turned to their state capitols for assistance. They continue to do so, of course, but the states themselves have had severe financial troubles for many years. Since the resources of the states are limited, municipal authorities have been looking more and more to Washington for help. It is this desire to tap federal resources that accounts for the present interest of city officials in revenue sharing.

Where does the money come from to finance urban governments? Some, as has been indicated, comes from the state and federal governments. But the great bulk comes from general revenue from the locality's own sources. The largest single source of locally originated tax money is the property tax, which accounted for some 85 percent of the revenue of cities and other local governments in 1970. The remaining 15 percent was obtained from a variety of miscellaneous taxes, including local sales taxes, levies on utilities, and, in a few cities, taxes on incomes or payrolls. During the 1960's, income from local taxes doubled, and reached $40 billion in 1970–71.[19]

As the above figures show, the general property tax remains one of the cornerstones of municipal finance. But this tax has always been unpopular, partly because of inequitable tax rates, partly because tax payments must ordinarily be made in a large lump sum. There are, in addition, legal limitations in all but seven states on the amount of property taxes that can be levied by local governments. Politicians have therefore sought to lessen the dependence of cities on the property tax by creating new and more flexible taxes. In addition to extending local sales taxes, they have looked with some favor on city wage taxes. Philadelphia, in 1939, was the first city to tap this source of income. In recent years the movement has been spreading.

But no matter how ingenious the cities may be in devising new taxes, they are running out of tax resources. Part of this is due to the increases in the costs of urban government. An even larger part is because many central cities are decaying and the taxpaying middle classes have moved out. Mayor Thomas J. D'Alesandro explained Baltimore's worsening fiscal crisis in terms of population shifts. In Baltimore in 1971, he said, only about one-third of the city's residents paid any income tax and about one-third of that third had an income of $3,000 or less per year. Out of a total of 905,000, he said that the city had only 118,000 substantial tax-payers. To raise city taxes any further, he declared, would be to risk driving this thin rank into the suburbs.[20]

Where does the money spent by cities and other local governments actually go? The most costly operation is the school system, which claims nearly half of the total. In 1970, the schools cost $41 billion, of which $35 billion was paid for locally, mostly from property taxes.[21] Welfare is the next most expensive item, and is followed by police and fire protection, then by streets and highways. When health services, sewage and garbage collection, parks and recreational facilities, and interest on debts are added up, they account for a total of $15 billion.

On a per capita basis, there are wide variations in expenditures. The cities spend far more per capita for police and fire protection, sanitary services, parks and recreation, and public welfare than rural areas. Public welfare, in fact, is the most costly item in New York City's budget. It is not in the least surprising that the mayors of New York and of other large cities would like to see most welfare responsibilities assumed by the federal government.

Although urban finance is an uncertain area, two tendencies can be cited as inevitable: 1) the costs of government operations will continue to increase; 2) the ability of the cities to finance such operations on their own will continue to decline.

CITIZEN PARTICIPATION

Citizens participate in government in two principal ways: voting in elections, and acting as members of interest groups. The purpose of the following paragraphs is to indicate the general structure within which such activities take place. The activities themselves form the substance of several succeeding chapters.

The Electoral Process

The electoral process includes the nomination and election of public officials, the popular recall as a means of removing officials, and direct voter participation in legislation through use of the initiative and referendum.

Choosing elective officials involves two distinct steps: 1) the nomination of candidates for office; and 2) the selection of the winners through an election. Four methods of nomination exist in the United States. Under the first of these—the caucus—members of the party simply get together and nominate one of their number for office. The system is informal and quick, but it became discredited because meetings were often unrepresentative of party rank-and-file membership. A second system calls for the use of conventions, which have also fallen into general disfavor as a means of selecting party candidates. The institution still survives in Connecticut as it does, of course, in the nomination of national presidential candidates.

The most widely-used nominating technique at present is the direct primary election. Devised to combat the abuses of caucuses and conventions, the intent of a primary is to permit a party's regular members to make the selection of the party's candidates. All states now make use of primaries. In the case of Connecticut, a primary is held only if a candidate defeated in a convention who received at least 20 percent of the convention's votes demands a primary.

There are two general categories of primary—open and closed, the difference being in the presence or absence of a test of party affiliation. In the open primary, there is no such test, and any registered voter may participate, at his option, in the primary of any party. In contrast, the purpose of the closed primary is to limit the nominating process to voters who are affiliated with the party. In most states, this is enforced through a challenge system or through prior registration as a member of a particular party. Because this type of primary discourages raiding, it tends to promote a sense of party responsibility. About three-quarters of the states have adopted this method.

But it is also possible both to nominate and to elect candidates through the nonpartisan method. The use of nonpartisan primaries and elections is quite common in many cities and school districts. Members of the state legislatures of Minnesota and Nebraska are chosen through this method. Several very large cities choose their city councils in what are technically nonpartisan elections, although every voter knows the party affiliations of the candidates and tends to vote accordingly.

In addition to nomination by caucus, convention, and direct primary, nomination is also made by petition. This is done by securing the signatures of the number of citizens required by law for a valid petition, and the name of the candidate is then placed directly on the general election ballot. While this method is thought of as being supplementary, it may also be regarded in a democratic sense as a safety valve to be employed if the major parties fail to take into account major public trends.

Election administration is handled locally in accordance with state laws. A host of activities is involved, including the designation of voting precincts, assignment of polling places, provision for distributing and tabulating the ballots, and the appointment of supervisory officials. The results of elections must be certified by an appropriate canvassing agency, and certificates of election are issued to the winning candidates.

Voting in American elections is now done on what is called the Australian ballot—which means that it is officially prepared by the government and that it is secret. In terms of its method of listing candidates, a ballot may group all candidates of the same party in a separate vertical column (the party-column ballot), or it may group the candidates by office (the office-group ballot). About two-thirds of the states use the party-column form.

In some areas, especially in the large urban centers, voting machines have replaced paper ballots. As modern technology goes, the machines are not particularly complicated, and they make possible almost instant reporting of election results. The machines are used both for primaries and for general elections. What astounds even such hardened observers as political journalists is the relative frequency with which machines used only two days a year break down, especially in key wards.

If an enrolled voter knows he will be absent from his place of residence on election day, he can usually arrange to cast an absentee ballot. While absentee voting is normally not decisive in determining election results, there have been cases in recent years, for example, in Rhode Island, where the absentee vote has swung the balance from one candidate to another.

A special form of election results from application of the recall principle. Under this procedure, a required number of voters may by petition demand and secure a special election to determine whether a particular official should be allowed to continue in office until the expiration of his term or should be removed immediately. The recall was first adopted by Los Angeles in 1903 and was first applied to state officers by Oregon in 1908. The most widespread adoption of this method has been, however, at the municipal level, and about three-quarters of the states permit recall elections in some or all of their cities.

In addition to choosing elective public officials, voters may participate in government through the approval or rejection of propositions relating to matters of public policy. Where state law so authorizes, voters may do this through the devices of the initiative and the referendum. The initiative allows a specified number of voters, through a petition, to propose a law or ordinance and to secure its submission to the electorate for adoption or rejection. The referendum is also activated by petition. This device enables voters to force a law enacted by a legislative body to be submitted to the electorate for determination as to whether it shall or shall not take effect. Both the initiative and the referendum provide a type of direct control on the part of the electorate over the legislative process.

Usually coupled together, both the initiative and the referendum are widely used in American municipalities. They constitute something of an American version of the slogan, "Power to the people."

Party Politics

Even in cities where local elections are held on a nonpartisan basis, political parties exist, whose main function in such cases is to contest state and national offices. In cities where the elections are on a partisan basis, there is apt to be a one-sidedness of such an extent that the second major party practically never wins. The two-party system, so extolled at the national level is something of a rarity in America's cities, as it also is in very many of the states. There are many reasons for this; for instance, concentrations of like-minded voters, tradition, political skill, and gerrymandering, among others.

It is customary to refer to political parties as extralegal organizations. In so far as the national parties are concerned, this is very largely true. But state party organization—and therefore that of the state's subdivisions—is very highly regulated. Unlike national parties and their committees, the committees of state and city parties are in reality the creatures of state law. This means that politicians who want to control local politics can do so by capturing the party machine.

The specifics of party organization in any city can only be determined by detailed examination of the practices of that city and the laws of the particular state. Yet some generalizations may be helpful before that type of examination is undertaken. As a general rule, party organization follows that of the existing political units. But the smallest unit of party organization—the precinct—is not governmental but merely a registration and a polling area. Following the precinct, the next largest unit is the ward. Commonly, committeemen and committeewomen chosen by primary or caucus in each precinct combine to form the ward committee. City organization is based on ward organization.

The system works in pyramid fashion, building upwards on a basis of committees chosen by the party's faithful. The highest level of organization of the city party is the city central committee, and its chairman is the official party leader.

In practice, the party organization may be far less democratic and responsive to rank-and-file pressures than the system of layers of committees implies. Some ward leaders or chairmen are obviously more important than others, that is, influence is not distributed equally among them. In addition, the analogy with military organization is misleading. Studies have shown that in some cities, for example, there are almost always sizeable vacancies at the lowest levels of the party organization. In Minneapolis it has been possible for many years for any one with a handful of friends to be chosen precinct committeeman for certain precincts by simply registering a few favorable votes at an open meeting. In many other cities, party organizations are much more formidable in tables of organization than they are in reality.

Liaison between city central committees and county and state organizations is built into the system, since the local committees form the base upon which the others are constructed.

Party committeemen are provided by state law and they are assigned some official duties. But the bulk of their work consists of efforts on behalf of the party: maintaining the organization, raising money, campaigning. The private nature of most of the work of these party officers is underscored by the fact that they receive no public salaries for their services.

A hundred years ago, the local party leader had a good deal more to offer his supporters than he does today. But his ability to control patronage appointments was severely curtailed by the civil service reform movement which resulted in selection on the basis of merit as shown in competitive examinations. Furthermore, what he had to offer in the nature of private welfare services has been largely overshadowed by the rise of government-sponsored welfare programs. An occasional bucket of coal may have been the price of a family's vote a century ago, but the price has gone up in the age of the welfare state.

The city political machine as described by Lord Bryce in *The American Commonwealth* in 1888 has disappeared. It has been largely a victim of social change. The old-time machine leaders were able to hold their organizations together because they could offer something in return for the efforts of ward and precinct leaders. Today the problem has completely shifted. Rather the question has become: What does a city organization have to offer in return for the support it needs to function effectively? This is not an easy question to answer.

Interest Group Politics

In the next chapter we shall deal with the "model" of group politics. First, however, it is useful to see how the parties and interest groups are interrelated. In some of the technical literature of political science, political parties are said to perform the function of "aggregating" interests, that is, of pulling different interests together. At the same time, interest groups are said to perform the function of "articulating" interests, that is, of making it possible for group values to be formulated and expressed. The distinction is useful, among other things, because it permits a functional contrast between the two types of political institutions.

The role of a party in urban America is to choose candidates and to try to elect them to office. Interest (or pressure) groups rarely engage directly in the electoral function. Rather, their concern is to influence public policy through contact with lawmakers, executives, and even judges. Interest groups therefore tend to be built on specific aspects or issues of public policy.

American urban politics furnishes a wide panorama of interest groups. These range from groups set up to deal with a one-shot issue, for example, a hospital bond proposal, to those which reflect a permanent interest in the community, for example, labor unions.

Even though no classification of interest groups is completely satisfactory, a rough breakdown would include several obvious categories. The most completely organized groups are usually those associated with business. Labor organizations, too, may achieve a high degree of effectiveness. There are various professional groups which can wield great influence, especially the bar and medical associations. In every large urban area there are so-called good-government groups which sponsor certain types of reform programs. These would include the highly successful League of Women Voters and the National Municipal League. There is a vast number of groups based on race, ethnicity, or religion. Veterans' organizations are often powerful forces in municipal politics. The least effective groups of those which are drawn from wide "sections" of the population are those which represent consumers.

The interest group process has been an integral part of American urban politics from the beginning, and its importance is hard to over-estimate. Two trends in interest group politics are having an influence in the political arena. The first is the emerging importance of neighborhood associations in urban politics. These are more numerous and are growing in political sophistication and punch. The second important trend is the unionization of municipal employees, and their increasing militancy in politics. Both of these developments are affecting the nature of the urban political "game."

Now that we have examined the legal framework and political institutions of urban America, let us take a look at the American "model" of urban politics.

CHAPTER
NOTES

1. John F. Dillon, *Commentaries on the Law of Municipal Corporations* (Boston: Little, Brown, 5th ed., 1911), Vol. 1, sec. 237.

2. On this point, see Clyde F. Snider, *American State and Local Government* (New York: Appleton-Century-Crofts, 1965), p. 355.

3. See Carl A. McCandless, *Urban Government and Politics* (New York: McGraw-Hill, 1970), p. 59.

4. See Belle Zeller and Hugh A. Bone, "The Repeal of P.R. in New York City—Ten Years in Retrospect," Vol. XLII *American Political Science Review* (Dec., 1948), pp. 1127–1148.

5. Snider, *op. cit.,* p. 401.

6. On these points, see Snider, *op. cit.,* p. 406.

7. *Ibid.,* p. 361.

8. *Ibid.,* p. 379.

9. Cited in Snider, *op. cit.,* p. 385.

10. Cited in Thomas A. Flinn, *Local Government and Politics* (Glenview, Ill.: Scott, Foresman and Co., 1970), p. 15.

11. Thomas R. Dye, *Politics in States and Communities* (Englewood Cliffs, N.J.: Prentice-Hall, 1969), p. 311.

12. *U.S. News & World Report,* July 26, 1971, p. 74.

13. Gladwin Hill, *Our Troubled Waters: The Fight Against Pollution* (New York: Public Affairs Committee, Public Affairs Pamphlet No. 462, 1971), p. 11.

14. *Newsweek,* April 26, 1971.

15. Quoted in J. Clarence Davies, III, *The Politics of Pollution* (New York: Pegasus, 1970), p. 33.

16. Davies, *op. cit.,* p. 33.

17. *New York Times,* May 1, 1971, pp. 1 and 67.

18. Maxwell S. Stewart, *Money for Our Cities: Is Revenue Sharing the Answer?* (New York: Public Affairs Committee, Public Affairs Pamphlet No. 461, 1971), p. 3.

19. *Ibid.,* p. 5.

20. *New York Times,* April 23, 1971.

21. Stewart, *op. cit.,* p. 8.

part two

THE OFFICIAL

MODEL

4

The Official

Model

of Urban

Politics

The American model of democracy rests essentially on the doctrine of pluralism, and on the dichotomy of community/state. Since the application *par excellence* of the pluralistic model of democracy has been in the area of urban politics, it is important to discuss the origins and features of both. This chapter and those which follow apply the pluralistic model to the urban political setting. The objective is both to use the model for the insights it may provide and also to test its adequacy. If the model, on the basis of the empirical situation, should be found to be deficient, it should be possible to specify in our analysis at which points.

THE AMERICAN DOCTRINE

Modern socio-political analysis of the state had its origins in Europe and in Britain, but came to its fullest fruition on American soil. In itself, this is not surprising, for the American environment—because of the American emphasis on pragmatism—was and is more receptive than most others to the temper of social science. Along with the process of acculturation—or, in this case, of Americanization, came one of accommodation. A characteristically American view of the operations of a democratic state resulted which eventually assumed the status of orthodox doctrine.

What are the essential elements of this doctrine, and why may it appropriately be called "orthodox"? The claim of orthodoxy rests upon the widespread agreement among social scientists, especially political scientists, concerning the nature of American democracy.

Of course, the development toward consensus occurred over a sizeable period of time, but in 1947, with the publication of a brilliant work, *The Web of Government*,[1] by the noted Scottish-American sociologist and political philosopher, Robert M. MacIver, this consensus on the "orthodox" definition of the concept of democracy was generally endorsed by the academic community.

The approved formulation contained no new ingredients. Rather, the utility and value of the new definition lay in its ingenious re-structuring of well-known components. Specifically, MacIver focused attention upon two aspects of democracy—the distinction to be drawn between the community and the state, and the multi-group nature of modern society. Because this emphasis was both useful and timely, it succeeded in re-directing a good deal of academic thinking about democracy.

MacIver's classical presentation on the relationship between the community and the state makes these principal points:

1. "Man builds himself an invisible world of institutions. By them his life is ordered."[2] This is so even if man perceives these institutions very imperfectly.
2. "We live in communities; we do not live *in* states."[3] Many of the controls men live under, for example, are not governmental controls. Everywhere men distinguish in real life between the community and the state.
3. Assuming that the distinction between the community and the state exists universally, how is this related to the question of democracy? "The answer is simple. Democracy, and democracy alone, gives a constitutional sanction to the universal principle."[4] In contrast, to-talitarian governments explicitly deny the distinction.
4. The community or the people, in a general way, control the government in a democratic system.[5]
5. "Democracy is founded in the free responsiveness of the state to the community."[6] There is a democratic liberty *against* the government, as shown in free elections, an uncensored press, and so on.
6. The fundamental law, in a democratic state, "elevates the community above the state."[7] Constitutions restrict what the state is permitted by the people to do.
7. Democracy is a form of government. It is not helpful to try to define it as "a way of life."[8] In fact, the United States has gone through various economic and social transformations while adhering to democratic principles.

8. All dictatorships are alike in that they sever the state from the community. "Dictatorship ignores the community. The order it sets up is not harnessed to the communal frame of order. It arrogates to itself complete independence from that frame. It has no abiding rules, no fundamental laws."[9]

What difference does it make if a community, through its fundamental law, limits what the state (or government) may do? The accepted answer is that the difference is crucial for the survival of democratic government. In placing certain activities off-limits to government, for example, religion and the press, the community (or people) has indicated that these activities should be carried on by non-governmental groups and associations. As a rule of thumb, anything protected by the First Amendment would usually fall into this area. The right of association (implied though not in fact specifically mentioned in the First Amendment) is held to be a fundamental freedom.

In contrast, modern totalitarian regimes deal definitively with the concept of freedom of association by simply abolishing it. Trades unions, universities, newspapers, business groups, and churches find themselves "co-ordinated" by the state authorities. When totalitarianism runs its full course, the old distinctions between what is an affair of the community and what is an affair of the state are completely abolished. Art, for instance, must further the class struggle, or literature must espouse "Aryan supremacy."

Schematically, the differences between democratic and totalitarian regimes are illustrated in Figure 4.1.

After emphasizing the importance of the community-state distinction, MacIver examines the nature of the society in which a modern democracy can exist. He notes that the outstanding characteristic of such a society is that it is composed of many groups. Whether a man joins one or another group is ordinarily his own business. Any attempt to force him to give his sole devotion to any one group, including for this purpose the state itself, is a step away from the democratic principle. "The conception of the all-inclusive all-regulating state is as it were a pre-Copernican conception of the social system. It appeals to the primitive sense of symmetry."[10]

Here, again, is found a basic difference between democratic and totalitarian states. On the assumption of power, a totalitarian regime destroys the private character of groups and makes them into virtual quasi-governmental agencies. The many groups, which previously had their own values and beliefs, now find that they

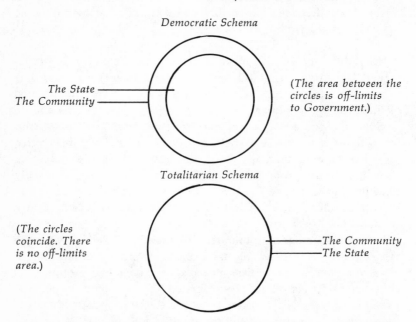

FIGURE 4.1
*Democratic and Totalitarian States
Compared*

Democratic Schema

The State
The Community

*(The area between the
circles is off-limits
to Government.)*

Totalitarian Schema

*(The circles
coincide. There
is no off-limits
area.)*

The Community
The State

have only one set of values and beliefs—the state's. In a modern democracy, in contrast, the principle of a multi-group society is accepted both as a social reality and as a constitutional right.

As a result of the writings of MacIver and others, a reasonably coherent and up-to-date theory of the modern democratic state was created by the end of the 1940's. It was a theory which was extraordinarily useful in making operational distinctions between democratic and totalitarian states. It provided the basis for meaningful contrasts, first, between the Allied democracies and their German and Japanese opponents, and later, between the United States and the Soviet Union in the era of the Cold War. Yet for all its undoubted utility, this general theory of democracy suffered because of its very generality. It failed to provide an adequate conceptual basis for understanding the political process *inside* a country such as the United States.

Now to be sure, American political scientists have long been skilled in offering explanations about the operations of the political system. In general, prior to the 1940's, these explanations tended to be grounded in history, law, or philosophy. Notably absent were theories of politics based on sociology or psychology. During the Second World War, these disciplines left the campus and demonstrated their usefulness to the war effort, for example, in selling war bonds and in psychological warfare. In this sense they "arrived," and joined the older social science of economics as practical subjects which practical men in government and industry could employ for practical purposes.

All of these developments had a profound effect on political science. In some respects a discipline in search of fundamental concepts, political science was at a decisive stage of its evolution. It could adhere to its traditional methods, and probably slowly wither away. Or it could adapt itself to the mood and thinking of the emerging behavioral sciences and, in so far as possible, become itself part of the behavioral movement. For the alternatives to be stated so bluntly is, of course, to oversimplify a very complex situation. But the decision as to the future direction of the discipline obviously involved important if ill-perceived consequences. With the hindsight of two decades, it is now clear that the pro-behavioral group of political scientists began to be influential in the early 1950's, that their influence steadily increased, and that their point of view became the dominant one in the profession during the 1960's.

The most notable contribution of the behavioralists was the creation of a theory of political action. Known as the group theory of politics, this explanation was particularly helpful when applied to the political process in the United States. The group interpretation of political behavior also nicely filled the vacuum in the general democratic theory developed by MacIver.

Stripped down to its essentials, the group theory holds that the basic political relationships are those which occur between and inside groups. As Aristotle noted long ago, man is a social animal. This means that what man accomplishes he normally does in association with other men. Generally, this involves some kind of organization. Hence, observation of what men do can ordinarily be best examined from the perspective of the activities of groups.

There are, of course, many different kinds of groups, but the political scientist is concerned mostly with those which have an actual or a potential influence on the political process. Such groups are usually referred to as "interest groups." David B. Truman has put it: "As used here 'interest group' refers to any group that, on the basis of one or more shared attitudes, makes certain claims upon other groups in the society for the establishment, maintenance, or enhancement of forms of behavior that are implied by the shared attitudes."[11] The interest group, then, may be viewed as the basic building block of the political process.

For American political scientists, the group theory of politics held and holds extraordinary fascination. It does so for several reasons, among which are the following: 1) The theory is consistent with the findings of voter behavior studies, which stress the influence of group attitudes and values upon individual voting habits. 2) The theory assumes a continuity in human action ranging from individual psychology at one end of the spectrum to the sociology of institutions at the other. 3) The theory supplies an explanation in the form of group conflict for the dynamism and movement of modern politics. 4) The theory focuses attention on the role of interest groups and offers an explanation for the normally weak role of political parties in the United States. 5) The theory is obviously consonant with the pluralistic character of American society.

Truman's *The Governmental Process* was published in 1951. Almost immediately it became the "Bible" of the group theorists. Within a few years it also enjoyed the distinction of being—in all probability—the most frequently cited post-World War II book on political science to be authored by an American. It would be difficult to overstate the importance of this treatise. At the conceptual level, the group theory offered a sophisticated series of propositions about the political process. It seemed to prepare the foundations of a genuinely empirical political science. At the operational level, the theory provided keys and clues for the understanding of political conflict. For all of these reasons the group theory was widely endorsed by political scientists, and a new direction was provided to the discipline.

In a few years, the group interpretation became the standard explanation of the American political process. It thereby became an essential part of the "official" theory of American politics. The formulation of an official, or "orthodox" theory of politics, was now complete.

THE AMERICAN MODEL

In the social as well as in the natural sciences, it is useful to develop models intended to help explain the operations of large-scale systems. Plato's *Republic* established a model of an ideal state as, with very different implications, did Hobbes' *Leviathan*. From the writings of Marx, Engels and Lenin, it is easily possible to construct a model of a certain type of Communist state. Similarly, models have been built of Fascist dictatorships, Latin American military oligarchies, and, of course, modern democracies.[12]

The dominant model of American politics has been derived from the prevailing doctrine of how American democracy operates. The lengthy process by which this happened need not be traced here. It did, however, take place well within the typical American tradition of development through experience (the United States is not by accident the home of pragmatism). Included in this experience is the total American political tradition: significant leaders whose decision-making gave the system its tone and temper, as well as the interpreters and the communicators of the basic decisions. At a certain point in time the tradition in a sense becomes codified, usually either by the intellectual elite, or the mass media.

The end result of this train of developments was that the American model of government was put into fairly sharp focus. This accepted model rests on the two basic elements of doctrine already underscored, the community/state dichotomy and the group theory of politics.

The community/state distinction quite logically supports the notion that the political conflict should occur within a clearly limited arena. This area is limited by the Constitution as well as by custom and tradition. Because of this, the role of government comes under definite restrictions. At the same time, relatively free rein is given to private associations and organizations. In the political area the most significant of these associations are the political parties and the interest groups. Because the areas open to political solution are limited, the intensity of political conflict tends to be low.

The first deduction from the model is, then, that the area of politicization is confined within definite boundaries, and there is a relatively low level of politicization generally.

In the prevailing American version of the democratic doctrine, the second major element is the group interpretation of political behavior. The group is considered to be the basic unit in understanding the political process. From this concept comes the idea that group competition in the political marketplace is the norm. Group competition is held to be the chief catalyst in stimulating political activity. Clearly, such competition would not take place in a political marketplace characterized either by monopoly or by oligopoly.

The second deduction from the model is, accordingly, that competitiveness among groups is the usual and expected condition of the political marketplace.

The pluralistic model of American democracy, while generally and broadly accepted, has come under scholarly scrutiny. This criticism is understandably diffuse, and ranges from charges of ambiguity in the model itself to assertions that the system upon which the model is intended to cast light is not working very well. To develop anything like a complete catalogue of the alleged defects would require a lengthy listing, and the result would probably be of small value. But a briefer and more general typology set within the framework of the principal elements of democratic doctrine does permit comparisons. Such an arrangement has an analytical as well as a symmetrical advantage. Of the four principal categories in the typology, the first and the last are somewhat peripheral to our immediate interests. But they need to be dealt with because they affect the degree of acceptance of the orthodox pluralistic model.

I. The model is derived from a theory which is ambiguous at points, and therefore comes under a shadow of suspicion.

The principal proponent of this argument is Professor Robert A. Dahl, who published in 1956 a short but important work bearing on the immediate problem. The purpose of the book, which was entitled *A Preface to Democratic Theory*,[13] was to analyze two of the principal theories of democracy, to challenge them, and to present the beginnings of an alternative construct. Dahl begins with a discussion of the check-and-balance or compromise theory of democracy, which he refers to as the "Madisonian" theory. He defines this as ". . . an effort to bring off a compromise between the power of majorities and the power of minorities, between the political equality of all adult citizens on the one side, and the desire to limit their sovereignty on the other."[14] He continues: "As a political system the compromise, except for one important interlude, has proved to be durable. What is more, Americans seem to like it."[15] When pushed to its extreme premises, the familiar argument of James Madison could become undemocratic. But Madison did not push his argument so far.[16]

Dahl follows the same method in analyzing "populistic democracy," the theory under which popular sovereignty, or majority will, rules.[17] He has little difficulty in demonstrating that this theory of democracy contains logical contradictions within itself. Because of this difficulty, the meaning of the theory is by no means clear.

After stressing the deficiencies in both the Madisonian and the populistic theories of democracy, Dahl develops an alternative construct which he calls "polyarchal democracy."[18] As the term implies, the emphasis is placed on a system with many centers of power. In this theory, the perspective from which the analysis proceeds tends to be more social than legal. As Dahl puts it: "Whether we are concerned with tyranny by a minority or tyranny by a majority, the theory of polyarchy suggests that the first and crucial variables to which political scientists must direct their attention are social and not constitutional."[19] It is likely that real polyarchal democracy could occur only under most unlikely conditions.[20] Yet the theory may be a step toward the development of a more complete theory of democracy.[21]

Concerning the reality of modern America, Dahl asserts that none of the three models offers a totally adequate explanation for American democracy. In practice, that democracy is something of a "hybrid." In the "normal" American political process, ". . . there is a high probability that an active and legitimate group in the population can make itself heard effectively at some crucial stage in the process of decision."[22] But this does not mean that any particular group should expect to find its cause adopted as governmental policy. On the contrary, there will usually be rival groups. "Thus the making of governmental decisions is not a majestic march of great majorities united upon certain matters of basic policy. It is the steady appeasement of relatively small groups."[23] Even the majority put together through the electoral process is best conceived of as merely a transient arithmetic expression.[24] Decisions, in fact, are made on the basis of seemingly endless bargaining." . . . perhaps in no other national political system in the world is bargaining so basic a component of the political process."[25]

The constantly changing character of American society under the pressure of time and events is another factor which helps to account for the difficulty in constructing a definitive model of the American political process.[26] Yet, despite the theoretical difficulties inherent in the undertaking, Dahl insists that it is necessary to continue to try to perfect a democratic model as part of the effort to increase our understanding of the political process.

II. The model is deficient in that the distinction between community and state sometimes breaks down.

The pluralistic model of democracy postulates a clear dichotomy between those activities which are managed by government and those which are under private control. Logically, this distinction could be eroded in either of two ways. To begin with, the private, associational, communal sphere could be "invaded" by government. In the conventional wisdom of Rotary Clubs and Chambers of Commerce, this is thought to happen with deplorable frequency. In this view government is constantly whittling down the role of private organizations, especially in the economic area. Eventually, the pessimists hold, government will swallow up the communal sphere, and there will be no real difference in this respect between the United States and the Soviet Union. To this point in American history the fear that the "Leviathan" will swallow the rest of society has been unsubstantiated. Logically, however, the possibility exists.

Conversely, there is the logical possibility that non-governmental organizations and associations could invade the sphere of influence normally assigned to government. It is easy to imagine various hypothetical, even humorous, instances of such an enlargement of private authority: 1) Government might make a contract with General Dynamics to take over the Postal Service. 2) Government might leave the regulation of drug abuses to the American Medical Association and the pharmaceutical industry. 3) Government might turn over the operation of public schools to the churches. 4) State governments might get out of the business of automobile regulation and leave vehicular matters to the conscience of individual drivers. 5) The Department of State might dissolve itself and turn over the management of foreign affairs to the United Nations. All of this might be thought of—with apologies to the Marxists—as an American version of the withering away of the state. Figure 4.2 illustrates three possible relationships of this type.

Some political scientists insist that, at least in certain areas, there has been an erosion of governmental power; that a vacuum has been created, and that the void has been filled by private power, such as the situation illustrated in item III.

This point is made by Robert Engler in his monumental casestudy of the oil industry. With careful documentation, Engler

FIGURE 4.2

I. Normal Relationship Between Community and State

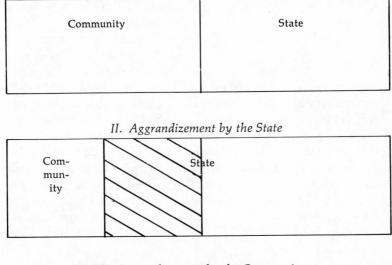

II. Aggrandizement by the State

III. Aggrandizement by the Community

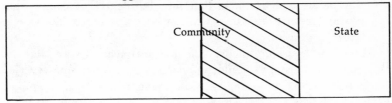

examines ". . . the private government that controls most of the petroleum resources of the world and the impact of this control upon American political life."[27] He shows how, at numerous points, the distinction between private and public has been obliterated. In most important aspects, the oil industry is not only self-regulating, it is self-governing. It performs many functions which would ordinarily lie within the governmental sphere. It transcends national lines, becoming in the process a kind of private world government.

Does it make any difference if the oil corporations operate as political institutions and become governments? Engler believes that it does. He feels that such a vast concentration of power, immune from governmental controls, is not only undemocratic but threatens the survival of liberal democracy. "It is folly," he says, "to allow the development of energy resources—the mainspring of modern civilization—to be determined by choices and conflicts rooted in the power-profit motives of a few."[28] Furthermore: "What is required is public planning, not just of oil, but of all energy resources."[29]

Another warning against the dangers of private control of American political life comes from Grant McConnell. Pluralism, he warns, can and often does lead to a species of private government. To illustrate his thesis McConnell examines the trade unions.[30] By all of the usual criteria, he finds the unions more or less undemocratic. But the phenomenon extends beyond the area of trade unions to include many other groups. The principal problems of politics relate to reconciling differences and to limiting power. Yet, McConnell concludes, "The record of private associations in dealing with these problems gives little justification for the wishful view that the private association is the natural home of democracy."[31]

III. The model is deficient in that the high degree of competition postulated in group theory often does not occur in the real world of politics.

According to group theory, the political marketplace, like its economic counterpart, should be characterized by a high level of competitiveness. Continuing with the economic analogy, one might expect to find occasional situations of political monopoly. Or, in other circumstances, a situation might show the characteristics of political oligopoly. In orthodox economic thought, monopolies, except where inevitable because of the nature of the industry,—as in the case of public utilities—are generally thought to be undesirable. To a lesser extent, this is the judgment also passed on oligopolies. The ideal is a high level of competition in the marketplace. For the competition to have any real meaning, the units in competition with each other should ideally have some approximation of equality.

In the world of politics it is perfectly feasible to measure the level and the intensity of competition between political parties. Such measurement has become, in fact, a rather highly developed art. But in group theory, the political party is merely a very large and not an especially cohesive group.[32] The most significant struggles are those which occur among interest groups. Group conflict, however, need not be limited to competition among interest groups. The struggle among competing elites is also included within the framework of group theory.

Whether there is, in fact, a struggle among competing elites is one of the problems explored by C. Wright Mills in his controversial and seminal book, *The Power Elite*.[33] It was Mills' contention that a triumvirate of forces—the political directorate, the corporate rich, and the ascendant military—make the key decisions affecting contemporary American life. Far from being in conflict with each other, these "higher circles" are staunch allies in the task of running the country. Almost by definition, the idea of elites competing for power is ruled out of the discussion. In any event, Mills cannot find any evidence of real competition. Rather, the reverse is true—brought about by a harmony of interests, purposes, and objectives.[34]

Mills also finds the theory of political competition wanting. "Not wishing to be disturbed over moral issues of the political economy," he writes, "Americans cling to the idea that government is a sort of automatic machine, regulated by the balancing of competing interests."[35] This idea, which is a carry-over from the official image of the economy, gives the impression that an automatic equilibrium is reached both in the economy and in politics. In both cases, the result is supposed to come from the "pulling and hauling of many interests."[36]

How does this affect pluralism, or what Mills calls the "theory of balance"? Mills' reply is that the theory had a good deal of validity some while ago—say, in Andrew Jackson's time. During that era both economic and political interests operated competitively and on a small scale. But—and this is one of Mills' key points—as the class basis of the economy evolved, so did the class basis of political action. "Nineteenth-century America was a middle-class society, in which numerous small and relatively equally organizations flourished."[37] Continuing, he adds: "If at times it was not a world of small entrepreneurs, at least it was always a world in which small entrepreneurs had a real part to play in the equilibrium of power."[38]

But the situation has changed. Why? Mills' answer is that the old independent middle class, upon which the former economic and political system of balance was based, has lost its importance. "The independent middle class became politically, as well as economically, dependent upon the machinery of the state."[39] As a case in point, farmers—once noted for their sterling qualities of individualism—have become virtual wards of the state under federal subsidization programs. In addition, the new middle class is largely a dependent class of white-collar employees. "The old middle class for a time acted as an independent base of power; the new middle class cannot."[40] For a while there was some hope that organized labor, a new group on the scene, might develop into an independent political force in politics. As it turned out, Mills says, labor's influence on important political decision-making has been minimal.[41]

Mills concludes by stating that in so far as the old model still operates, it does so only at the "middle levels" of power. When it comes to top level decisions of national power, it is the power elite—not the middle-echelon politicians and interest groups— that gives the commands people obey.[42]

In telescopic form, this is Mills' critique of pluralism. It is an analysis which has been hotly criticized and vehemently condemned, as it is obviously both provocative and suggestive. But because of its all-embracing, global nature, the thesis is virtually impossible to prove or disprove by the usual empirical methods.

Running counter to Mills' idea of one transcendent elite is the concept of competing elites. Suppose, as Dahl suggests, that America in reality is a polyarchal society. Suppose that there are many centers of political as well as of economic power. Would this necessarily guarantee the competitive political marketplace the pluralists picture? One recent writer, citing particularly the study of New York City by political scientists Sayre and Kaufman, thinks not. Political theorist Peter Bachrach declares: "A pluralism of elites does not necessarily produce a competitive situation among elites."[43]

IV. The model rests on economic assumptions and analogies which are less and less valid.

Social scientists have long tended to view ideology as an official system of thought which rationalizes an existing social and economic order. It has therefore been a short jump to anticipate that changes in the economic order will be followed by transformations in the ideological explanation of that order. In all of this there is often a considerable time lag, so that the ideology may be out of date with reference to the society it is intended to explain.

This is one of the principal points made by Theodore J. Lowi in *The End of Liberalism*.[44] Liberalism was the term given originally to the classic economic doctrine of laissez-faire capitalism, which placed its emphasis on a self-regulating mechanism based on the marketplace. This doctrine has now changed, Lowi notes, to group competition regulated through politics. In the process, the old laissez-faire doctrine has become passé in fact and conservative in character. It has been replaced by "statism," the principle of government intervention and direction.[45] In this way, the "new" liberalism embraces the notion of positive government action in economic affairs.

A related development—a new public philosophy—led to pluralism, "the intellectual core of the new liberalism."[46] Called by Lowi "interest-group liberalism," this philosophy is an amalgam of capitalism, statism, and pluralism.[47] It is this concept which Lowi analyzes and finds contrary to the observed facts of present-day American society.

Specifically, Lowi indicts the ideology of interest-group liberalism on four counts: 1) It "corrupts democratic government because it deranges and confuses expectations about democratic institutions."[48] 2) It renders government "impotent," because liberal governments cannot plan.[49] 3) It "demoralizes" government, "because liberal governments cannot achieve justice."[50] 4) Finally, interest-group liberalism "corrupts democratic government in the degree to which it weakens the capacity of government to live by democratic formalism."[51] (For instance, citizens do not really believe that the government will impartially fulfill its many promises. They distrust the formal processes, which seem less effective than the informal, personal, "insider" methods.)

So far as pluralism is concerned—the intellectual component of interest-group liberalism—Lowi is equally pointed. His bill of particulars includes three charges: 1) Pluralism assumes that a system "built primarily upon groups and bargaining is perfectly self-corrective."[52] But this, he says, is not so. 2) Pluralism does not deal with the problem of political oligopoly.[53] 3) The pluralist paradigm "depends upon an idealized and almost totally miscast conception of *the group*."[54]

To replace interest-group liberalism, "the enemy" of democracy, Lowi proposes a system which he calls "juridical democracy."[55] It is beyond the scope of the present analysis to consider the advantages and drawbacks of the proposed system. It is clear, however, that Lowi's criticism of the liberal democratic model has much in common with earlier criticisms, especially those of C. Wright Mills.

THE OFFICIAL MODEL AND
URBAN AFFAIRS

Despite some minority reservations about the adequacy of pluralist doctrine, political scientists in general continue to accept the pluralist model as a useful explanatory device. When changes have been suggested, they have usually been changes of degree rather than of kind. But on balance, the pluralist model still bears the imprimatur of acceptance, which is to say, of orthodoxy.

One feature of the model described so far warrants underscoring—its close relation to international (MacIver) and national (Truman) political analysis. Both in the quoted expositions and critiques of the doctrine there has been a relatively high-level perspective. Because of this distance from events, there tends to be a good deal of imprecision in the application of the model to actual political situations. At the national level the paradigm has been most suggestive and serviceable in analyzing group conflicts in the Congressional arena. The group interpretation is central to the modern analysis of Congressional behavior, as the works of Bertram Gross and others have shown.[56] As applied to Congress, the acceptance of the pluralist model has been almost total. On the judicial level, the effort has been less successful. The same observation holds true for the presidency and for the bureaucracy. The judicial and executive branches lend themselves to group interpretation far less precisely than does Congress.

The pluralistic model has however gained its readiest acceptance in the field of urban politics. It has been especially valuable in helping to interpret metropolitan conflict situations such as voting bloc versus voting bloc, class versus class, ward versus ward, whites versus Blacks, one ethnic group versus another, and similar confrontations. In all of these instances the pluralist model has been generally considered to be an aid in advancing understanding of the political process. The reason, of course, is the obvious relevance of the model to the problems.

The relevance of pluralism is especially noteworthy in explaining the highly visible conflict that is characteristic of urban politics. No one tries to keep it a secret if voters of Italian ancestry are out to wrest control from an Irish-dominated machine. So-called reformers may deplore the attempt to mobilize voters along religious lines. But if this is in fact what is happening before everyone's eyes, there is not much to be gained by denying it. Certainly political reporters for the urban press frequently make extensive use of the pluralistic model to explain politics to their readers.

Thus, pluralism, as applied to metropolitan politics offers a comprehensive explanation. It is relatively easy to identify the principal groups and actors in the political struggles. And it is quite feasible to chart the moves of the actors over a long period of time. Any good metropolitan political reporter, for example, maintains a file which is virtually a running history of the area he covers for his paper. At the national level, it is obviously much more difficult to do this. For one thing, information is often lacking, or is made available only sporadically. For another, the situation may be so complex that it would take an army of investigators to identify the actors, figure out their plays, and evaluate the results with any degree of certainty. When a national interest group has foreign policy concerns, the problem becomes even more complicated.

ANALYTICAL TOOLS

The pluralistic model supplies the conceptual framework for the study of contemporary urban politics. This framework helps to indicate what is worth examining in detail and what may be put aside with no great loss. At the same time the conceptual scheme points to the priority of some elements within the framework over others. With this assistance it becomes possible to explore closely the field of urban politics without becoming lost in some formless urban haze.

Bear in mind that the dimension of the analysis is always *political*, rather than administrative. For example, the politics of education refers to the resolution of educational policy matters through political means. The technicalities of educational administration, while of first-rate importance, are beyond our frame of reference. Or, again, the politics of law and order is to be distinguished from the techniques of police administration. To train a candidate so that he will become an excellent detective is obviously a concern of police administration, but the decision as to which laws will be enforced, and against whom, is essentially a political determination.

Another distinction worth underscoring is that between "political" and "partisan." The latter term, of course, is employed when referring to a political party. But "political" decisions may and do encompass a much larger area of decision-making. A great many of the cities in the United States employ a non-partisan election in selecting mayors and city councils. In electing members of school boards the non-partisan method is overwhelmingly predominant. Yet it is obvious that the decisions made by these non-partisan bodies represent authoritative allocations of power, i.e., they are political decisions.

Lastly, it may be objected that "there is no Republican or Democratic way to pave a street. There is only a right way and a wrong way." Even though the truth of the proposition may be conceded, the statement remains relatively useless, for the decision as to *whose* street to pave and *when* to pave it is, of course, a political one. In short, when governmental agencies make binding decisions, these decisions—no matter on what basis they were made —become "political."

In testing the pluralistic model in the contemporary urban political environment, certain analytical tools are available. Because they are universally present, these tools make it possible to analyze any metropolitan area with a good deal of precision. There is also the opportunity to examine different areas on a comparative basis. It is convenient to list these tools under the following seven categories:

1. Census Data

The Bureau of the Census, located in the United States Department of Commerce, is a basic source of primary data for the study of urban politics. In addition to the decennial Census of Population, the Bureau publishes other compilations relating to business, manufactures, mineral industries, and housing. *The Statistical Abstract of the United States*, another continuing publication of the Bureau, presents the latest available summaries of important economic, social, and demographic data. In developing any chart of social change over time, for example, the *Statistical Abstract* is indispensable.

2. Public Opinion Data

A second important analytical tool is the public opinion poll. Properly designed and interpreted, a sample survey is essential in determining the current condition of public opinion. By comparing surveys taken on the same issues over a period of time, it is possible to chart the extent to which public opinion has changed. It is also useful to superimpose a chronology of important events over a chart showing trends in public opinion. While the juxtaposition does not prove a cause and effect relationship, a high correlation between event and opinion is presumptive if not conclusive evidence.

It is true, of course, that the public surveyed in a standard Gallup-type poll may in some respects be distinguished from the public which participates in the electoral process. But as a practical matter, public opinion and the electorate normally are in general agreement. Certainly where universal suffrage is the norm and not the exception, the differences would hardly be worth arguing about. To the extent that the suffrage is limited, the electorate would correspondingly be less representative of the general public.

There is likely to be some difficulty when the two universes to be examined—the public of the pollsters and the public of the voters—differ greatly in size and in geographical area. The Gallup-type survey is, of course, national in its scope. To correlate national opinion with national electoral results is, in this case, relatively simple. But a problem arises when national opinion trends are applied to smaller electoral divisions. In such situations it is useful to have breakdowns in terms of states, or large cities, or class, or some other basis. Often state-wide or even city-wide polling data are available and may be utilized to meet this problem.

3. Electoral Campaign Data

Whether local public opinion data are available or not, there is always information about the state of public opinion to be learned from following a campaign in progress. It is a reasonable assumption that the candidates for office discuss and emphasize issues which, in their opinion, are of concern to the electorate, that is, the public. The best source of such material is the local press and the local broadcasting stations. Besides the mass media, other forms of communication—such as gossip, rumors, hand-outs, and billboards—also indicate areas of campaign emphasis.

4. Election Results

Electoral returns give a further indication as to what the public wants. Sometimes an election may revolve around the proposition of "throwing the rascals out." In this case what is involved is exchanging one team for another, and there will probably be very little indication of public policy preferences. But in another election the emphasis may have been on the personalities of the various candidates, with the winners those who projected the most attractive "image." In yet a third type of situation the results may reflect a high degree of issue-orientation on the part of the voters. One candidate defeated another because a majority of the voters approved of the positions the winner took. In this instance it is possible to establish a fairly direct association between public opinion on issues and public selection of officials.

It is most likely that issue-oriented elections in metropolitan areas will be perceived when the contests take place in so-called "off years." When national, state, and local offices are contested on the same ballot, it is difficult to separate national from other considerations. Even when the ballot is limited only to state and local offices, the problem of distinguishing state from metropolitan issues remains troublesome. But in those years when the only posts of any consequence to be filled are local, it is feasible to weigh the impact of party as against personality as against issues in assessing the final result.

Because of the deliberate factoring out of national and state contests, it follows that off-year elections furnish the most useful data for an examination of urban politics.

5. Policy-Data

All the sound and fury of elections means nothing unless there is eventually a policy out-put in the form of legislation. For it is policy formulation which is expected to lie at the end of the long process that begins with the articulation of public opinion and its aggregation through nominations, campaigns, and elections. There is a variety of ways to determine whether the legislative out-put is reflective of public opinion and if so, to what degree. But the most usual method is one of common sense observation. If the law and order candidate won the election, was he later able to change the legislation relating to the maintenance of law and order? Once in office, did he change the procedures and emphases in law enforcement?

To answer such questions for every standard metropolitan statistical area in the United States would be a gigantic undertaking. It is easier to come up with more manageable evidence by using a selected number of metropolitan areas. Yet there is no reason why an interested citizen, given access to his city hall and his local library cannot make a reasonably well-informed judgment of the public opinion-legislative out-put relationship that prevails in his own locality.

6. Political Simulation

In the last few years a way has been devised whereby students, union members, and persons in civic organizations may obtain an understanding of political processes, including elections, by the use of a new educational tool. Called simulation-gaming, this method simulates a "realistic, although artificial, representation of the world."[57] The principle involved is that one learns by doing.

Included among the advantages of learning by the use of simulation exercises are the following: 1) They are an excellent learning experience, even better, in many cases, than would be true of real life situations. 2) Simulations may be much faster than the real life equivalent, and can be repeated if the lesson is not fully understood. 3) Simulations can help people to become highly motivated and intensely involved in learning to play well. 4) Though in real life errors in judgment may be costly, in simulation exercises the risks are not actual ones. Therefore more innovation and experimentation are likely to be present. 5) "Finally, simulations have an additional advantage because they lend themselves well to ex post facto analysis."[58]

Originally used in political science primarily in international relations situations, political simulations have been developed in other fields. James S. Coleman has prepared an election game that has been utilized at Johns Hopkins University and in Baltimore high schools. Under the direction of Dale Garvey, a national political game has been tested at Kansas State Teachers College. An American government game has been developed under the supervision of Robert Alperin. A presidential election simulation has been prepared by Marvin Weinbaum and Louis Gold.[59]

Of all the various games, the Woodbury Political Simulation is perhaps the most relevant to urban politics. Developed by H. Robert Coward, Bradbury Seasholes, Marshall H. Whithed, and Robert C. Wood, the Woodbury game is a mock election in a hypothetical community of 500,000 (Woodbury). Student participants are given background data concerning the ethnic characteristics of the population in each of the wards of the city. Information about past voting trends, potential bases for campaign issues, and the mass media are also made available.

The Woodbury Political Simulation differs from ordinary mock elections in that statistical controls are provided. For each ward, there is an umpire, who calculates, on the basis of the vote distribution worked out beforehand, the effect of various moves on the vote of the ward. There is, thus, a statistical outcome to the election: one candidate wins and the other loses.[60] In its computerized version, the computer replaces the human umpires. To play the game through the twenty-one simulated campaign days requires about 200 separate moves and takes approximately nine hours. But the result is the best substitute yet devised for actual high-level participation in a real electoral situation.

It is also possible to apply the technique of simulation to actual elections. In their De Kalb model—based on the actual city in Illinois—Whithed and Clifford N. Smith were able to compare simulation results with the actual results of an election held four days after the simulation run. There may therefore be a predictive value to simulated elections under some circumstances.

For undergraduate teaching, simulation games may be superior to the use of case studies. In addition, they have an advantage over real electoral campaigns in that the games may be played at any time of year.[61] But its teaching utility aside, the Woodbury game magnificently illuminates the brokerage characteristics of modern urban politics. The outcome of the election is decided by the dominant combination of forces bringing about an electoral majority. These forces include those which are evident during real campaigns: ethnic and class solidarity, socio-economic groupings, influence of the mass media, and the appeal of particular issues.

It is possible to view the urban political conflict from different perspectives. A hundred years ago, it was the fashion to concentrate upon the electoral contests. Political leaders—"bosses"—were a special focus of attention. In the early years of the present century, the emphasis turned toward the institutional aspects of urban politics. Reformers, particularly, viewed institutional changes as the necessary means of achieving honest and effective government. In our day, the emphasis has changed once again, and the perspective which is usually employed—and which is employed in this book—is the behavioral one. Since an understanding of this viewpoint is now essential in studying modern urban politics, a few paragraphs about the rationale, background, and characteristics of the behavioral perspective seem appropriate at this place.

7. The Behavioral Perspective

In examining the forces and events which shape the modern urban political conflict, it is imperative to have some understanding of the social, economic, and cultural milieu within which the action takes place. It is also desirable to have at one's command a working knowledge of the administrative and judicial structures of the area being explored. At the same time, a viewpoint which was limited to legal and administrative perspectives would tend to be one-dimensional and, to that extent, incomplete. What would be lacking in such an analysis is the element of movement.

Here is where the behavioral emphasis, so prominent in today's social science, increases one's appreciation of the total scene.[62] The analogy is with the theater. Action is said to take place on the political stage. Committees and other organizations are viewed as continuing and recurring patterns of action and interaction. Inside a committee a distinction is made between the roles of the different actors. For instance, the role of the chairman is distinguished from that of the ordinary members. Then there is also the question of the audience, and of its reactions to the players.

From the point of view of behavioral analysis, certain leading questions arise. All of them may profitably be applied to the study of urban politics.

a) What precisely is the stage of political action? Is it constant in size, or has it been expanding? If it has been expanding, why is this the case?

b) If the political arena has been enlarged, has this expansion affected the roles of the actors? How and why?

c) Has the expansion of the stage resulted in the appearance of new actors? What are their roles, and how do these roles affect the parts played by the old actors? How does the sheer presence of the new actors affect the performance of the old actors?

d) As the stage has expanded, and as new actors have been added, have the expectations of the audience—the electorate—changed? In the real theatrical world, there is now a "living theater," in which the audience is often encouraged to participate in the action along with the actors on stage. Has the enlargement of the political stage changed the role of the electorate from passive watching to active participation? If so, with what results?

e) Have the changes in the scope of the action and the participation in it altered in any serious fashion the "game" of politics? Have the "rules of the game" been rewritten to accommodate to the new situation?

These questions, and related ones, ferret out answers which place the political struggle in a behavioral context. When viewed through a behavioral lens, that struggle gains a dimension of clarity and depth that it is otherwise missing. Groups are seen not only to be in competition with one another, but the coalition of groups varies over time.

The behavioral approach is, clearly, congenial to the thinking of the group theorists. Indeed, most group theorists would call themselves behavioralists in terms of outlook and methodology.

Reverting to the pluralistic model of urban politics, it will be recalled that the two basic elements are the community/state dichotomy and group theory. One would expect to find certain types of behavior when the model is applied to actual politics. In our examination of urban politics along this model in the following chapters we will be concerned with such issues as whether the size of the political arena is remaining constant and how extensive group competition actually is. If the model should call for one type of behavior and we find another type in practice, then the model in this respect would seem to require redefinition. When the evidence has been assembled and subjected to rigid analysis, perhaps we will be able to make a judgment on such issues.

CHAPTER
NOTES

1. Robert M. MacIver, *The Web of Government* (New York: Macmillan, 1947).

2. *Ibid.*, p. 192.

3. *Ibid.*, p. 193.

4. *Ibid.*, p. 196.

5. *Ibid.*, p. 197.

6. *Ibid.*, p. 201.

7. *Ibid.*, p. 204.

8. *Ibid.*, p. 206.

9. *Ibid.*, p. 225.

10. *Ibid.*, p. 421.

11. David B. Truman, *The Governmental Process* (New York: Knopf, 1951).

12. For an excellent analysis of the uses as well as the abuses of models in the social sciences, see Eugene J. Meehan, *The Theory and Method of Political Analysis* (Homewood, Ill.: Dorsey Press, 1965), pp. 149–150, 162–163.

13. Robert A. Dahl, *A Preface to Democratic Theory* (Chicago: University of Chicago Press, 1956. Phoenix [paperback] edition, 1963).

14. *Ibid.*, Phoenix edition, p. 4.

15. *Ibid.*, p. 4.

16. *Ibid.*, p. 32.

17. *Ibid.*, pp. 36–37.

18. *Ibid.*, p. 63.

19. *Ibid.*, p. 83.

20. *Ibid.*, p. 75.

21. *Ibid.*, p. 84.

22. *Ibid.*, p. 145.

23. *Ibid.*, p. 146.

24. *Ibid.*, p. 146.

25. *Ibid.*, p. 150.

26. *Ibid.*, p. 150.

27. Robert Engler, *The Politics of Oil* (Chicago: University of Chicago Press, 1961. Phoenix [paperback] edition, 1967). Citation, p. 1, Phoenix edition.

28. *Ibid.*, p. 488.

29. *Ibid.*, p. 488.

30. See Grant McConnell, *Private Power and American Democracy* (New York: Knopf, 1966), especially Chapter 5, "Private Government," pp. 119–154.

31. *Ibid.*, p. 154.

32. On this point, see Truman, *op. cit.*, pp. 532–533.

33. C. Wright Mills, *The Power Elite* (New York: Oxford University Press, 1956. Galaxy [paperback] edition, 1959).

34. *Ibid.*, Chapter 12, "The Power Elite," pp. 269–297, Galaxy edition.

35. *Ibid.*, p. 242.

36. *Ibid.*, p. 242.

37. *Ibid.*, p. 259.

38. *Ibid.*, pp. 259–260.

39. *Ibid.*, p. 260.

40. *Ibid.*, p. 262.

41. *Ibid.*, p. 262.

42. *Ibid.*, p. 268.

43. Peter Bachrach, *The Theory of Democratic Elitism* (Boston: Little, Brown, 1967), p. 37. See also, Wallace Sayre and Herbert Kaufman,

Governing New York City (New York: Russell Sage Foundation, 1960), pp. 719–720.

44. Theodore J. Lowi, *The End of Liberalism* (New York: W. W. Norton, 1969).

45. *Ibid.*, p. 29.

46. *Ibid.*, p. 29.

47. *Ibid.*, p. 29.

48. *Ibid.*, p. 288.

49. *Ibid.*, p. 288.

50. *Ibid.*, p. 289.

51. *Ibid.*, p. 291.

52. *Ibid.*, p. 294.

53. *Ibid.*, p. 295.

54. *Ibid.*, p. 296.

55. *Ibid.*, pp. 297–314.

56. See especially, Bertram Gross, *The Legislative Struggle* (New York: McGraw-Hill, 1953).

57. William A. Coplin and Leonard Stitelman, *The American Constitutional Convention, A Simulation Exercise* (Chicago: Scientific Research Associates, 1969), p. 1. See also, William A. Coplin, *Simulation in the Study of Politics* (Chicago: Markham, 1968), and John Raser, *Simulation and Society* (Boston: Allyn and Bacon, 1969).

58. Coplin and Stitelman, *op. cit.*, p. 2.

59. See Marvin G. Weinbaum and Louis H. Gold, *Presidential Election: A Simulation with Readings* (New York: Holt, Rinehart, and Winston, 1969). The background information on simulation games is taken from a paper prepared by Marshall H. Whithed, "The Implementation of a Political Simulation: The Woodbury Model," for the April 24–26, 1969, meeting of the Midwest Political Science Association at Ann Arbor, Michigan.

60. The Woodbury Political Simulation is described in a mimeographed paper prepared by Marshall H. Whithed under the date of August, 1969. The description in the text is taken from that document. The De Kalb model, which grew out of the Woodbury one, is described by Marshall H. Whithed and Clifford N. Smith in a paper entitled "An Urban Political Simulation: The De Kalb Model," which was presented at the 1969 Institute of Electrical and Electronics Engineers Systems Science and Cybernetics Conference, Philadelphia, Pa., October, 1969.

61. See the paper by Frederick Hartwig, "The Use of Simulation Games in Undergraduate Teaching," (Schenectady, N.Y.: Union College, no date).

62. On the relationship of behavioralism to the more traditional approaches in political science, see Meehan, *op. cit.*, pp. 4–5, 162–163. See also, James C. Charlesworth, ed., *The Limits of Behavioralism in Political Science* (Philadelphia: The American Academy of Political and Social Science).

part three

OLD STYLE

POLITICS

5

Old Style

Politics:

I—Brokerage

Politics

Senator Plunkitt is a straight organization man. He believes in party government; he does not indulge in cant and hypocrisy and he is never afraid to say exactly what he thinks. He is a believer in thorough political organization and all-the-year-around work, and he holds to the doctrine that, in making appointments to office, party workers should be preferred if they are fitted to perform the duties of the office. Plunkitt is one of the veteran leaders of the organization; he has always been faithful and reliable, and he has performed valuable services for Tammany Hall.

Charles F. Murphy, onetime leader of Tammany Hall, in 1905.[1]

The preceding chapter examined the pluralistic model of American democracy, and suggested that the best application of the pluralistic model has been in the area of urban politics. The theoretical concern of Chapters 5 and 6 is to test the adequacy of the pluralistic model of urban politics. To this end Chapter 5 explores the application of the model to the past. Chapter 6 considers its contemporary applicability and speculates on its future usefulness. In evaluating the model from a theoretical point of view, two principal problems require attention. It is first necessary to determine under what conditions the pluralistic model did (or does) work. A second problem is to learn the extent to which such conditions prevail today and are likely to prevail in the near future.

From a more down-to-earth perspective, the focus in Chapter 5 is on the actual workings of the pluralist system of urban politics. In contrast, Chapter 6 is largely devoted to an evaluation of the system itself.

THE BROKERAGE STYLE

The traditional urban political system was—and where it survives—is characterized by a brokerage system of politics. In a manner somewhat akin to a commodities exchange, sales and purchases are handled by specialists operating under carefully drawn procedures. No one is required to engage in the acquisition, trading, or selling of the commodities. But if he chooses to do so, he places himself under the accepted rules and regulations of the exchange.

The so-called traders are also not equal in the resources at their disposal; some are more powerful than others. No matter how carefully the fact may be concealed by such phrases as "people's capitalism," the truth is that the ownership of the commodities is highly concentrated. A few people own a great deal, and many people individually own very little. In this the exchange may be fairly typical of other social organizations. Robert Michels' "iron law or oligarchy" applies to more than political parties. The great German sociologist formulated his "law" in 1911 in *Political Parties* in these words: "Who says organization says oligarchy."

In the brokerage system, the broker is a key figure. As a person who brings buyers and sellers together—for a fee—the broker is in a position to affect the play of the game in numerous ways. Without his presence, in fact, the game could not take place at all, for there would be no rules, simply the chaos of an Hobbesian jungle. Above all else, the broker endlessly supervises bargaining, trading, and negotiating, so that all parties may at least have the illusion that the best arrangement under the circumstances was consummated. The deals which are made—the decisions—come about not as the result of abstract appeals to justice or freedom but in response to the realities of the marketplace.

In its political manifestation, the brokerage system is built around a leader and his organization. Persons or interests desiring to arrange a political accommodation must do so through the cooperation, intervention, and assistance of the dominant political group. In working out a solution to a problem—for example, does a community group, a factory, or a school get the use of a particular piece of land?—the political organization provides the means and the milieu for the bargaining of the different interests to take place. There is a quid pro quo, a trade-off, as in the commodities exchange system.

Brokerage politics places a high premium on organization, as Charles F. Murphy rightly noted in his paean to Plunkitt. And, conversely, disloyalty to the organization is the cardinal sin. In Plunkitt's words: "There's no crime so mean as ingratitude in politics, but every great statesman from the beginnin' of the world has been up against it."[2]

In Plunkitt's time (1842–1924), the role of the political organization was quite clearly defined. Indeed, up to the outbreak of World War II, this role—even when deplored, as by the early 20th century upper-class Reformers—was well understood. Only in recent times has the position of the organization seemed ambiguous.

To this point in our discussion of the urban political organization, no mention has been made of the political party as such, and the omission is deliberate, because whether the particular urban system under study is partisan or nonpartisan in its electoral aspects is not very significant. Underlying this assertion are two basic considerations. In the first place, the core cities of the largest metropolitan areas tend to be overwhelmingly Democratic, and divisions inside core cities along party lines are simply not very important politically.[3] In contrast, the suburbs tend to register a high preference for Republicanism, although the distribution tends to be spotty and exceptions are numerous. Cleavages do occur, of course, in elections for city offices. But with respect to party, as Banfield and Wilson have pointed out, the cleavage is "artificially created" and ". . . cuts across all other cleavages and often supersedes them in importance."[4]

The second reason for emphasizing the urban political organization instead of the political party is the widespread acceptance of nonpartisan elections. It is estimated that about 60 percent of all cities are nonpartisan.[5] To this it must quickly be added that most of the largest cities (over 500,000 population) adhere to the practice of partisan elections. These are Baltimore, Buffalo, Chicago,[6] New York, New Orleans, Philadelphia, Pittsburgh, and St. Louis. Cities in this same population category which are nonpartisan are Boston, Cincinnati, Cleveland, Dallas, Detroit, Houston, Los Angeles, Milwaukee, San Antonio, San Diego, San Francisco, and Seattle.[7]

To say that a city holds nonpartisan elections for city offices may not reveal more than a fraction of the truth about the character of the city council. In Boston, for example, successful council candidates are almost always publicly identified as members of the Democratic party, as is the mayor. It is the electoral system, not the candidates or voters, which is nonpartisan. People do not change their stripes very easily; for instance, a Boston Democrat who casts his vote in a city election for a Democrat running on a nonpartisan ballot is more than likely to cast his vote for Democratic candidates on the partisan ballot used in choosing state legislators. What is important is not the presence or absence of a party label, but the strength, tenacity, and endurance of the dominant local political organization. In some cases, as in Boston, that organization is, of course, the local Democratic party operating on a nonpartisan ballot for local elections. In other cases, as in Cincinnati and other "reform" cities, the dominant local organization is really a locally-based political party. The City Charter Committee has no official relationship with either of the two major parties which dominate state and national elections in Ohio. Nonpartisanship, then, can mean a variety of things, depending on the political environment in which it occurs.

Although many dissimilarities exist in the political structure of urban America, some important similarities in the political systems of large cities have been noted by Edward C. Banfield.[8] Banfield in 1965 made a comparative study of the political systems in Atlanta, Boston, Detroit, El Paso, Los Angeles, Miami, Philadelphia, St. Louis, and Seattle. He found "several striking similarities" including "honesty," improved "quality" of government, "conservatism," ability to manage "conflicts," and the absence of "extremism."

What factors accounted for these similarities in the political systems of the large cities? Banfield suggested three considerations. First, there was the increasing professionalization of city employees.[9] Secondly, there was the separation which existed in most cases between the local political system and the state and national systems.[10] And lastly, and most importantly, there was the electoral process itself.[11] This process tended to create a situation where only two serious candidates opposed each other. Consequently, a contest to win the votes of a majority of the electorate developed. As in any two-party system the result was a politics of relative moderation. The support for this kind of political structure came from coalitions of moderates.

THE TWO SUBDIVISIONS OF BROKERAGE POLITICS

The old style, or brokerage, politics has two general subdivisions—the "machine" type and the "reform" type. Although they began in different time-periods, they both continue to exist. In any particular community, elements of both types may persist side by side, although in most cases one or the other category is usually dominant.

It is the machine type which has, historically, attracted the greater amount of public attention—for obvious reasons. From the founding of the first New York Society of Tammany in 1785 until the present, the tactics, antics, and personalities of the Democracy of New York have delighted journalists, scholars, and presumably the voting public. Even the Indian symbolism of the Society—a Grand Sachem, twelve lesser Sachems, the use of an Indian calendar in correspondence—pleased an electorate in search of political trimmings in a drab, republican country.

Starting as a patriotic society, Tammany rapidly developed into a private political club. Toward the end of George Washington's Administration, it became the principal exponent in New York City of Jefferson's doctrines. Under the leadership of Aaron Burr, the first real leader of the Society, the Republicans (Jeffersonians) carried New York State in 1800. By 1815, Tammany obtained complete control of the state, as well as of the city.[12]

The Golden Age of Tammany took place following the Civil War, when it was under the leadership of William M. Tweed. The son of a prosperous chairmaker, Tweed received a fair education for the times. He entered politics as a volunteer fireman, became better known, and then joined in ward politics. Working his way up in the Democratic organization, Tweed became a Sachem of the Tammany Society and in 1857 was elected to the New York County Board of Supervisors. He then sold his chairmaking business and devoted his full time to politics.

In 1859 the first Tweed Ring, based on the Supervisors, was founded for the purpose of controlling for the Democrats the appointment of inspectors of elections. Subsequently, the Tweed Ring enlarged its sphere of operations. In 1861 Tweed was elected chairman of the Tammany General Committee. Shortly thereafter, he was chosen Grand Sachem, and became known as "the boss." In 1863, he became Deputy Street Commissioner, a post which permitted him to recruit thousands of followers. In 1868, he became a state senator, a position which made it possible to give personal supervision to the operations of the state legislature in Albany. Tweed's real estate holdings—by 1869—had risen from zero to a total value of $12 million. The next year Tweed secured from the legislature a new charter for New York City. Reported to have cost around a million dollars in bribes, the charter was worth every

penny: it relieved the ring of accountability to any state governmental authority.

By 1870 the fortunes of the Tweed Ring were on the decline. The
immediate causes of the exposure of the operations of the Tweed
Ring were accidental. In December, 1870, Watson, one of the chiefs
of the Finance Department, was fatally injured in a sleigh-riding
accident. He was succeeded by a new man, and in the subsequent
job turn-overs Matthew J. O'Rourke became County bookkeeper.
O'Rourke amassed considerable evidence of fraud and presented
his evidence in the summer of 1871 to the *New York Times*. The
charges were printed in full, and the collapse of the Ring was under
way.

Tweed himself was arrested and held on $1 million bail. After
being indicted for a felony, he was removed as Grand Sachem. In
November, 1873, he was found guilty on three-fourths of 120
counts, and sentenced to Blackwell's Island. After a year's imprisonment, he was released because of a legal technicality. He was
promptly tried again, but managed to escape while on a visit from
the penitentiary. For two days he hid in disguise in New Jersey and
later he reached Florida, from where he escaped to Cuba in a fish-
ing smack, and finally to Spain.

But it was not possible for Tweed to escape New York justice. Upon the request of the United States Secretary of State,
Hamilton Fish, Tweed was arrested by Spanish authorities and
returned to the United States on the man-of-war *Franklin*. Sent
to the Ludlow Street jail, he occupied the warden's parlor at the
cost of $75 per week. While dying, he said to the matron's
daughter: "Mary, I have tried to do good to everybody, and if I
have not, it is not my fault. I am ready to die, and I know God
will receive me." His hearse was followed by only eight carriages
—a decidedly unimpressive number. The remaining members
of the Ring fled the country, or were imprisoned. It is estimated
that the total plunderings of the Ring amounted to about $200
million.

As the archetype of the classical machine, the Tammany Society
was imitated in large cities throughout the country. But toward the
end of the 19th century, the machine as such came under increasing
attack from two different influences. There was—as we shall see—
a concerted effort by the Reformers to take politics out of municipal
government. Secondly, there was an effort to bolster city government through devices like merit civil service, professionalization,

and the impartial administration of the law, all of which weakened the machine.

The classical machine of the 19th century is now dead, but machine-type politics is still very much alive. It has, in fact, been remarkably persistent. In the recent past—the period since World War II—the machine type of political organization has lost a good deal of ground. But as Mark Twain is reported to have remarked at his own death, "the whole matter was greatly exaggerated."

A high peak in the mortality rate of traditional machines occurred during the years 1947–51. On June 17, 1947, Frank Hague resigned as mayor of Jersey City. His successor and nephew, Frank Hague Eggers, was defeated in the election of May 10, 1949, by a rival ticket headed by John V. Kenny. In November, 1949, City Clerk John B. Hynes defeated James M. Curley in a bitter battle for the Boston mayoralty. The Republicans lost Philadelphia in the 1950 gubernatorial race by 75,000. In the next year they lost control of the city itself, as the Democratic candidate for mayor of Philadelphia, Joseph S. Clark, Jr., won by more than 100,000 votes. The Democratic Party lost the New York City contest for mayor in 1950 to Vincent Impellitteri, an Independent. All in all, it was a bad season for the political machine.

The ouster of the McFeely organization in Hoboken, N.J. in 1947 illustrates the mood of the period. Located across from lower Manhattan on the New Jersey side of the Hudson River, Hoboken in 1947 was a city with a dimly romantic past and a depressing present. It was characterized by wharves, factories, warehouses, bookie parlors, 254 bars, and bleak blocks of ancient brown-stone houses. Some 50,000 people lived in its one-square mile.

For 22 years Bernard McFeely had been undisputed boss of the city. The son of a butcher, he had quit school at the age of nine. He had driven a dump wagon, and later left that job for ward politics. After becoming top man in the Democratic organization, McFeely made his brother Edward chief of police and his nephew Thomas superintendent of schools. At one time 79 McFeelys were on the city payrolls.

There was nothing very complicated about McFeely's methods. Prior to the McFeely reign, the city paid $36,000 a year for garbage disposal. Under the new regime the McFeely Contracting Company was awarded the business and the annual price rose to $112,000. Contractors found they could not get permits unless the Company did their hauling for them. An old Sunday-closing law was enforced against theater-owners, unless they contributed $600 a year to the organization. For saloon-owners, the price of staying in business was $200. On the average, the machine collected $100,000 a year and spent $15,000 on elections. McFeely himself handled the funds. Although his salary never topped $5,000, his wealth in 1947 was estimated at $3 million.

In addition to fees assessed against various kinds of businessmen, the machine exacted 3 percent salary kickbacks from city employees. The machine received the cooperation of the AFL leaders who controlled the votes of dock workers. There was a working alliance with Jersey City's Mayor Hague.

Despite all of this activity, prosperity seemed to bypass Hoboken during the McFeely years. The population fell by one-fifth, taxes soared, and no outsider prophesied a happy future for the city. Unlike most bosses, McFeely himself staged no circuses. Nor did he make any public speeches—his grammar was simply too atrocious. A bachelor, he lived in a frame house across from an automobile scrap yard. He never went to Florida, or to Europe, or to the horse races. He hated Italians (persons of Italian ancestry comprised 65 percent of the population), and did his best to make their lives miserable.

On May 13, 1947, a Reform ticket defeated the organization. There were three principal factors which caused the downfall. The state, for the first time in Hoboken's history, had installed and actually used voting machines. Some policemen, who were World War II veterans, opposed the machine in a referendum, and they were successful. Veterans and others simply got out the anti-McFeely vote. The magnitude of the upset was shown in the composition of the new city commission: 3 persons of Italian descent; 1 Irish policeman whom McFeely had persecuted; 1 CIO union leader. What took place in Hoboken also occurred, in less dramatic fashion, in other cities across the nation—it was a period of general municipal housecleaning.[13]

The idea that an entrenched in-group ought eventually to be thrown out of office and replaced by an out-group—the principle of "throw the rascals out"—is, of course, as old as American city politics. Often the principle is accorded more recognition by out-of-power partisan candidates than it is by the electorate. In the case of Philadelphia, for instance, the Republican organization controlled the city for an uninterrupted period of 68 years. The GOP dominance was ended only in 1951. For the last generation the Demo-cratic organization has been in control.

In rotations of this sort, the shift of power was, and was intended to be, from the hands of one party organization to those of its rival. It remained for the Reformers to introduce the concept that politics as such should be removed from municipal government. The Re-formers left a very marked imprint on the structure of American city governments, although they were less successful in changing the behavior of the electorate. Yet enough of their work was suffi-ciently enduring so that one may speak of the Reform type of poli-tics as the alternative to the more widely publicized machine type. Both types may currently be observed in operation in urban America. Together the machine type and the Reform type form a type of sub-classification under brokerage—or old style—politics.

The Reform movement coincided with and grew out of the loss of political power by the old elite which had controlled northern cities prior to the Civil War.[14] Outgunned by the new dominant class of businessmen and entrepreneurs who wanted special favors from local government, outvoted by the new immigrant groups, and outraged by the newly formed political machines, the old elite retreated to the community service organization. This kind of or-ganization included hospitals, charitable groups, and civic-reform associations. Today it includes foundations. From this strong point it launched its appeals for municipal reform, and called for a politics serving the public or general interest instead of the various private interests.

In calling for a politics of the public interest, the Reformers as-sumed that the task of local government was basically a technical matter; for example, the best informed citizens would establish policy, while qualified technicians would carry out its administra-tion. Because the Reformers concentrated on fundamentals, politi-cal parties were held to be both superfluous and evil, at least, for municipal government. For the same reason, it was felt that group competition, on the part of interest groups, should be held to an absolute minimum. The principal strategy was to put into office "those best qualified to serve."

To the Reformers, the programs of the National Municipal League—discussed later in this chapter—served as models. With its emphasis on nonpartisan elections, the city manager plan, the short ballot, the League set patterns and standards which were avidly followed wherever the Reformers could set the style of local government. They were notably successful in smaller, middle-sized cities. While the larger cities adopted features from the municipal program of the League, these same cities never accepted the total program.

In their evaluation of the Reform movement, Banfield and Wilson were struck by several "anomalies":

1) ". . . although reformers have lost most of their battles for power, they have in the main won their war for the adoption of particular measures of structural and other change."[15] All cities have adopted a good deal of the reform program.

2) ". . . although reform has won its war, victory has not yielded the fruits for which the reformers fought."[16] The Reformers expected to gain efficiency and to eliminate corruption. In general, modern city governments *are* a good deal more efficient than they used to be. At the same time, they continue to be plagued with repeated scandals over housing contracts, welfare and poverty programs, and gambling operations. In addition, the elimination of patronage positions has had unanticipated results. In Philadelphia, as a case in point, the Reform Democratic officials—Joseph Clark and Richardson Dilworth—soon found they needed patronage in order to keep their own organization together. In this they were not very much different from the Republicans whom they ousted in 1951.

3) "Although reform measures have not produced the effects that the reformers have anticipated (and have indeed often produced opposite ones), those desired effects are being produced by other causes."[17] That city government is much more honest than it was a generation ago is not an achievement of the Reformers. As Banfield and Wilson see it, the measures and improvements that have occurred "are both effects of a common cause: the steady diffusion in our culture of the political ideal of the Anglo-Saxon Protestant middle-class political ethos."[18] This is a way of saying that changes in municipal government have come about because of changes in the political culture.

In an absolute sense, both reform and machine classifications of politics should be regarded as "pure" or "ideal" types. Winnetka, Illinois and Scarsdale, New York may indeed be "pure" types of reform politics, but they are exceptional. At the same time, Hoboken and Chester (Pennsylvania) may have been brilliant examples of the machine type. But, again, they are unusual in this respect. For the most part, the cities of America include elements of both political types, yet the blend is rarely perfect; one type usually is dominant and the other correspondingly subordinate. In the Philadelphia of Mayor James H. J. Tate, the style of government was distinctly of the machine type, as is also the case in the Chicago of Mayor Richard J. Daley. The government of New York City in the Wagner era emphasized machine politics, while the second administration of John Lindsay (elected as a Liberal) stressed the Reform style. Highly decentralized Los Angeles is, in the ordinary sense, hardly governed at all. Despite the Reform-type rhetoric of Mayor Samuel W. Yorty, the city cannot be included in the Reform camp. Yet Los Angeles has adopted, of course, many elements first proposed in the golden age of the Reformers. In short, the major American cities represent in practice a mélange of machine-type and of Reform-type politics.

The policy out-put seems to be independent of the type of politics which is dominant; since both types, in actual operation, are characterized by a system of brokerage politics. And brokerage politics—in relation to the urban problems which require attention —is Old Style.

THE MACHINE TYPE: NATURE, FUNCTIONS, SOCIAL BASE

The traditional urban political machine has been studied in depth, and from the wealth of studies some general observations as to its nature have emerged. Of all of the investigations undertaken during the last three decades, one of the very best remains Dayton D. McKean's 1940 appraisal of the Hague organization in Jersey City.[19] Because the main points developed by McKean have a wide applicability, they are cited with the understanding that what was true of the Hague machine in its heyday is more or less typical of the style of machines in general.

For the Hague organization, the cardinal tenet was self-interest. What was good for the organization was assumed to be good for Jersey City, Hudson County, New Jersey, and, ultimately, the nation. With reference to Mayor Hague, McKean states: "The central principal of his thinking is that what benefits the political organization is desirable and therefore right; what damages it is undesirable and therefore wrong."[20] A philosophy of this sort has the virtue of making it quite simple to establish operational priorities. Moral considerations that might trouble some people can be dismissed—within the Hague frame of reference—as being irrelevant.

In line with this conviction, decision-making in the Hague machine was confined to the uppermost echelon. The concept of grass-roots democracy in the sense of ideas flowing upward for execution and implementation was alien to the mayor's thinking. Writes McKean: "The nature of political leadership, as he [Hague] conceives it, leaves little room for the formation of policy anywhere except at the top of the organization; while the party workers keep the citizens in line by all the variety of means at the disposal of a well-built machine, the leader decides what is good for the people."[21]

Had he been aware of the Hague organization, the great German sociologist Max Weber would have admired its dedication to the bureaucratic principles of discipline, hierarchy, and line of command. City commissioners or legislators under Hague's control were expected to vote as they were instructed and to present a united front toward the outside world.[22] "Complete obedience is necessary from the bottom to the top; officials are not supposed to have ideas on public policies, but to take orders."[23] Successful though this tactic was in producing solidarity in the ranks of the organization, it failed lamentably to produce strong individuals who could appeal to voters in other sections of New Jersey.

So far as spoils, patronage, and taxes were concerned, Mayor Hague was consistent with his basic principles. Patronage appointments and spoils were considered fundamental facts of political life. It should be noted, however, that the machine had its puritanical side: brothels were not tolerated in Jersey City, nor was burlesque. But the city was generally considered to be the national headquarters for horse-racing gambling.[24] On taxes, McKean notes, the Hague attitude was straight-forward. "The Mayor's position on the question of taxes is clear and consistent. He favors a continually increasing public revenue."[25] How the funds were raised did not matter to the mayor.[26]

Do the leaders of political machines have any characteristics in common other than political success? This question was posed by J. T. Salter in his 1935 study of the Republican organization—then dominant—in Philadelphia. After noting that no two politicians are alike, Salter goes on to list certain attributes of the successful ones. They are those who "(1) stick everlastingly at it, (2) know that the kingdom of heaven is taken by violence, (3) live decades among their people and learn to judge their wants, (4) have a flair for getting along with people, (5) have problem-solving ability, and (6) understand that politics is the science of the possible."[27] Surely George Washington Plunkitt would have agreed!

If machines performed no function other than to enrich themselves, it seems unlikely that they would have remained for so long on the political scene. In fact, such organizations serve a variety of purposes which society—or some elements of society—want fulfilled. It has long been realized that the boss fulfills the function of providing some measure of centralized direction in the largely decentralized administration of American municipalites. Given the vast formal dispersion of power among the mayor, the council, scores of boards and agencies, some one has got to serve as a unifying force. When the official apparatus of government could not so operate, it became the historical function of the boss to provide the needed centralized leadership. Even the rise of strong-mayor local governments has not obviated the need for unofficial methods of bringing about centralized direction. In many cases, the mayor has taken on this function—not because of his position as mayor, but because of his additional strength as "boss." The power of Mayor Richard J. Daley in Chicago, for instance, rests both on his legal base as mayor, and even more importantly, on his extra-legal base as party chief. In combination, these bases of support make it possible for Daley to control the Chicago municipal government with a firm hand.

But machines also fulfill social functions that other agencies in society tend to neglect. Even where the services provided by the machine and by other agencies may be identical—as in certain types of welfare referral—the machine often provides its services in a more satisfactory manner. For the subgroup receiving these services, this difference in style or manner may be all-important. In his famous essay on the functions of political machines, the sociologist Robert K. Merton observed that the politician may be closer to understanding the needs and doing something about them than the "impersonal, professionalized, socially distant and legally constrained welfare worker."[28]

One might, of course, choose another illustration to make the same point. What Merton is emphasizing is that the "deprived classes" constitute one subgroup "for whom the political machine satisfied wants not adequately satisfied in the same fashion by the legitimate social structure."[29]

A second subgroup identified by Merton is that of "business." Here the political organization provides "those political privileges which entail immediate economic gains."[30] Big businesses seek, of course, political dispensations which will enable them to increase their profits. The machine provides a degree of economic security. If guarantees needed to limit competition and maximize profits cannot be obtained through the conventional channels, then they are obtained through the efforts of the machine.

A third subgroup whose needs may be met by the machine consists of those whose social mobility has been blocked. For such persons the machine provides a means for getting ahead which would otherwise not exist. One thinks immediately of Irish and other immigrant groups. Denied access to satisfactory niches in the economic and social structure, they turned to politics, and were notably successful. Other "disadvantaged" groups would include the professional criminal. Viewed in functional terms, the racketeer or gambler ". . . has basic similarities of organization, demands and operation to the subgroup of the industrialist, man of business or speculator."[31] From the economic point of view, "legitimate" and "illegitimate" businesses are about the same. "Both are in some degree concerned with the provision of goods and services for which there is an economic demand."[32] For both groups, the function of the machine is to prevent undue interference from the government.[33]

Salter, in his Philadelphia study already referred to, also stresses the service nature of the machine. The party organization resolves such "fellow-creature wants" as jobs, food, and taxes.[34] Even if the machine of today is of less importance in these areas than in Salter's time, Salter's conclusion remains valid: "The party is, basically, an intermediary between the citizen and the state."[35] The party is a service institution, ". . . and service means favors."[36]

Besides the sociological functions noted by Merton and the service functions underscored by Salter, a third type of function has been stressed by Harold F. Gosnell. After a careful study of Chicago politics from the late 1920's to the mid-1930's, Gosnell was struck by the conciliating role of the Democratic machine. He asserts: "Some of the submerged groups may not be so appreciative; but the fact remains that during the years 1930–36 the city was comparatively free from violent labor disputes, hunger riots, and class warfare."[37] While Chicago had plenty of troubles during the great economic crisis of the period under study, "On the credit side of the ledger should be placed the success of the bosses in softening class conflicts."[38]

The essential mass base of the traditional machine was the immigrant population. The reason is that the machine rendered certain services which an immigrant clientele considered important. In exchange for these services, this clientele gave its electoral support to the organization. So long as immigration was a continuing process, it was possible for the machine to replenish its strength indefinitely. With the virtual cessation of large-scale European immigration during the 1920's, this source of machine strength gradually dried up. ". . . it was the succeeding waves of immigrants that gave the urban political organizations the manipulable mass bases without which they could not have functioned as they did," notes Elmer E. Cornwell, Jr.[39] But since the 20's there have been two additional forms of immigration: Negroes from the rural south and Puerto Ricans have moved in a steady stream to northern and western population centers. To this extent the immigrant base for urban organizations continues to renew itself.

When viewed through a socio-economic lens, the traditional machine appears as a lower-class based organization. It is from this class that its principal support has always come. This is the case today in those cities such as Philadelphia and Chicago where machine-type politics remains the norm. The class base of this type of politics is also evident from the attitude of machine supporters toward civic reform movements. Banfield and Wilson, after a careful survey of the literature, concluded that middle-class culture is fundamentally opposed to machine politics. At the same time, there is a high correlation between "lower class immigrant culture" and the machine's "private-regarding" objectives.[40] To put the matter differently, machine-type politics thrives in a lower-class milieu, while Reform-type politics flourishes in a middle-class environment. Given this condition, one would expect changes in the type of politics as the socio-economic culture undergoes change.

THE REFORM TYPE: NATURE, FUNCTIONS, SOCIAL BASE

In order to realize their ideals of good government, the civic reformers supported certain concrete measures. These included the initiative, referendum, and recall; the direct primary and proportional representation; nonpartisan municipal elections held in odd-numbered years; the council-manager form of government; and at-large elections. The objective of these proposals was to destroy the political machines and "return" governing power more directly to the people.[41]

It was the National Municipal League, founded in 1894, which served as the intellectual center for the Reform movement. The League adopted its first municipal program in 1900. In its current version, this program may be found in the latest (1941) revision of the Model City Charter. The Charter continues to stress the council-manager form of municipal government, nonpartisanship, and election by proportional representation.[42]

Even though the Reformers emphasized certain common objectives, the movement itself has assumed several different forms. James Q. Wilson has identified five types of reform movements: citizens' associations, candidate screening committees, independent local parties, blue ribbon leadership factions, and intraparty reform clubs.[43] A citizens' association usually operates outside the party structure. It performs such functions as reviewing the record of elected officials and making recommendations regarding expenditures and taxes. The League of Women Voters is an illustration. Candidate screening committees, prominent in certain nonpartisan cities, examine prospective candidates, make recommendations, and raise funds for the persons they endorse.

On occasion reform movements assume the form of an independent local party. One such type of party is the Fusion party which helped elect mayors of New York City in 1901, 1913, and 1933. This party represented a temporary alliance with the Republicans. A more continuing type of local party is the independent good government organization, of which one of the most famous examples is the City Charter Committee in Cincinnati. In every sense this is a permanent, local party.

A "blue ribbon" leadership faction sometimes emerges when a reform movement occurs within the ranks of a major party. Here the emphasis is on purging the existing party leadership. In such cases, the objective is to oust machine-oriented leaders and to replace them with a reform-oriented elite. Often there is a very pronounced class difference between the two contending factions. The Clark-Dilworth seizure of power in the Democratic party in Philadelphia during the early 1950's illustrates the blue ribbon type of reform.

Finally, there is the intraparty reform club. Members of these clubs consider themselves "amateurs" when compared to the professional politicians. Reform clubs tend to be issue-oriented and, relative to the regular organizations, somewhat ideological. Reform Democratic clubs are scattered throughout the Upper West Side of Manhattan and in Greenwich Village in New York City. They also exist in other big northern and midwestern cities.[44]

Unless one has had personal involvement in Reform politics, it is difficult to appreciate the fervor the movement generates. In her excellent case study of Toledo, Jean L. Stinchcombe recaptures the dedication of Reform politics in that city during the last seventy years. Under such colorful figures as Samuel M. "Golden Rule" Jones and Brand Whitlock, the Reformers took control of Toledo early in the century. In spite of continuing challenges, the movement has succeeded in dominating Toledo municipal politics until the present time.[45] In the process—it must be added—the original enthusiasm of the Reformers has given way to a good deal of weariness and lassitude. But the *forms* devised by the movement remain embedded in municipal politics and government.

In Toledo—and elsewhere—one of the lasting contributions of the Reform movement was nonpartisanship. Thomas R. Dye notes that nearly ". . . two-thirds of America's cities use the nonpartisan ballot to elect local officials."[46] Nonpartisan local elections are held in large as well as smaller cities. In the former category are found Boston, Chicago, Cincinnati, Cleveland, Detroit, Los Angeles, Milwaukee, San Francisco, and Seattle. There appear to be several distinct types of political systems in the various nonpartisan cities. In one type, for example, the parties operate quite openly with the exception that party designations do not appear on the ballot. Chicago is an illustration. In another type of local political system, the parties disguise themselves behind other formal organizations. Where this occurs—as in Detroit or Dallas—no one is deluded by the deception. In the smaller cities, there tends to be a third type of nonpartisanship: the parties play no role at all in local contests.[47]

Political scientists have long been interested in the effects of nonpartisanship on the vitality of the political parties. While some consequences have been found, it is difficult to establish firm general relationships. In some cities, nonpartisanship does not seem to have affected the vitality of party politics—Boston, Chicago, and Detroit are examples. In other cities—such as Toledo—the effect seems to have been the reverse. Given the present state of information on the subject, it is necessary to examine a particular city over time in an effort to judge the relationship. The general belief, of course, is that, all things being equal, nonpartisanship ought to weaken the local base of the national and state party organizations. But the caveat is an important one, as the experience of Cincinnati and other strongly partisan cities (in national and state elections) shows.

There is a good deal of hard evidence, and therefore more agreement, as to the social base of the Reform movement as a whole. One careful student of municipal politics, Duane Lockard, has concluded: "Efforts to initiate or to maintain 'nonpolitical' operations in municipal government tend to divide communities along class-status lines with upper-class elements favoring and lower-class elements opposing these procedures."[48] But a problem arises. If there are more lower-class than upper-class voters, why have the cities adopted so many elements of the Reform program supported by the upper-class? Lockard's answer is that a much higher proportion of upper-class voters goes to the polls in all elections, including referenda. Thus, the strength of the upper-class group proportionately is magnified.[49]

As has been emphasized in this analysis, the Reform movement was highly successful in getting many of its specific proposals accepted by municipal governments. But what have been the general consequences in terms of public policy? This is, after all, the substantive result—the pay-off—that the Reformers wished to achieve.

In an effort to come to grips with this question, Robert L. Lineberry and Edmund P. Fowler made a careful study of spending and taxing in 200 American cities. They found that reformed cities do, in fact, tend to spend less and to tax less than unreformed municipalities. Even more significant was the finding regarding the responsiveness of the two kinds of cities to the composition of their populations: "the more reformed the city, the less responsive it is to socio-economic cleavages in its political decision-making."[50] Reformed cities are relatively unresponsive in their tax and spending policies to distinctions in income, education, and ethnic characteristics of their populations. In contrast, the unreformed cities take these factors into account when arriving at such decisions. Another way of looking at this is to note that reformism tends to diminish the impact of ethnicity, education, home ownership, and religion in city politics. Unreformed cities (those with mayor-council governments, partisan elections, ward as opposed to at-large constituencies) reflect in their public policies a more pronounced response to socio-economic divisions.[51]

In her study of Toledo, Jean Stinchcombe was able to test certain hypotheses about reform politics against the actual record. She had posited the hypothesis that the "compatability of reform institutions with middle-class civic ideals would encourage participation by business leaders."[52] But this proved to be false. In actual fact, "The community participation of executives is confined to good works and isolated issues of direct concern to business."[53]

Another hypothesis tested in the Toledo study was that the reform movement would enhance the influence and interests of business and middle-class groups at the expense of lower-class and minority groups. However, "This hypothesis is not completely true. Although the role of lower-income groups has been restricted, the participation of other groups has not increased."[54]

Finally, Mrs. Stinchcombe weighs the values of reform against the needs of Toledo, and finds an unbridgeable chasm between the two.[55] "The values of reform," she declares, "are in fact antithetical to the character of the large industrial city."[56] Abstract reform ideals are of little use when it comes to resolving such issues as racial discrimination in education, housing, and employment. Toledo does not have a political machine, but neither does it have effective political leadership. "Toledo's experience," she concludes, "suggests that the ethos and institutions of reform can have debilitating consequences in populous, industrial cities."[57]

More studies of the Toledo kind are needed in order to develop a body of high-level generalizations applicable across the country. But it is clear that the Reform-type of politics has not turned out to be the panacea its founders had expected. Nor have the structural changes engineered by the Reformers brought about any basic changes in the rules of the game.

OPERATIONS OF BROKERAGE POLITICAL ORGANIZATIONS

In the course of their continuing operations, political organizations—whether of the machine or of the Reform type—have three guiding principles. The degree to which this observance is deliberate is a matter for conjecture, but the principles themselves are more or less beyond debate, for they are an essential part of the rules of the game or system in which the organization functions.

The first principle is that the organization responds to demands made on it in proportion to the relative strength of these demands. Since the resources available to a municipal government almost always are less than the demands presented to it, some method must be devised for choosing one option over another. Besides the problem of supply vs. demand there is the added factor that rival groups often each claim exclusive rights—monetary and otherwise —in the same area. For example, several community groups may be in contention for recognition as the exclusive bargaining agent in a given section of the city. In such cases, the municipal authorities must decide not only whether the function itself deserves public support, but also which group should receive the funds and authority, if they are in fact granted.

As a system, this mode of decision-making is apparently quite active. Even the most casual newspaper reader can hardly fail to be impressed by the clamor with which claims are put forward by the leading organized interests in his community. The presentation of demands and the mustering of support for them comprise the active side of the picture. Yet, on inspection, there is also a decidedly passive side: it is evident in the role of the political organization (i.e., the authorities), who tend to sit back and adopt the stance of a referee or mediator. Preferably, the interests themselves work out a compromise, which can be ratified by the organization in the name of a "consensus."

In the absence of this form of agreement, the organization has certain options. In the unlikely event that there is a perfect stalemate, the authorities can presumably elect to do nothing. But since in the real world such a perfect balancing of forces would be unusual, the organization more probably would decide to go along with the interest with the broadest and most intensive support. Thus, in brokerage politics, demands work their way up the ladder of political attention, and only those which survive in the elimination contest are recognized as entitled to support. In the process the organization does not really lead; it acts as a moderator, or broker.

A second leading principle of brokerage political organizations is that they tend to concentrate on the solution of problems which are essentially administrative in nature. On this point some elaboration may be in order. Political organizations do, of course, give attention, from time to time, to great questions of public policy. But these are issues which, on the whole, they prefer to avoid. The reason is that such decision-making is apt to be divisive and, hence, costly to the organization in terms of electoral support. But organizations are usually quick to react to problems involving matters of personnel and patronage. What is at stake here is the party apparatus itself. Personnel management is therefore a top priority of the organization.

As an illustration, consider the situation in Philadelphia during February, 1970. After the unexpected resignation of Streets Commissioner David Smallwood, Mayor James H. J. Tate appointed a police official, Chief Inspector Joseph F. Halferty, as his successor. This appointment was immediately followed by a series of unofficial slow-downs by the sanitation workers, nearly all of whom were Black. As a result, trash collection in the city fell seriously behind schedule, and the possibility of a health emergency loomed. It was the mayor's position that he could name whomever he pleased—in this case an Irish police official who had served the city faithfully for many years—to the streets commissioner post. It was the preference of the sanitation men, led by Sanitation Local 427, State, County, and Municipal Workers (AFL-CIO) that a Negro drawn from their own ranks should occupy the job. It was also asserted by the union that it would be offensive to the sensibility of the Black workingmen to come under the authority of a former policeman. But the union men were alternatively prepared to accept a "qualified engineer" as their superior.

While the fracas was at its height, Philadelphia was confronted by the very real threat that its public and parochial schools were facing imminent bankruptcy. Urban renewal had largely come to a halt. The streets were characterized by a record number of deep and dangerous potholes. Gang warfare among juvenile groups continued. The school construction program was cut back and virtually abandoned. The city's hospitals faced a financial crisis. Despite all this, the Democratic organization and Mayor Tate concentrated on the solution to the personnel situation created by the resignation of Smallwood. No issue, large or small, was permitted to interfere with their most intensive concentration on this question. In the discussions, and in the columns of newsprint, no one bothered to raise the simple question as to whether Halferty was qualified for the streets commissioner post. In fact, no one raised the question as to whether there were any merit-type qualifications for the job at all.

This predominant issue of Philadelphia Democratic politics was solved by the resignation of Halferty on February 25, 1970. Mayor Tate, in announcing the resignation, said that it had taken place at the request of Halferty. The ex-inspector had held his new position for ten days. The union had won a smashing victory.[58]

The third guiding principle in brokerage politics is that the sphere of governmental activity should be limited. Within the sphere itself, there may be and often is a high level of action. But this action is confined to the very narrowly defined area of what is considered proper for municipal governments to do. As a consequence, brokerage political organizations place great importance on the private sector of the community.

At first glance it may seem strange that a political organization would voluntarily agree that the area reserved to the public sector of the community should be restricted. For the self-interest of the dominant organization would appear to lie in the direction of increasing the governmental sphere. Socialism—or government ownership—would then be a logical demand of local organizations. With his customary clarity, George Washington Plunkitt put the case this way: "I am for municipal ownership on one condition: that the civil service law be repealed. It's a grand idea—the city ownin' the railroads, the gas works and all that. Just see how many thousands of new places there would be for the workers in Tammany! Why, there would be almost enough to go around, if no civil service law stood in the way. My plan is this: first get rid of that infamous law, and then go ahead and by degrees get municipal ownership."[59]

As it turned out, the voters of New York City were not disposed to pursue their love affair with Tammany to the point where that organization took over the entire regional economy. But the Society had other ways of maintaining itself, even in temporary periods of great adversity. In the election of 1901, the Reform candidate Seth Low defeated the Democrats, who presumably lost most of their traditional patronage. This was a hard but by no means a fatal rebuff.

Plunkitt explained: "I acknowledge that you can't keep an organization together without patronage. Men ain't in politics for nothin'. They want to get somethin' out of it.

"But there is more than one kind of patronage. We lost the public kind, or a greater part of it, in 1901, but Tammany has an immense private patronage that keeps things goin' when it gets a setback at the polls.

"Take me, for instance. When Low came in, some of my men lost public jobs, but I fixed them all right. I don't know how many jobs I got for them on the surface and elevated railroads—several hundred.

"I placed a lot more on public works done by contractors, and no Tammany man goes hungry in my district."[60]

It is obviously very advantageous to the organization to control the kind of private patronage which Plunkitt so engagingly describes. But this does not answer the broader question as to why municipal governments in very extensive areas of community concern utilize the services of private agencies to perform public tasks. In New York City, for example, it has been customary for the city (and the state) to finance religiously affiliated organizations in the field of child adoption. The operations are kept in private hands, but the funds come mostly from the public treasury. In very many areas of social welfare this practice is followed throughout the country.

To explain why the Americans have adopted this particular amalgam of public and private interests would require a lengthy excursion into cultural history. But the prevalence of this practice has had the effect of limiting the direct operations which political organizations can undertake.

PSYCHOLOGICAL PERSPECTIVES OF THESE ORGANIZATIONS

The psychological outlook of brokerage organizations is another factor which both defines and limits their role. Though at times the traditional organization might seem to reflect a petty bourgeois bias, this is not really a very accurate description. "Petty bourgeois" is more than a term of stratification in the social system; it also implies an inherent and petty conservatism which does an injustice to the more flamboyant and successful American machines. In any event, the term has the drawback of Marxist origin in a country which goes to great lengths to avoid Marxist terminology.

It is more accurate, under American conditions, to regard the brokerage political organization as possessing a trade-union mentality. The parallels are striking. Both the political organization and the labor union tend to have a cadre of permanent careerists. Both are dependent for success on the occasional support of a much larger group of followers. Both solicit sympathy and understanding from the general public. Yet the most notable similarity lies in their approach to proclaimed goals. Just as labor unions stress short-range objectives, so do political organizations emphasize the here and the now. Trade unionism in the United States means a "bread and butter" approach. In itself, this is not much different from the political concept of awarding a "slice of the pie" to an important interest. What the unions and the political organizations have in common are strictly limited objectives. Because of this, both the union and the organization are as nearly shorn of ideology as it is possible to be. They may cover their nudity with layers of pronouncements and declarations and demands, but underneath there exists stark ideological bareness.

Though the political organizations adopt a trade-union outlook in opting for limited objectives, they entertain a capitalistic perspective when it comes to economic matters. But it is a particular kind of capitalism which is involved. The machines do not especially favor the psychology of large-scale industry, though they may grant favors to such businesses. Nor do the political organizations share the point of view of the cooperative movement. What they do subscribe to is the individualistic economic outlook of middle-scale competitive enterprises, including both individual businesses and professionals who work for themselves. The ideal is the middle-sized company and the lawyer who works in a small law firm. It is this kind of marketplace capitalism that the political organization understands and finds congenial. Under the circumstances the "deal-me-in-too" philosophy—so evident in the actions and words of urban political leaders—appears as natural as the city debt.

The political organization tends to accept the middle-class values which other large social organizations also possess. Though these values may not be achievable in fact, they are endorsed as part and parcel of the American "way of life." For example, one such value is held to be home ownership for the average family, although this may be in the process of losing its impact. Another is the conviction that it is better to work than to be idle, in other words, too much leisure is an evil. Except for those few cities such as Milwaukee and Bridgeport which had Socialist governments for a number of years, the middle-class value system has been largely and automatically adopted by urban political organizations. And even in the Socialist cities, the governments were much more of the Reform type than they were "Socialist."[61]

SOCIAL RESPONSES

The response which a political organization gives to a particular demand will depend largely on its assessment of the intensity, imminence, and depth of the demand. In this respect a political organization follows the bureaucratic formula of all large organizations. What distinguishes the political from other organizations, however, is not only the exercise of public power—there is also the element of continuous publicity. It is often possible for a corporation, as it used to be possible for a university, to keep its deliberations secret. But a reigning political organization finds itself constantly in the public spotlight. Because of this, it tends to develop an awareness of public opinion not characteristic of other types of organizations. The ability to gauge public reactions is among the most highly prized of the political arts.

It is not by chance that successful political leaders have an unusual ability in the area of public relations. In the hands of the best practitioners, this skill goes far beyond the capacity to explain actual or proposed programs. It includes the element of winning public favor in a score of ways. When there was a newspaper strike in New York City, Mayor LaGuardia endeared himself to millions of fellow citizens by reading on the radio the otherwise unavailable daily comics. When Soviet Prime Minister Khrushchev was in Los Angeles, Mayor Yorty publicly insulted the visitor in an effort to cater to anti-Soviet Los Angelenos. More recently both Mayor Lindsay of New York and Mayor Daley of Chicago, both mayors of cities with large Jewish populations, announced that French President Pompidou—whose government had sold warplanes to an enemy of Israel—would not be publicly welcomed in their cities. While Mayor Daley subsequently relented, Mayor Lindsay did not.

Yet proclamations of a city's foreign policy and other acts of showmanship by the political leaders all tend to obscure the limitations under which these leaders and their organizations operate. For there exists a whole category of demands to which the organizations are simply not in a position to give any meaningful response. Aside from international and national matters which are obviously beyond the ability of a municipality to handle, there are extremely important urban concerns with which brokerage political organizations find it virtually impossible to deal. Most of the urban crises of our time—race relations, education, housing—fall into this classification. To put the issue in a different perspective, urban political organizations have shown little capacity to cope with the results of large-scale social change. Partly, of course, this is because the resources needed to solve the problems exceed the capacity of any one urban complex. But it is also in part due to the political system itself. Brokerage politics provides a limited-response mechanism. Its nature prohibits it from responding to the most pressing demands growing out of massive social change.

AN APPRAISAL OF THE
PLURALISTIC MODEL

As an analytical device, the pluralistic model of urban politics has served admirably. The model has been extraordinarily helpful in explaining the political systems of the large cities. It has enabled analysts to study the types of group competition and the scope of their struggles. It has provided a functional rationale for the existence of "bosses" and machines. At the same time, the model has illuminated the style of urban politics. The emphasis on an administratively-oriented politics emerges not as a plot or conspiracy but as a natural by-product of the system itself. Whether the model will continue to be so useful in a changing political environment is a question to be examined later. But there can be no doubt that the paradigm has been indispensable for the historic understanding of urban politics.

CHAPTER
NOTES

1. William L. Riordon, *Plunkitt of Tammany Hall* (New York: E. P. Dutton, paperback edition, 1963), p. xxvi. The book was first published in 1905.

2. *Ibid.*, p. 33.

3. For an illustration, see Edward C. Banfield and James Q. Wilson, *City Politics* (New York: Vintage, 1963), p. 45. Table 4 lists cities over 500,000 population ranked by Democratic percentage of the 1960 Presidential vote.

4. *Ibid.*, p. 45.

5. *Ibid.*, p. 44.

6. For mayor and other Chicago city officials, the election is partisan. For members of the city council (aldermen), the election is non-partisan in form. In practice a successful candidate must have the active backing and endorsement of one of the two major parties.

7. *The Municipal Year Book, 1968*, p. 65.

8. Edward C. Banfield, *Big City Politics* (New York: Random House, 1965), p. 11.

9. *Ibid.*, p. 14.

10. *Ibid.*, p. 14.

11. *Ibid.*, p. 15.

12. The principal source on Tammany Hall is Gustavus Myers, *The History of Tammany Hall* (New York: Boni & Liverright, 1917). See also, Edwin Patrick Kilroe, *Saint Tammany and the Origin of the Society of Tammany or Columbian Order* (New York: Ph.D. Thesis, Columbia University, 1913).

13. The sources on Hoboken and the McFeely machine are *Life* Magazine, May 22, 1947, and *Time* Magazine, May 26, 1947.

14. The account follows generally from Banfield and Wilson, *City Politics, op. cit.,* pp. 138–150.

15. *Ibid.,* p. 148.

16. *Ibid.,* p. 148.

17. *Ibid.,* p. 149.

18. *Ibid.,* p. 150.

19. Dayton David McKean, *The Boss, The Hague Machine in Action* (Boston: Houghton Mifflin, 1940).

20. *Ibid.,* p. 268.

21. *Ibid.,* p. 270.

22. *Ibid.,* p. 271.

23. *Ibid.,* p. 271.

24. *Ibid.,* p. 218.

25. *Ibid.,* p. 278.

26. *Ibid.,* p. 279.

27. J. T. Salter, *Boss Rule, Portraits in City Politics* (New York: Whittlesey House, 1935), p. 9.

28. Robert K. Merton, "Some Functions of the Political Machine," pp. 72–82 of a longer article, "Social Theory and Social Structure," in *American Journal of Sociology* (1945). The section of the article relating to machines is reprinted in Garold W. Thumm and Edward G. Janosik, eds., *Parties and the Governmental System* (Englewood Cliffs, N.J.: Prentice-Hall, 1967), pp. 25–32. The citation is at p. 27 of the Thumm and Janosik collection.

29. *Ibid.,* p. 27.

30. *Ibid.,* p. 27.

31. *Ibid.,* p. 29.

32. *Ibid.,* p. 30.

33. *Ibid.,* p. 31.

34. Salter, *op. cit.,* p. 18.

35. *Ibid.,* p. 18.

36. *Ibid.,* p. 224.

37. Harold F. Gosnell, *Machine Politics: Chicago Model* (Chicago: University of Chicago Press, 1937), p. 183.

38. *Ibid.,* p. 183.

39. Elmer C. Cornwell, Jr., "Bosses, Machines and Ethnic Groups," *The Annals,* Vol. 353, May, 1964, pp. 27–39.

40. Banfield and Wilson, *City Politics, op. cit.,* p. 235.

41. For an elaboration of the Reformers' objectives, see Jean L. Stinchcombe, *Reform and Reaction: City Politics in Toledo* (Belmont, California: Wadsworth, 1968), p. 27.

42. The history of the National Municipal League and the details of the Model City Charter are skillfully summarized in Thomas A. Flinn, *Local Government and Politics* (Glenview, Illinois: Scott,Foresman, 1960), pp. 136–141. The League itself publishes a substantial library of technical materials.

43. James Q. Wilson, "Politics and Reform in American Cities," in *American Government Annual*, 1962–63 (New York: Holt, Rinehart & Winston, 1962), pp. 37–52.

44. For an interesting study of nonprofessionals in politics, see James Q. Wilson, *The Amateur Democrat* (Chicago: University of Chicago Press, 1963).

45. Stinchcombe, *op. cit.*, especially the concluding chapter.

46. Thomas R. Dye, *Politics in States and Communities* (Englewood Cliffs, N.J.: Prentice-Hall, 1969), p. 273.

47. For a detailed account of the kinds of nonpartisan political systems, see Dye, *op. cit.*, pp. 275–276.

48. Duane Lockard, *The Politics of State and Local Government* (New York: Macmillan, 1963), p. 247.

49. *Ibid.*, pp. 247–252.

50. Robert L. Lineberry and Edmund P. Fowler, "Reformism and Public Policies in American Cities," Vol. LXI, No. 3, *The American Political Science Review* (Sept., 1967), pp. 701–16. Citation at p. 714.

51. See also the discussion in Dye, *op. cit.*, pp. 380–381.

52. Stinchcombe, *op. cit.*, p. 229.

53. *Ibid.*, p. 229.

54. *Ibid.*, p. 231.

55. *Ibid.*, p. 321.

56. *Ibid.*, p. 321.

57. *Ibid.*, p. 223.

58. Philadelphia *Evening Bulletin*, Feb. 25, 1970.

59. Riordon, *op. cit.*, p. 54.

60. *Ibid.*, p. 37.

61. The standard analysis of American values is found in Robin M. Williams, Jr., *American Society, A Sociological Interpretation* (New York: Knopf, 1957).

6

Old Style

Politics:

II—The Passing

of Brokerage

Politics

In the preceding chapter we noted that the nature of brokerage politics prevents it from being able to respond to contemporary urban crises—such as race relations, welfare, education, housing. Clearly, the Old Style brokerage approach is becoming less and less relevant to the needs of today. It has been repudiated, or is in the process of being repudiated, by significant groups in the community. This tendency is very apparent in the actions of the young, and other more or less alienated groups, including lower-class Blacks and certain upper-class whites.

What is there about the traditional system of brokerage politics that has led to its increasing discreditation? Why is it being rejected more and more? And, specifically, do the conditions which underlay the brokerage system when it was notably successful continue to prevail?

In coming to grips with this cluster of questions, the method employed in this chapter is to return to one of the two assumptions upon which Old Style politics is premised. One of the elements of the official model of urban politics—the idea that the arena of governmental action should be sharply delimited—will be examined later. At this point it is the other assumption—the concept of group competitiveness—which aids our analysis.

The group theory which furnishes one of the two basic postulates of the urban political model seems simple enough. At first glance, what is involved is mostly the clash of one interest group with another, with public policy the result of this and similar clashes. However, what is concealed, that is to say, what is implied operationally by group theory, will become apparent as the evaluation of this element of the urban model proceeds.

THE CHARGES AGAINST BROKERAGE POLITICS

To begin with, what are the principal charges against brokerage politics? They can be listed under four general categories, each of which will be examined in turn:

a) The system of rewards and punishments characteristic of brokerage politics has become ineffective.
b) Brokerage politics has failed to deal with the great urban social issues of our time—schools, race relations, crime, welfare, and housing.
c) The system has failed to meet the legitimate demands of lower-class Blacks and other excluded groups in the community.
d) It has likewise failed in its great function of social integration. In short, there is little sense of *civitas*. Anomie has increasingly replaced community.

To illustrate the traditional system of rewards and punishments associated with brokerage politics, one needs to think only of the proverbial bucket of coal given by Tammany to poor families during periods of severe winter cold. Or, again, there is the summertime outing on an East River steamer, permitting a pleasant combination of sunshine, beer, and Irish music. From the point of view of the consumer of such services, the quid pro quo of occasional support at the voting booths could easily seem a most advantageous exchange.

At the level of party officialdom, the payoff was in terms of a patronage job. Sometimes the reward for services would be petty, such as the appointment of a paid poll watcher. Or, the reward could be substantial, as with an appointment to a high civic office.

For reasons which do not require elaboration, the traditional system of rewards and punishments has become ineffectual. It has not disappeared, but its effects have become marginal. In an age of oil and gas heat, who really needs a bucket of coal? In an age when industrial and professional pay scales have been advancing rapidly, who really wants to hold a municipal patronage post? Thus, the traditional inducements which served brokerage politics so faithfully for many decades are now, to a great extent, uninviting.

A second charge levelled against brokerage politics is its failure to deal successfully with the great social problems of populous urban centers. The social critics, however, are by no means united as to the basis of their attacks. Some say that the cities have in fact made Herculean efforts to right urban wrongs, but have been frustrated by hostile state legislatures. The so-called Big Six Mayors of New York State—the mayors of the largest cities in that state— fall into this category. It is their contention that the Albany legislature discriminates, in a dozen ways, against the large cities. Because of this discrimination, it is held that resources which should go to the large cities have been diverted to smaller cities and towns. In passing, it should be noted that the case made by Mayor John Lindsay and the other embattled mayors of New York State is persuasive.

Other critics, going further, argue that federalism itself makes it unlikely that cities will ever, under the present constitutional arrangement, get an even break from state governments. What they propose, therefore, is some kind of new constitutional relationship between the large urban centers and the federal government.

Still additional critics take the position that a great deal can be done under the present ground rules, but that this will require time. They point to impressive achievements in urban renewal and in expressway construction. Give us more time, they say, and we will handle the question of urban revitalization to the satisfaction of all. The Urban Coalition, dominated by big business interests, is an exponent of this gradualist point of view.

The critics, however, are in solid agreement that brokerage politics has failed to deal *successfully* with today's most pressing urban questions even though they may differ as to how much has been done and how much could be done. Included in their indictment are the charges that the schools are bad and are getting worse; that transportation problems are mounting daily; that crime is rampant; that housing is inadequate; that the welfare system is self-defeating; and that race relations have reached the crisis stage. Even without the oversimplification implied by the use of these telescopic and journalistic clichés, the indictment is dramatically pointed and damaging.

A third charge against the system of brokerage politics is that it has failed to meet the legitimate demands of lower-class Blacks and other disenfranchised groups. Critics, of course, are not always sure which demands of this group are "legitimate" and which are not. This is especially true where the demands made at one time apparently run counter to the demands made at another time. For instance, under the doctrine of the great school desegregation case —*Brown* v. *Board of Education of Topeka* (1954)—the practice of having separate public school systems for Black and white children was outlawed.[1] But, a decade and a half later, respected voices in the Black community could be heard calling for what amounted to all-Black schools in the name of community control. It is, of course, easily possible to justify this shift in position, but such changes make a decision on the legitimacy issue more difficult.

This difficulty aside, it is evident that many demands whose legitimacy are unquestioned have not, in fact, satisfactorily been met; for instance public transportation. In city after city, the poorest neighborhoods are in greatest need of inexpensive, efficient public transportation. Yet these neighborhoods are the first to suffer when such transportation is abandoned or curtailed in favor of the privately owned automobile. From the riots and fires in Watts came at least this lesson. What appeared to white Los Angeles an unnecessary luxury—adequate public transportation— appeared to Black Los Angeles as an absolute necessity. In demanding a reasonable bus service, the citizens of Watts were actually asking for an opportunity, among other things, to get out of Watts and to and from work in other parts of the city. From the perspective of Watts, the inadequacy of the public busing service appeared to be an act of deliberate racial discrimination.

In addition to alleging insufficient public services of various sorts, Blacks and other lower-class groups often maintain that they are not proportionately represented on the public payrolls. They point to employment in big-city police forces and in the public school systems as illustrations. When it comes to the highest public positions, the employment of so-called minority group personnel is so exceptional as to become a major news event. Thus, the hiring in 1970 of former Air Force General Benjamin Davis as police commissioner of Cleveland under Mayor Carl Stokes, also a Black, was greeted as an impressive break-through. It may well have been, but the appointment also drew attention to the degree to which Blacks, Puerto Ricans, and others are tremendously under–represented in the higher civil service echelons. (Once in office, however, a gulf developed between General Davis and the ghetto Blacks, and he subsequently resigned from his post as commissioner.)

A fourth and final criticism of brokerage politics stems from the belief that it has failed in our time to perform its historic task of social integration. In dealing each new immigrant group into the political potpourri, the traditional political organization performed an act of political socialization. Along with public education and wartime military service, politics was historically considered to be the milieu in which socialization—or Americanization—was achieved. That the system worked reasonably well in achieving this goal for European immigrants is self-evident. That the system has worked far less well with regard to Negro and Puerto Rican immigrants to the big cities is now becoming equally apparent.

Beyond the increasing failure of brokerage politics to achieve the goals of socialization that earlier groups achieved, there is an even broader consideration. The urban political system in its present form has, to a very large extent, failed to inculcate in the minds of the newcomers a sense of civic-consciousness, which may be defined as a set of shared civic goals. The level of agreement is very low, between the more established sections of the metropolis and the more recently established areas. Furthermore, although the evidence is only partial, there is some indication that this failure in political socialization is self-generating; a situation that may deteriorate at an increasing momentum.

There is, finally, the charge that in the most deprived urban areas the brokerage politics system has succeeded in breaking down existing communities. Urban removal of persons preceding urban reconstruction is an obvious illustration of this charge. There is a good deal of documentation to the charge that "urban renewal" often means "removal of Blacks," whether intentional or through oversight.

Yet the most serious aspect of the alleged failure of brokerage politics to achieve the goals of political socialization goes beyond the question of physical removal and destruction of housing. It extends to the effects of these changes on the people themselves. With a sufficient sense of communal solidarity, a group can withstand and repel very severe hostile environmental and personal forces, as the history of urban Judaism has shown. However, if a community as a set of interrelated individuals is destroyed, anomie rather than a community develops. In such cases individuals do not purposefully relate to one another; they are discrete in their actions and behavior. There is considerable evidence that the spirit of anomie has replaced the sense of community in vast areas of America's urban slums and ghettos, partly because of urban renewal.

THE MORAL INDICTMENT

The moral and ethical indictment of Old Style brokerage politics takes many forms, but two themes are conspicuous among the various charges. First is the feeling that brokerage politics has failed, in one way or another, to achieve justice. The second is a widespread belief that the traditional politics has failed to create the quality of life that people expect.

In present-day urban America the leading exponents of social justice have often come from the extremes of society, not from the more complacent middle groups. When it comes to documenting the deficiencies of the system, however, authority and legitimacy must clearly be given to those few talented and courageous persons, mostly Blacks—like James Baldwin or Malcolm X—who have lived in, survived, and somehow transcended the slums.

The main thrust of Malcolm X, in his famous *Autobiography*, is his indictment of white American society.[2] But there is also a clear political dimension in the writings of the assassinated Black Muslim leader. In his public addresses, Malcolm X called for voluntary separation of the Negro from the white race in America. At the same time, he strongly rejected legal "segregation." Speaking on behalf of the Muslims, he declared in a standard speech: "The Honorable Elijah Muhammad teaches us that *segregation* is when your life and liberty are controlled, regulated, *by someone else*. To *segregate* means to control. *Segregation* is that which is forced upon inferiors by superiors. But *separation* is that which is done voluntarily, by two equals—for the good of both!"[3]

Malcolm X urged Blacks to follow the path of other groups in using social cohesiveness as a basis for advancement. "As other ethnic groups have done," he said, "let the black people, wherever possible, however possible, patronize their own kind, hire their own kind, and start in those ways to build up the black race's ability to do for itself. That's the only way the American black man is ever going to get respect."[4]

In assessing the impact of particular Black leaders on the white political and social system, Malcolm X singled out the importance of the ghetto hustler. "Why do I say this?," he asked. In answer to his question, he continued: "The hustler, out there in the ghetto jungles, has less respect for the white power structure than any other Negro in America. The ghetto hustler is internally restrained by nothing."[5] What makes him even more dangerous is the popularity of his image with "school-dropout youth in the ghetto."[6]

As an ex-hustler himself, Malcolm X was able to talk to ghetto youth more directly than were the middle-class Black leaders.

His readings of history had convinced Malcolm X that the European ethnic groups had developed political power—"clout"—by voting as blocs. He was especially critical of Blacks for dividing their votes between the existing parties. "Whenever any group can vote in a bloc, and decide the outcome of elections, and it *fails* to do this, then that group is politically sick."[7] Calling for a "black lobby," he summarized his thinking in these words: "The cornerstones of this country's operation are economic and political strength and power. The black man doesn't have the economic strength—and it will take time for him to build it—but right now the American black man has the political strength and power to change his destiny overnight."[8]

After his break with the Nation of Islam, Malcolm X organized a new mosque in New York City known as Muslim Mosque, Inc. He saw this as the working base for a political and social action program embracing all Afro-Americans.[9] How his program would have fared will always be a matter for conjecture for Malcolm X was murdered on February 21, 1965. However, his indictment of the existing social system for its failure to deliver justice—especially to Blacks—and his insistence on Black separation and unity as a form of social and political power, continue to live on among present-day Blacks and their leaders.

Two years after the death of Malcolm X, Stokely Carmichael and Charles V. Hamilton published a book entitled *Black Power*, which provided both a slogan and a new sense of direction to the Black political movement.[10] "Black power" means not only psychological power but a growing sense of community on the part of Blacks.[11] The social and political manifestations of "Black power" are premised upon a closing of ranks. Group solidarity is considered to be a necessary prerequisite to any activities involving an interaction between Blacks and other groups.[12] Among other things, this concept implies that Black-oriented organizations and businesses should be run by Blacks, not by white liberals and well-wishers.[13]

Of particular interest is the Carmichael-Hamilton idea of coalition politics. The authors do not oppose the formation of all coalitions which include Black groups, but they do insist that these participating Black groups possess a high degree of cohesion and of internal discipline. These qualities are important because, as issues change, coalitions will break up when their objectives are no longer shared by all of their constituent elements. Since this kind of development is inevitable, Black groups should be prepared for a constant reshuffling of any political coalitions they may choose to enter.[14] This is viewed not as a betrayal, but simply as a condition of political life in a pluralistic society.

One measure of the success of the doctrine of "Black power" is the ability of Blacks to be elected to public office. The recent record is both encouraging and discouraging. Spurred on by the Voting Rights Act of 1965, Black registration has soared in the south, and so has the election of Black officials. As late as 1965, the number of Black elected officials in that section was estimated at only 75. A 1970 survey indicated that the southern total had risen to 565. For the country as a whole, the same survey revealed that almost 1,500 Blacks were holding elective public office.[15]

Yet this figure—believed to be a substantial increase over that of earlier years—meant that Black officials still made up only three-tenths of one percent of the more than 500,000 officials elected in the United States. Blacks comprise about 11 percent of the total population.

So far as major cities were concerned, it was found that Blacks constituted the majority of the city council in Detroit and in Gary. Only in Pittsburgh was the percentage of Blacks on the city council significantly above the percentage of Blacks in the population. Blacks made up 21 percent of the population, but they held 33 percent of Pittsburgh's council seats. Jacksonville, Florida, which is 47 percent Black, was the only southern city in which Blacks were represented on the council in approximate proportion to their number in the population.

The second general moral indictment of the urban political system concerns the quality of urban life. While there are many approaches to the overall question, the main focus in recent years has been on the environment. In particular, considerations relating to noise, water and air pollution have been uppermost in the public consciousness. Tied in with these problems have been problems dealing with land use, including housing renewal, location of expressways, and parks and other recreational facilities.

Again, the demand for quality in the environment stems from a particular social class mainly middle and upper classes. In fact the parallels to the Reformers are striking. The movement to purify the environment comes largely from upper middle-class persons whose strongholds are the civic organizations. Using the weapons of publicity and exposure, the proponents of environmental improvement seek to persuade the other strata of society and to mobilize public opinion in the usual ways. However, their ability to command attention has not, to this point, been matched by their capacity to interest the political parties.

What mass basis there is for environmental reform has come from students, who during 1970, managed to stage some impressive rallies emphasizing their concerns. To some extent, the student phase of the movement competed for student energies with the more volatile subjects of Vietnam and civil rights. Yet there is no doubt that the student rallies evinced a considerable amount of genuine concern as to whether the cities of the future would be worth inhabiting.

Yet, in all the outcry for environmental improvement and control, one group has been notably silent—top management officials of the largest industrial enterprises. Though there have been some exceptions, as a class, the industrial directorate has proceeded to clean up waters and atmosphere polluted by industry only when absolutely forced to. The propelling forces, when they have been effective, have come from government, not from public opinion. The strategy of the present-day reformers is, therefore, to bypass big business and to put pressure on governments to enact punitive statutes regarding the polluters—often a remarkably difficult feat to execute.

FAILURE TO SET PRIORITIES

It is universally acknowledged that the United States has shown an extraordinary ability to establish and to meet wartime objectives. As Randolph Bourne indicated a half century ago, in a peculiar sense, "war is the health of the state."[16] By this Bourne meant that it was possible in wartime to establish priorities—economic and social as well as military—and to adhere to them in actual practice. But in peacetime, he pointed out, the state operated with far less assurance and decisiveness.

This characteristic of American public policy has also attracted the attention of the noted Swedish social scientist, Gunnar Myrdal, the author of *An American Dilemma: The Negro Problem and Modern Democracy* (1944). During the early 1940's when he and his associates were conducting their field work in the south, Myrdal was well-aware of the forces tending to encourage Black migration to the north and west.

Returning to the United States in 1970 during the course of one of his frequent visits, Myrdal expressed astonishment that

America's technical experts had done so little to prepare the government and the public in general to meet the migration problem. In an interview in connection with a lecture series at the University of Pennsylvania, he declared: "It was easy to see the strong push of the Negroes out of the South toward the northern cities, but it is amazing that the experts in the universities did not see what was coming. If they had seen, they would have asked for reforms that would have been infinitesimal compared to what is being demanded now. This problem and many of your other problems," he continues, "have been caused by the tendency in America to accept the cheapest solution."[17]

As an illustration, Myrdal cited the anti-poverty program launched by the Johnson Administration. The program was "under-dimensioned," he charged, because it ignored rural slums and white slums in the cities. It concentrated on Black slums because they appeared to represent the simplest problem to solve. In essence, Myrdal was saying that the approach of the Office of Economic Opportunity was unable to establish meaningful priorities, and that this constituted merely one example of a general tendency.

Even though Myrdal's observations relate primarily to the national scene, they are obviously equally applicable to the urban political scene. It has frequently been observed that a lack of direction is characteristic in the governance of the cities. As one observer has put it, "Cities are well run but badly governed."[18] In spelling out why this is so, Theodore J. Lowi cites two suppositions of the "prevailing ideology" that tend to confuse well-intentioned apologists for the system as it is.

His first point is that the suburban city fathers of America managed to fragment metropolitan regions by establishing autonomous suburbs around the great cities. Until about 1920, the typical large city simply expanded through the device of annexation. Later, the tendency increased for the suburbs to resist the jurisdiction of the cities. As a result, the "real city" finally developed into a metropolitan area of multiple governments. In the "city" of Chicago, for example, there are 1,060 governments, of which some 995 have the power to tax.[19]

As a second supposition of the current ideology, Lowi points to the belief that cities are now so technically competent that they require no overall direction. This belief holds that a competent bureaucracy can be self-directing and will produce an efficient and fair administration of public policy. While this thought is comforting, it is misleading. What is often served is the interest of the individual public agency to the detriment of any larger, more general—or public—interest. This may be so even if the particular agency is ferociously efficient. All that results is an especially efficient internecine war.[20] New York City, with its welter of unrelated bureaus and agencies, is an excellent example of the absence of overall coordination. But nearly every other large city will provide a good illustration.

The difficulties inherent in brokerage politics in the setting of administrative priorities form only one facet of the total problem. From the perspective of electoral politics, the difficulties are also striking. Who should be nominated? What moves should be made to attract new followers? What coalitions of interests are likely to increase voter support? These and similar questions go to the heart of the brokerage aspect of the electoral system. Unfortunately, it is not possible for any large number of persons to participate in formulating the important alternatives to be placed before the electorate. The average citizen can merely vote in the primaries and in the general elections—a relatively passive role. What he therefore learns about the negotiations, the give-and-take, the compromising of brokerage electoral politics he learns second hand. He learns, primarily, from the news media, not from personal experience.

At a more conceptual level, brokerage politics runs into another very serious difficulty: its incompatability with the public interest. This is not strange, for group theory denies that there is much substance to the concept. In David Truman's *The Governmental Process*—the handbook of the group theorists—the subject is not discussed.[21] This silence has been maintained by the principal writers who have followed in Truman's footsteps. It seems fair to conclude, therefore, that the omission is deliberate.

Why do the group theorists ignore one of the basic questions of traditional political theory? One reason may be the conviction that the policy outcome of group competition *is* identical with the public interest. In this view, the result of an election, the output of a legislature, the decisions of the courts would, in an operational way, define what is meant by the public interest. Alternatively, the question may seem unimportant to some group theorists. Another possible explanation is that the concept is not amenable to scientific research. It cannot be pinned down and investigated by the use of quantitative techniques. It may seem better policy under these conditions to avoid the question completely.

But the problem has a stubborn way of enduring. Ever since Rousseau distinguished between the General Will and the Will of All, men have been troubled by the difference between what ideally should exist as public policy and what in fact may exist. In Rousseau's vocabulary, the General Will of the community could never err. On the other hand, the Will of All—which simply meant counting up votes to determine the wishes of the majority—could and often did err. Rousseau never satisfactorily answered the question as to how men could actually determine the General Will by more certain means than voting. On this point, as on many others, his thinking was imprecise and often contradictory.

Yet the issue raised by Rousseau is resurrected almost daily by the actions of legislative bodies in America. Do people really believe that the most recent tax legislation enacted at Sacramento represents the general will—in modern terms, the public interest —of the people of California? Do people agree that urban renewal programs authorized by the city fathers of San Francisco necessarily reflect the public interest? It is palpably the case that very few citizens would automatically concur with the proposition that what a legislature—or an electorate—does is a reflection, in Rousseau's sense, of the General Will.

Under brokerage politics there is no prospect of an overall scheme for doing things, nor is there much hope of real coordination. The reason for this is that brokerage politics is unable to plan; it can only bargain and negotiate. It cannot set priorities and see to it that they are carried out; it can only set the stage for the group struggle and certify the results. Because of these factors, brokerage politics is incompatible with a politics of the public interest. Brokerage politics endemically has not, and cannot, develop a philosophy of the public interest. For above all else, a philosophy of the public interest requires the establishment of policy priorities and we have seen that brokerage politics functions in such a way that this is impossible.

SOME UNDERLYING CONDITIONS OF THE SYSTEM

Current indictments of the urban political system suggest, in part, that the system is based on outmoded assumptions—such as the group theory. In this connection, there are two general questions which must be explored. First, what are the assumptions which give structure to the system? Second, to what extent do these assumptions square with observed, present-day reality? As has been pointed out, a central feature of the brokerage approach to politics is that problems can be resolved through a process of accommodation. This accommodation is assumed to occur as the result of compromises worked out among competing groups. It is the group which articulates the demands, and it is the group which raises the cudgels on their behalf. In theory, the group could be a political party; in practice, the group is an interest group; and the party is a coalition of various interest groups. The initiative lies normally with the groups or coalitions. It is the function of the party, basically, to ratify what the more fundamental interests have decided upon.

Secondly, as we have already pointed out, group theory assumes that the most important political problems are essentially administrative in nature. They take place in a political milieu, but their solution, or resolution, is a technical matter. As an illustration, assume that a decision has been made to extend an interstate highway system through the center of a large city; a decision which was reached after the usual process of hearings, meetings, and public commentary. It is now time to implement the decision. Customarily, at this point, the affair is turned over to the federal and state highway experts, who proceed in a military-like fashion to bulldoze the highway through the city without much regard for people, historic buildings, or scenery. Unfortunately, this illustration is not a parody, as the downtown sections of Providence, R.I. and dozens of other cities sadly attest.

It is possible for this sort of thing to happen repeatedly because of a deep-seated American belief in the value of social engineering, which is much too involved to be discussed here. The theory is that if people can define the general nature of a problem, it can then be turned over to the experts for a definitive solution. The people therefore escape involvement, for the problem is seen as administrative, that is, technical and impersonal. The arrangement of priorities is therefore resolved automatically, according to the nature of the problem. This avoids giving the appearance that priorities are arranged by human beings in charge of the activities of other human beings. In brief, values are viewed as being allocated impersonally, not on the basis of judgment, preference, or whim. This, at least, is the implication of the faith in social engineering.

The third assumption of group theory is that the most vociferous group will be given a piece of the pie and thereby will be dealt into the system. There is ample documentation to this assumption; for instance attention has been given to the ability of Irish immigrants to advance rapidly through the political ranks and to become both an important part of and indispensable to the urban political system.

Yet the process of assimilation has not proceeded to the point where ethnic politics is passé. On the contrary, ethnic politics in the cities survives in a very vigorous fashion. Despite the eloquence of Edward Bok and others in praising the Americanization process, the fact remains that the assimilation has not glossed over nationality differences.[22] So far as religion is concerned, pluralism is even more in evidence. Religious pluralism undoubtedly reinforces cultural and nationality pluralism.

Judged purely on the basis of history, a group's chances for obtaining political power are related to such factors as its size, its geographical location, and its electoral solidarity. Where the conditions have been unusually favorable—as in New York City with regard to the Jewish population—it is possible for powerful veto groups to exist. The Arab vote in New York is conspicuous by its total absence, as is the Mormon vote in Boston.

Finally, there is a fourth assumption of group theory that has affected the suitability of the pluralistic model of urban politics— the concept of equilibrium. To the group theorists, the result of group action and interaction is the establishment of a condition of equilibrium. As forces come and go, the equilibrium in its particulars may vary from time to time, but usually some kind of a fairly stable balance will be maintained. (Group theorists would handle the question of a revolutionary situation in terms of the breakdown of a stable equilibrium. In due time, they would expect the creation of a new, and also stable, balance.)

Whether the equilibrium which is postulated will be intrinsically conservative because it tends to reinforce the status quo is a question of concern to political theorists. Although there is disagreement regarding the answer, it is difficult to see why there is any logical necessity for equilibrium theory to have a conservative bias.

But there is another aspect of the equilibrium concept in group theory that does present an immediate political problem. Once a balance of forces has been established to constitute a stable equilibrium, the groups concerned tend to equate the results with justice. They may feel, that is, that the equilibrium of which they are a part is essentially a concrete embodiment of a particular justice. According to this reasoning, a group which is included in the system has earned justice. On the other hand, a group which is excluded is deservedly out of the system. Justice is therefore in no sense offended by the exclusion.

From the point of view of the excluded groups, the situation is perceived entirely differently. The equilibrium is merely a fancy way of maintaining the status quo, and therefore is lacking in justice. For instance, it must not be imagined that the Indians praised the American system of equilibrium of groups in the same fashion as did the Irish. It all depends on whether a group is playing in the game according to the rules, or, on the contrary, is watching the contest from a segregated section of the bleachers.

So much for the assumptions of group theory. What are the present realities? To what extent do the conditions postulated in group theory coincide with what can actually be observed in the political world? In making an assessment along these lines, the concept of accommodation is a reasonable starting point.

It is possible to note today a decline in the belief that the most important political problems can be solved through the classical methods of accommodation. It has in some measure been replaced by a growing conviction that certain questions can only be resolved through the process of confrontation. This "politics of confrontation" can take many forms, extending simply from the peaceful presentation of "non-negotiable demands" to riots and the dynamiting of corporation headquarters. This is an all-or-nothing game with the total surrender by one side and the total victory by the other. In its purest form, the defeated side would not simply retreat, regroup, and return to the fray at some later time; it would be liquidated.

In this respect, confrontation politics can often quickly resolve problems. The events of 1789 did, of course, remove from the French political agenda a large number of difficult questions. But what may easily be overlooked by romantic confrontationists is that Bastille-like victories bring with them an inevitable complex of new problems. In the manner of the phoenix, the new issues arise and cast new men in the role of problem-solvers. And somewhere in the process the successful revolutionaries, having had their time on stage, pass from the scene to be replaced by the practical men of affairs. The dialectic of history is not immobilized by confrontation politics.

These comments aside, it is evident that in the America of the 1960's and 1970's the belief is fairly widespread that confrontation tactics can and sometimes do advance political causes. A case can be made that without outbreaks such as Watts, little would have been done to bring government programs to bear on immediate slum problems. There are, of course, limits to confrontation politics in a relatively non-revolutionary society. But it is not easy in the abstract to draw the lines between what is permissible and what is not. As in so many other areas, only the historical verdict will be decisive.

A second present-day reality of group theory is more emphasis on policy issues and relatively less concern with administrative and technical questions. Partly this is due to a feeling that the politics of accommodation fails to come to grips with the important issues of the time. Partly it is attributable to the increasing belief in the efficacy of confrontation politics. But besides these factors there is another factor which is deeply rooted in the nature of contemporary society—social change itself.

Social change in the United States, has been proceeding at a furious rate since 1945, and there is no let-up in sight.[23] The effect of large-scale social change is to bring to the forefront of public discussion various basic issues which can be solved, if at all, only through policy decisions—not through the traditional methods of accommodation politics.

As an illustration, consider the population question. Practically speaking, the United States has no population policy, but given a sufficiently large and continually increasing population, ensuing problems will arise which will bring about intense public discussion. In the long run, these problems may not be solved at all. But if they are, the solutions will be in terms of hard policy decisions. Other illustrations of the inevitable rise of policy issues can easily be drawn from such areas as conservation, pollution, housing, energy resources, transportation. In all of these fields, solutions will have to come, if at all, from a policy-oriented kind of politics which sets priorities, not through the brokerage politics style of accommodating rival interests.

A third observation on the relevance of group theory to present-day reality relates to the inclusion of various ethnic, racial, and social groups in the local political system. We have noted that the process by which a group moved from almost total exclusion to meaningful inclusion was considered among the outstanding achievements of the pluralist urban system. Not only was this hailed as a step in assimilation—or Americanization—of the group, it was also held to increase the stability of the political arrangement.

Since the process of assimilation has more or less been taken for granted, it shocks many Americans to realize that certain groups have effectively been excluded from meaningful participation in the political system. The emphasis is on the adjective "meaningful," for discriminatory legislation against voting by minority groups largely became a thing of the past with the passage and implementation of the Voting Rights Act of 1965. Under this act, hundreds of thousands of southern Blacks were registered and voted for the first time. As this was the purpose of the statute, it may be considered to have achieved its objective. Extended in 1970, the Voting Rights Act seems likely to have a permanent influence in enlarging the Black electorate.

Meaningful participation has not been resolved, however, by an extension of suffrage. It is quite true that recent Black gains have included winning the mayoralty in certain large cities—among them, Cleveland and Gary, and the vice-mayoralty in Atlanta. These achievements ought not to be minimized, but the percentage of Black members of city councils, to say nothing of state legislatures, remains proportionately very small. Too, the proportion of Blacks in the top-level appointive posts as well as judgeships of the large cities, is miniscule. These posts are disproportionately Irish and Italian, to the detriment of Blacks, Puerto Ricans, and WASPS, among others.

With profit one could extend the scope of meaningful participation to include school boards, special districts, and draft boards. In all cases, rather substantial minorities—Blacks, Puerto Ricans, and Spanish-Americans—are severely under-represented. The failure to include such groups in proportion roughly to their numbers in these aspects of the political process can be construed as a criticism of the process itself. It is essential to be able to vote, but that is only the beginning, not the end, of meaningful participation.

The deliberate separatism of some sectors of the population also runs counter to the tenets of group theory. In the official theory, it is easy to explain why certain groups have by law or custom been excluded from participation in the general political process— they have simply lacked power. Having obtained power or the threat of it, they have been permitted to enter the political arena. The rapid assimilation of the nationality groupings illustrates this situation quite vividly. But group theory can also explain why Indians on reservations, members of the military, women, the indigent, the elderly and the institutionalized have been denied the right to vote at various times.

The current efforts of some Blacks to operate within the political system have already been commented upon. But the fact remains that other Blacks have chosen a course of independency, even of separatism. There are both economic and political aspects to the separation movement. In the economic arena, there has been, understandably, an effort to establish "Black capitalism," especially in communities with heavy Black concentrations. This objective has had the support of the major Black organizations as well as civic associations such as the Urban Coalition. The path being followed may be paternalistic, but it is clearly within the traditional economic spectrum. There is nothing especially radical about wanting to have the stores in a community owned and managed by people who live in that community.

But it is in the political area that the established patterns of behavior have been overtly challenged. The challenges have varied in substance and style, but they have in common the conviction that the political system will not respond to the demands of Blacks in a manner satisfactory to Blacks. What the Black Muslims and the Black Panthers both believe is that the system will not treat them as it has treated the nationality groups. The road to salvation, in other words, is not to be found through politics. Given this attitude, it follows that ordinary political action is regarded with a good deal of cynicism. Instead of attempting to build coalitions with other groups, Black nationalists concentrate on seizing control of institutions and programs in their own neighborhoods. That there is a logic in this approach is undeniable. But it obviously constitutes a repudiation of the traditional political behavior.

Lastly, group theory tends to founder on the shoals of suburbia. Until the 1920's, the urban areas of the country were in general defined by city boundaries. This has become increasingly not the case. With the growth of the suburbs "metropolitan" politics became more and more something different from the urban politics postulated in the pluralistic model. The difference in terms of public policy has been noted by many observers. Thomas Dye, for instance, has drawn attention to the relationship between city-suburban social distance and public policy. In his intensive study of five metropolitan areas in Wisconsin, Dye found notable policy differences between the cities and their suburbs.[24]

But even if group theory could somehow be made to account for policy differences, it still runs into further difficulties when applied to the suburbs. There are, of course, many different kinds of suburbs. A steel worker's suburb is vastly different from the middle-class suburbs which also surround Pittsburgh. But the politics of a particular suburb is not ordinarily one of class versus class, nor is it likely to be dominated by shifting coalitions of ethnic groups. In many ways, the politics in the residential suburbs *is* the politics which the Reformers wanted—nonpartisan, low-key, civic-oriented, public-regarding. In analyzing this style of politics, the group competition element of the urban political model is not very germane.

CHAPTER
NOTES

1. *Brown* v. *Board of Education of Topeka, Kansas*, 347 U.S. 483 (1954).

2. Malcolm X, *The Autobiography of Malcolm X* (New York: Grove Press, paperback edition, 1966).

3. *Ibid.*, p. 246.

4. *Ibid.*, p. 275.

5. *Ibid.*, p. 311.

6. *Ibid.*, p. 311.

7. *Ibid.*, p. 314.

8. *Ibid.*, p. 315.

9. *Ibid.*, p. 316.

10. Stokely Carmichael and Charles V. Hamilton, *Black Power: The Politics of Liberation in America* (New York: Vintage Books, 1967).

11. *Ibid.*, p. 38.

12. *Ibid.*, p. 44.

13. *Ibid.*, p. 46.

14. *Ibid.*, p. 60.

15. The survey was conducted by the Metropolitan Applied Research Center, Inc., of New York and Washington, and the Voter Education Project of the Southern Regional Council in Atlanta. The findings are summarized in *The New York Times* of March 31, 1970.

16. Randolph Bourne, *Unfinished Fragment on the State* (1918), reprinted in *Untimely Papers* (New York: Viking Press, 1947).

17. Gunnar Myrdal, in interview with David J. Umansky, *Philadelphia Inquirer*, March 11, 1970, p. 43.

18. Theodore J. Lowi, *The End of Liberalism* (New York: Norton, 1969), p. 193.

19. *Ibid.*, p. 199.

20. *Ibid.*, pp. 200–201.

21. For a critique of this aspect of Truman's work, see Murray S. Stedman, Jr., "A Group Interpretation of Politics," *Public Opinion Quarterly*, Vol. 17, No. 2 (Summer, 1953), pp. 218–229.

22. For a classic account of the assimilation process, which ends as a success story, see Edward W. Bok, *The Americanization of Edward Bok* (New York: C. Scribner's Sons, 1921).

23. The impact of social change on American political institutions is discussed at length in Murray S. Stedman, Jr., ed., *Modernizing American Government* (Englewood Cliffs, N.J.: Prentice-Hall, 1968).

24. See Thomas R. Dye, "City-Suburban Social Distance and Public Policy," *Social Forces*, Vol. 44 (September, 1965), pp. 100–106.

7

The

Politics of

Suburbia

We have noted that one of the most interesting findings of the 1970 Census was that more than half of the population of metropolitan areas was located in the suburbs. This shift in the balance of metropolitan populations from the central cities to their suburbs has obvious consequences in a large variety of fields, including marketing and distribution of goods, communication of ideas, finance and banking, and governmental services. In focusing attention on the importance of the suburbs generally, the Census also suggested their importance in specific sectors, including the political; interest in the politics of suburbia is clearly at an all-time high.

In this chapter, two aspects of political behavior as it relates to suburban politics will be examined. One is theoretical, the other empirical, and both may conveniently be expressed in the form of questions.

The first is: Does suburban politics bring into question or does it sustain the competitive element of the pluralistic model which was analyzed at length in Chapter 4?

The second is: As a "system," is politics in the suburbs different in any significant ways from what it is in the central cities?

In chapter 2, we presented some of the qualities which distinguish core cities from suburbs. It should be noted here that the term "suburb" encompasses a wide variety of actual localities. Sociological research has quite clearly established that it is an error to treat the suburbs as if they were all the same. There are a number of clichés associated with the suburbs, for instance that they are dormitories for well-to-do executives who work in the cities, and for their families. But there are other types of suburbs, one of which is the industrial suburb—which provides jobs for its own residents as well as others. As far back as 1925, H. Paul Douglass advised his fellow sociologists to distinguish between the "suburb of consumption"—the residential type, and the "suburb of production"—the industrial type.

More recent research has thrown a great deal of light upon the socio-economic differences in American suburbs. These are considerable and cover a very wide range, as the study of 154 suburbs undertaken by Frederick M. Wirt has shown.[1] What emerges from his study is a continuum of suburbs, each with its own socio-economic composition and its own life style.

People move to the suburbs—stay there and raise their children there—for a wide variety of reasons. Looking into the causes of the post-World War II migration, Peter Rossi found that people were both "pushed" and "pulled." The "push" forces were crime in the cities, fear of crime, bad schools, deteriorating housing. But the "pull" forces were also important: the desire for more space, "to own our own home," and the attraction of superior suburban schools.[2]

Whether or to what extent the people who have willingly moved from central city to suburbs have achieved their objectives is not readily determinable. What is clear is that the great social problems of education, housing, crime, health care, and drug addiction are becoming increasingly more serious in metropolitan areas outside the central cities.

As has been noted earlier, fragmentation is one of the characteristics of government in the non-central city areas of the metropolis. Suburban governmental services are provided by a large and diverse number of governmental units—municipalities, counties, towns, and overlapping special districts. There are usually several layers of government. As a result, a citizen is likely to receive his public services from several different local governments.

Robert C. Wood has observed that governments in a metropolitan area serve as catalysts to promote a sense of separate identity and community consciousness for their inhabitants.[3] He has also questioned some of the values commonly held in suburbia, and its indifference to the metropolitan world about it. He contends that grass roots values—said to be prized in the suburbs—are not always identical with democratic values.[4]

Despite the differentiation among suburbs, and the political fragmentation which characterizes suburban political systems, there is one theme which pervades the politics of suburbia—the politics of accommodation.[5] Popularized by Princeton political scientist Michael N. Danielson, the term "politics of accommodation" is useful in suggesting an emphasis on reaching widespread agreement as opposed to conflict for its own sake. The general objective of the politics of accommodation has been to retain suburban autonomy in the face of steadily rising pressures for more goods and services. The desire to retain autonomy is related to the very high value placed on self-government. The solution to the general problem has been found in the creation of a system of accommodations based on the use of specific devices to achieve this purpose, such as special districts to supply such services as water or sewage disposal for contiguous suburban municipalities. Intermunicipal cooperation is also a very common method for providing goods and services. This ranges from informal agreements to specific contractual arrangements. As has been noted earlier, counties are often able to help suburbs adjust to new situations brought about by urban growth and social change. The greatest development along this line has taken place in California, where the urban county has played an important role in helping the suburbs to provide for increased public services. In addition, the suburbs take advantage of growing state and federal involvement in their efforts to cope with new pressures.

The politics of accommodation has in fact preserved local autonomy, and is therefore viewed by most suburbanites as a decided success. But a price is paid for the maintenance of this autonomy. The increasing use of special districts and other devices—a form of functional autonomy—has resulted in shifting broad areas of public policy from locally elected officials to relatively autonomous and distant functional agencies, which are insulated from the local political process.

The effects of functional autonomy over local control are limited by several factors. The most important local concern is land use, and functional autonomy only rarely affects this area. In addition, most of the relationships are voluntary, and a suburb can withdraw from them if it can afford to pay the price of proceeding on its own. A community can also accommodate by refusing to act at all on particular problems. This may adversely affect the residents of the non-acting suburb, but it is a legitimate instance of the politics of accommodation.

REPRESENTATION OF THE
SUBURBS IN CONGRESS:
NEW TRENDS

Congressional representation is
rapidly shifting in favor of the suburbs. In 1966, some 171 congressmen came from rural areas and small towns, while the remaining 264 congressmen were from districts that were predominantly
metropolitan. Of these metropolitan districts, 110 were located in
central cities, 98 were dominated by the suburban areas surrounding the central cities, and 56 districts contained a mixture of central
city and suburban populations along with a minority of rural
residents.

By 1972, the effects of reapportionment under the 1970 Census
will begin to be felt. By the time of the 1972 general elections, it
is estimated that some 291 congressmen will come from metropolitan areas, and 144 districts will be located in rural areas. Of
the metropolitan congressmen, 100 will come from districts dominated by the central cities, 129 will come from predominantly
suburban districts, and 62 congressmen will represent districts that
are mostly composed of central city and suburban voters but with
a minority of rural residents.[6]

This shift means that the suburban portions of metropolitan
areas are expected to pick up some 31 new congressmen between
1966 and 1972. For the first time in American history, suburban
representation in Congress will be greater than that of the central
cities. More congressmen will come from suburban areas than from
either cities or rural districts.

According to Robert Lehne, the ideological effects of the new
congressional alignment will be to create a Congress "slightly more
liberal" than that of the 1960's.[7] This is because the suburbs—
though conservative in relation to the voting behavior of the central cities—are definitely liberal in comparison to the rural districts.

Nonpartisanship

In contrast to contests for na-
tional and state office, many elections for suburban offices are
conducted on a nonpartisan basis. The use of nonpartisan elections
is, of course, widespread in the smaller and medium sized communities of the country. As we have seen earlier, nonpartisanship is
accepted in form in some of the largest cities, but in practice

partisanship easily pierces the disguise. In such cities politics is nonpartisan in name only. But the popularity of the genuine nonpartisan approach is especially noteworthy in the suburbs. In approximately 60 percent of the suburbs nonpartisanship is officially recognized in the electoral system. There are, as one would expect, suburbs which are fiercely partisan, but the main thrust is in the other direction. As Robert C. Wood has pointed out, suburban nonpartisanship may take several forms.[8] Sometimes it is simply a means to add another party to the local scene to show local independence from the dominant regional party, as in the Washington suburbs. Or it may take the form of inclusion of members of the minority party in local councils, as happens in suburbs in New York and Connecticut. But most frequently nonpartisanship takes the form of no association at all between local politics and the established parties. Public affairs are considered to be the province of various civic organizations whose goals are said to be "what is best for the community."

Many communities which are not suburban also emphasize local politics, but it is important to distinguish between the no-party pattern common to suburbia and the one-party localism which occurs in many small towns. Under one-party localism, there is apt to be a good deal of intra-party fighting within the organization, and as is shown by the primaries. After the primary, it is expected that the ranks will close and that party regularity will prevail. Party per se is valued.

But the characteristics of the no-party politics found in many suburbs are quite different. Wood has identified three of them. In the first place, there is what he calls "an outright reaction" against partisan activity. The emphasis in local elections is on consensus, not conflict. Many suburbanites seem to delight in cultivating a politically independent state of mind. A second aspect of suburban nonpartisanship is the acceptance by the suburbanite of an obligation to participate extensively in civic affairs. This may be demonstrated in a number of ways, including serving as an elective official on a part-time, amateur basis. And thirdly, there is the belief that the citizen himself knows best. He does not need leaders or parties, but will follow his conscience in the belief that this will result in the common good.

Criticism of the nonpartisanship found in suburban politics takes two forms. In the first place, skeptics contend that the Jeffersonian type of citizen postulated as the ideal can only infrequently be found in the flesh. Most citizens, it is said, have neither the time nor the energy to master increasingly complex governmental problems. The second line of criticism employs the party-responsibility argument. It is alleged that the political party is the best way to hold administrators responsible to the electorate. It is said that in this respect a civic organization is inferior to a party organization.

Despite these adverse charges, there is no indication that nonpartisanship in the suburbs is about to vanish. On the contrary, both as a practice and as an ideology, it seems here to stay.

There is one claim made on behalf of nonpartisanship, however, which requires examination. It is the statement that nonpartisanship succeeds in removing "politics" from local government. Whether this is true depends on how one defines "politics." If "politics" is equated with "partisanship," then, to be sure, nonpartisanship probably removes some party influences from local government. But if "politics" is defined as conflict over public policy, then the mere elimination of party labels has not eliminated politics.

Economic Correlates of
Suburban Voting

For some years now, social scientists have noted a close relationship between economic indices and partisan voting. For example, an association has been found between persons with high incomes and those who vote Republican. Even though psychological factors may depress any one-to-one ratio between economic factors (rent, income, occupation) and voting behavior, the association between the two remains statistically high.[9] In other words, suburban political variety is related to variety in the suburban economic base.

To translate these general propositions into the political behavior of a particular suburb presents obvious hazards, for the propositions are based upon aggregate data. Nonetheless, suburban political leaders have usually assumed the existence of some general correlation between economic characteristics and voting behavior. Their hunches have now been largely supported by scientific data.

From a partisan point of view, what does all this portend for the suburbs? It is likely that the suburban fall-out from "the exploding metropolis" will to some extent duplicate the patterns in the central city, where there are working class, mixed, and silk stocking wards. Since the out-migration consists only in small part of upper-class Republicans and in large part of middle-class and lower-class Democrats, the expectation is that the Republican margins in suburbia will be progressively reduced. What we know about political socialization implies that the new migrants to the suburbs will retain their previous party affiliations, which are probably largely Democratic. Although there may be some reverse migration of rich Republicans into fashionable city sections, on balance the continuing migration ought to help the suburban Democrats.

POLITICAL ISSUES

Observers have long noted that much of suburban politics is concerned with family-related issues. In particular, questions concerning the schools and housing attract continuing interest and attention. Of almost equal prominence is the perennial problem of taxes. Occasionally in the limelight are such additional subjects as the police, recreational facilities, and "corruption." In short, the politics of small communities tends to be focused on local issues. Local government in the suburbs usually pays very careful attention to the interests of its constituents.

Schools

Everywhere in America, education is a prominent issue in local politics. But it is especially stressed in the residential suburbs, since, as we have noted, one of the reasons people move to the suburbs is because of the presumed superiority of suburban over central city schools. While suburban school systems come in all shapes and forms, there is no doubt that those found in the more affluent suburbs are at the top of the educational pyramid. Presumably this is because of the high socioeconomic status of the residents.

In the nonpartisan atmosphere of suburban politics, a sharp distinction has been traditionally drawn between politics and education. The task of the citizens was to see to it that the necessary funds were raised for school operations, and to attend P.T.A. meetings from time to time.

In recent years, the schools have increasingly been the subject not only of public interest but of public controversy. The reasons for this development are quite clear. To be blunt, the costs of school operations have soared in relation to the incomes of many taxpayers. At a certain point requests for larger educational appropriations are refused, and bond issues for educational purposes are voted down. By 1970 what had long been suspected became an actual fact: a taxpayers' "revolt" was in process and it was seriously affecting school budgets. The continuing inflation, coupled with a sharp business recession, made matters worse.

Besides strictly financial problems, suburban schools in recent years have also found it difficult to deal with the growing unionization of their teachers. In some communities there were teachers' strikes which, no matter how short-lived, provoked violent reactions on the part of many parents.

But there is a further issue on the horizon which potentially could influence emotions even more than fiscal or unionization problems. This is the issue of busing students from poor, mostly Black, central city districts to the schools in suburban districts. On an experimental basis, such busing was tried in a very limited number of school systems in the late 1960's. In most of them a good deal of hostility was evident on the part of parents in the receiving districts. Whatever the educational value of busing may be, it remains an emotionally charged political issue. The suburbs —for various reasons—are likely to remain committed to the neighborhood school principle.

Nonetheless, in spite of suburban objections, the movement to end segregation in the public schools through a city-suburb linkup has been gaining momentum. While the center of activity obviously shifts from time to time, a major focus of activity was Detroit in the fall of 1971. An order by a federal district court to the Detroit and the state boards of education for a plan ending segregation in the city's schools pointed toward a "metropolitan" solution to the problem. If the city schools were integrated totally, Blacks in each school would approximate a majority of 65 percent —a situation many, if not most, white parents would oppose. But under the metropolitan plan suggested by Judge Stephen J. Roth, the school district would be extended to a radius of twelve miles from downtown Detroit. Under this proposal—which involved 61 school districts—white students would have a 60 percent majority. It was generally assumed by the proponents of the larger district plan that state funds would be necessary to implement the proposal.[10]

Housing and Land Use

Problems of housing and of land use generally are in the forefront of suburban political controversy. This is not strange, since one of the leading *raisons d'être* of the residential suburbs is comfortable housing with adequate surrounding space. These considerations go to the very heart of suburban living.

The sharpest disagreements over land use arise when a change in the zoning ordinances is proposed. For example, a proposal that undeveloped land be zoned so that the minimum area in any one plot is three acres has obvious social consequences. Conversely, a proposal to downgrade an existing residential area in order to permit the presence of light industry equally has social implications. Why are such land use controversies apt to be especially bitter? For individual families, the stakes are very high. As the realtors constantly remind any one who will listen, the purchase of a house (or perhaps a condominium, as well) is the largest single investment a family will ever make. A family which has committed its earning power for a lifetime does not view lightly any action by the zoning commission which is likely to jeopardize that investment. Whatever action is or is not taken, the impact on an individual family is highly personal.

Other Issues

Occasionally, a suburb may be stirred by charges of the "corruption" of those in office, although this is unusual and is out of keeping with the predominant nonpartisan suburban ethos. Ordinarily, an opposition group will merely maintain that it could, if in power, administer public affairs more efficiently than the current in-group.

In the suburbs, as elsewhere, the public may be aroused by issues related to police administration or to police policy. But these issues are much more limited in scope than in the big cities. For example, overt defiance of the gambling and vice laws would not be permitted in the affluent residential suburbs. Yet how the police handle traffic jams and how well they control out-of-town "rowdies" may become sources of political, i.e., policy conflict.

Taxation

The great bulk of money needed to finance suburban governmental services, including the school system, is raised through property taxes. The impact of these taxes is usually a dormant issue in suburban politics, but in periods of recession it often becomes salient.

For decades, the property tax on real estate proved a reasonably reliable source of revenue for the residential suburbs. The income was constant and, if insufficient, the council and the school board could increase their incomes by raising the tax rate. In a time when the market value of real estate was almost automatically increasing—and when the assessed value was only a portion of the market value—real estate was a satisfactory tax base.

The inflationary trend in the national economy in the 1960's and early 1970's tended, however, to make the property tax less and less attractive because, for all its virtues, it was relatively inflexible. Inflation coupled with a business recession often resulted, as has been noted, in the refusal of suburbanites to accept raised rates on their property taxes.

As was the case with the central cities, the suburbs, too, found that the state had pre-empted for itself the most lucrative sources of tax funds. Faced with relatively constant revenues and spiraling costs, the suburbs confronted a Hobson's choice. They could try simply to hold their level of services constant—which meant in fact letting them decline and which defeated the main point of suburban living in the first place. Or, they could try to raise the tax rates on real property—which meant at some point incurring formidable taxpayer resistance. The continuing impact of the fiscal crisis of the late 1960's and early 1970's varied from suburb to suburb, but even the richest community was subjected, probably for the first time, to very serious financial difficulties.

To bolster their revenues, some suburbs displayed great ingenuity. One solution—humorously called the "ball bearing factory solution"—was to rezone some undeveloped land at the border of the community for the use of light industry. The idea was that a nice, clean, ball bearing factory located at the edge of the residential area would produce badly needed taxes. At the same time, the workers employed in the plant would live in the neighboring suburb across the line, which would be responsible for educating the workers' children. If every suburb in the area attempted the same "solution," it is evident that this approach to financial salvation would be more or less self-defeating.

Nondecision-making in the Suburbs

In an analysis of community power, Peter Bachrach and Morton S. Baratz suggested in 1962 that power was exerted when a person or group could prevent the public airing of policy conflicts.[11] They believed that there was always a chance that some person or association could limit decision-making to relatively non-controversial matters. This might be accomplished, for example, if community values largely precluded discussion on an issue. A current example might be covert and implicit community resistance to plans of the federal government to construct low-cost housing in a highly affluent suburb. There simply might be no public discussion of the proposal at all, but this "nondecision" would have, of course, very profound consequences to the community.

Conrad J. Weiler, Jr. has applied the concept of non-decision-making to the local governments in the metropolis.[12] He found that nondecision-making is very widespread in suburban communities. Some important assumptions are not challenged and some potential issues are not discussed. This nondecision-making is the result, Weiler said, of the fragmented political structure of the metropolitan area, not the consequence of a plot or conspiracy.

SOME POLITICAL DIFFERENCES BETWEEN THE CENTRAL CITIES AND THE SUBURBS

Voting Behavior

The overall socio-economic differences between central cities and the suburbs were discussed in an earlier chapter. The political importance of such distinctions is that they furnish a rationale for explaining differing political patterns. As applied to voting behavior, this is fairly clear-cut. The prevailing theory of voting behavior in America holds that differences in voting preference are primarily related to differences in socio-economic status, and this status, it may be noted, includes religious affiliation as one of its elements.

The most obvious illustration of voting differences explicable on socio-economic grounds comes from state-wide elections. Here, where the ballot is ordinarily partisan, there is the opportunity to compare the central city vote en masse with that of the surrounding suburbs. As we have seen, in the big cities outside the south, this tends to establish a Democratic/Republican contrast. But this is only the aggregate part of the picture. For when voting behavior in state-wide elections of rich city wards is compared to the voting behavior of rich suburbs, the results are comparable.

Political Systems

The political differences between central city and suburban political systems are only partly explained on general socio-economic grounds, for differences are exacerbated by the relative autonomy of the suburban systems. In order that there may be complete understanding of this point—and at the risk of some repetition—it may be well to repeat what has been said earlier.

The theme expressed in Chapter 2 and reiterated in the present chapter is that there is a measurable degree of economic, cultural, and social cohesiveness inside any particular metropolitan area. This cohesiveness is not simply a sleight-of-hand of the Bureau of the Census—it exists. The precise degree of cohesiveness can be determined, of course, by means of statistical gradation.

But even though there is ordinarily a relatively high degree of economic cohesiveness within an American metropolitan area, the outstanding political fact is the very high degree of diversity. This differentiation is due, clearly, to the very large number of independent municipalities existing within a given metropolitan area. The result, as has been underscored, is that the politics of the suburbs possesses an autonomy of its own. In any particular metropolitan area, there are many different suburban political systems, and they show a very great degree of independence from the political system of the central city.

By way of illustration, what this means is that Cook County, Illinois, has a political system, Chicago has a political system, Winnetka has a political system, but the Chicago metropolitan area does *not* have a political system.

Effects of Demographic Trends

The effect of population increases has already been to shift considerable political power from the central cities to the suburbs. This has been attested to in the increasing importance of the suburban vote in state-wide elections and in the increases in suburban representation in Congress. Besides sheer population increases, analysts are giving particular attention to the question of shifts in race, which will affect political developments in many ways. For example, if the central cities become more and more Black, and the suburbs continue to increase their white populations very rapidly, then metropolitan consolidation schemes would appear unlikely to succeed. Such plans, if carried out, might threaten Democratic control of the central cities, and challenge Republican control of suburban counties.

Issues

Cities and suburbs also reflect their social differences in divergent public policies. The evidence indicates that the suburbs spend more money per pupil on educa-

tion than is the case in the cities. In the large central cities the operating expenditures per capita run substantially higher than in the
suburbs. Tax bills, though climbing in the suburbs, are likely to be
somewhat lower than in the central cities.

Lastly, policy differences between city and suburb in the smaller
metropolitan areas are not so great as those in the larger metropolitan areas. This is presumably because the social differences between the city and the suburbs in the smaller metropolitan areas
are less marked than in the larger areas.

Political Attitude
and Activity Patterns

For many years, political analysts
have assumed that both the attitudes toward politics and the patterns of political activity differed rather sharply as between cities
and suburbs. In an effort to find out more precisely the extent of
such differences, Joseph Zikmund, using interview data from the
Survey Research Center, studied this problem in seven major
metropolitan areas.[13] For each area interviews included both cen-
tral-city and suburban samples taken during the 1952, 1958, 1962,
and 1964 national election polls. The findings of the Zikmund study
have necessitated a considerable revision in the traditional view of
suburban-urban differences.

It was found that these differences were less great than had been
previously suspected. For example, one attitude question was
this: "Do you believe or not that 'hardly any' people running the
government are crooked?" Of the urban sample, some 22
percent agreed; of the suburban sample, some 27 percent. The
differences were not statistically significant. So it went with other
responses.

When questions relating to political activity were put to the respondents, some statistically significant differences emerged. These
appeared in answers concerning party identification, party loyalty
in past presidential elections, and split-ticket voting. But even here,
the differences were not monumental. For instance, in response to
the question: "Did you vote for candidates of 'different' parties
in past presidential elections?" 33 percent of the urban sample
said "yes," while 39 percent of the suburban sample said "yes."
This is statistically, but not practically, significant. The data further
indicated that there were greater differences among people from
separate metropolitan areas than among people from the central
city and suburbs of the same metropolitan area. In explaining
urban and suburban data patterns, it was found that the nation-wide

urban-suburban division was the least rather than the strongest of the influencing forces.

For Zikmund, the implication of these findings was that future research might most fruitfully focus on particular metropolitan areas considered as separate entities. Suburban phenomena would then be studied within the framework of an individual metropolis, and the national urban-suburban division so commonly used in the past would be downgraded.

Earl M. Baker conducted research along these lines when he examined the place of the political party in community political systems, specifically, in 73 suburban Philadelphia localities.[14] He was especially interested in learning how some 215 elected legislators serving on the governing boards at the municipal level perceived the political party. The findings indicated that most of the elected officials placed no value whatsoever on the role of the party in policy matters. On the other hand, as would be expected, the same officials credited the party with an important role in the recruitment and nomination processes. Baker further found that there was a direct relationship between positive party perceptions and urban development. Competition was found, however, to be negatively related to positive perceptions. This suggested that those officials who came from the least secure party environments had the smallest commitment to their respective parties.

SUBURBAN EXPERIENCE
AND COMMUNITY CONTROL

Proponents of community control frequently cite suburban political experience to bolster their own cause. The question is therefore raised as to how valid these references are in the light of what we actually know about the suburbs and their political behavior. In order to do this, we must make some distinctions.

The suburbs differ from local neighborhoods inside the cities in a number of important ways. In the first place, the suburbs are self-governing as a matter of law. They are independent municipal corporations with relatively stable boundaries. Many of them have been in existence for a long time, for example, as we have noted, the principal suburbs of many eastern cities are older than many western cities.

Secondly, the suburbs are basically self-supporting financially. In general, they are able to pay their own way, and they do.

Thirdly, the suburbs have a tradition of self-reliance which is hard to find in modern cities. There is very little such tradition in the largest cities, and practically none in the urban ghettos.

If this were the whole story, then the answer would have to be that suburban experience would be of little help to persons advocating local community control inside the cities. But it is not the whole story. If the citizenship participation aspect of suburban experience is stressed—rather than legal separatism—there is much in that experience from which local neighborhoods might learn.

There is, further, the idea in the suburban experience that certain institutions should be close to the people. This concept specifically includes such areas as education, land use, and the police—all of which are likely areas for neighborhood control in large cities. In these areas, the experience of the suburbs may have much to offer. At least it is worthy of detailed investigation.

THE FUTURE OF THE SUBURBS

Most writers on metropolitan affairs—including this author—would like to see both the central cities and the suburbs survive. Because of this preference, people often overlook or minimize evidence which suggests that the suburbs might well survive even if the cities do not. They seek elaborate reasons for contesting the prediction that most large cities will, sooner or later, follow the downward path of Newark.

Personal preferences aside, there appear to be two reasons for the confusion which often surrounds writing about the future of suburbia. In the first place, some of the evidence is contradictory. It is often possible to cite opposing trends, depending on which metropolitan areas are selected for study. And much of what passes for evidence has been carefully sifted by chambers of commerce on the one hand or by reform groups on the other in order to lead to a particular conclusion. From a scholar's point of view, the area is booby-trapped, and one must proceed warily.

But there is a second—and probably more profound—reason for the difficulty. It stems from the failure to distinguish sharply between two models of the metropolis. As a result, the analysis is often less focused than it could be.

The *historic model* stresses the linkages between the city and its suburbs. The impression is given that most suburbanites are directly dependent upon the city for their economic survival. At the same time, the social and cultural dependence of the suburbs on the city is also emphasized.

The basic objection to the historic model in the 1970's is that it is outmoded. While it is still applicable to certain of the smaller and medium-sized metropolitan areas, it is rapidly becoming obsolescent in the largest such areas, especially in the east and in the middle west.

The *emerging model* emphasizes the autonomy of the suburbs. It suggests that the suburbs of New York City, of Boston, of Philadelphia, and of St. Louis—to take a few prominent examples—will in all probability survive no matter how desperate the condition of the central cities becomes. The emerging model—which is an *actual* model for many of the largest metropolitan areas—acknowledges that the suburbs have become increasingly independent of the cities economically and socially as well as politically. More and more jobs are located in these suburbs, as is shown by the spate of weekly announcements of firms and stores moving from downtown to suburban areas. Fewer and fewer suburbanites have any reason to come into the city at all as life in the suburbs comes increasingly self-sufficient.

At the heart of the situation is the question of function. The problem can be approached by asking: "What does the city today do better than some other place?" To confirmed urbanites, the answer may well be discouraging, for the big cities have been losing many of their historic functions. They are becoming less important, for example, both as manufacturing and as commercial centers. And ever since the coming of the automobile—about 1910 —they have been losing out to the suburbs as attractive places in which to live.

The entire picture is further complicated by the racial bifurcation that seems firmly entrenched in the largest metropolitan areas. Wherever one turns in examining the politics of central cities and suburbs, he runs into questions related to race. Yet it is important to realize that the emerging or actual model of the metropolis was not created solely or even mostly by the heavy migration of Blacks to the cities and the migration of whites to the suburbs. It is quite probable—as George S. Sternlieb has contended—that the Black migration merely speeded up the departure of whites which would have taken place anyway.[15]

In speculating as to economic, social, and political trends in the suburbs, it is useful to have a rather clear idea as to which of the two metropolitan models the particular area under examination more nearly corresponds. The chances are that more and more metropolitan areas will approximate the conditions postulated by the emerging model.

SOME CONCLUSIONS

It will be recalled that one of the concerns of this chapter is to relate the politics of suburbia to the theory of pluralism. More specifically, the problem is whether suburban politics sustains or questions the group competition element in the pluralistic model of American politics. According to this model, competitiveness among groups is the usual and the expected condition of the political marketplace.

On this point, the experience of the suburbs is revealing, for it shows that the competitive element is minimized in a number of ways. Competition is not highly prized but, on the contrary, is regarded with some apprehension. How does this come about?

First, as we have seen, the prevailing tradition in local politics is one of nonpartisanship, whether party labels exist or not on the ballots. There is, relative to the cities, a lack of competition along partisan lines. The suburban ethos places a premium on consensus arrived at by individual agreement, not on decisions arrived at through party conflict.

Secondly, suburban politics is notable for its relative absence of class warfare. The political struggle, such as it is, is centered on individual disagreements, not on profound class differences. The class struggle, so often just beneath the surface in big-city politics, is muted or eliminated.

Thirdly, the general level of homogeneity inside particular suburbs does work toward a consensus type of government. This homogeneity is much more than merely economic. It tends to have social and religious dimensions as well.

Fourthly, the public airing of certain key questions is very often avoided or prevented. Nondecision-making, in this sense, means that decisions are made by individuals or groups but not by elected bodies.

The net effect of these four factors is to keep competition at a low level. On balance, then, it may be concluded that suburban political experience fails to sustain the competitive element of the orthodox pluralistic model. On the contrary, this experience suggests that the model is not especially relevant to current suburban political practice.

In addition to this theoretical concern, a second question was raised at the start of this chapter. It was asked whether politics considered as a "system" is different in any significant ways in the suburbs from what it is in the cities.

After examining the available evidence, we found that there are substantial differences with regard to emphasis on public issues. There are also wide differences in electoral patterns. The actors tend to be of differing types. Even the conditions of the "system" are to some extent different, for example, the suburban emphasis on the nonpartisan ideal. All this adds up to the conclusion that there are important differences between city and suburban political systems. These are sufficiently marked so that we can say that the city and suburban systems are separate, and that the autonomy of the suburban political systems is increasing.

CHAPTER
NOTES

1. Frederick M. Wirt, "The Political Sociology of American Suburbia: A Reinterpretation," *The Journal of Politics*, XXVII (August, 1965), pp. 647–666.

2. Peter H. Rossi, *Why Families Move* (New York: Free Press of Glencoe, 1955). See also, Leonard Goodall, *The American Metropolis* (Columbus, Ohio: Merrill, 1968), ch. 2.

3. Robert C. Wood, "Metropolitan Government, 1975: An Extrapolation of Trends," *American Political Science Review*, LII (March, 1958), p. 121.

4. Robert C. Wood, *Suburbia: Its People and Their Politics* (Boston: Houghton Mifflin, 1959), p. 260.

5. For further discussion of the idea of accommodation in suburban politics, see Michael N. Danielson, ed., *Metropolitan Politics: A Reader* (Boston: Little, Brown, 1971), pp. 191–195.

6. The calculations are presented in Robert Lehne, "Warming Up for 1972," *Trans-Action* (Sept., 1971), pp. 75–79.

7. *Ibid.*, p. 79.

8. Wood, *Suburbia, op. cit.*, pp. 153–158.

9. Especially, see Wirt, *op. cit.*

10. *U.S. News & World Report*, Oct. 18, 1971, p. 36.

11. Peter Bachrach and Morton S. Baratz, "The Two Faces of Power," *American Political Science Review*, LVII (Dec., 1962), pp. 947–952.

12. See Conrad J. Weiler, Jr., "The Metropolis as a Political System," paper delivered at the 1971 meeting of the American Political Science Association, Chicago, Illinois, Sept. 7–11, 1971.

13. Joseph Zikmund, "A Comparison of Political Attitude and Activity Patterns in Central Cities and Suburbs," *Public Opinion Quarterly*, XXXI, No. 1 (Spring, 1967), pp. 69–75.

14. Earl M. Baker, *Community and Party: Perceptions of the Political Party Among Local Legislators* (Washington, D.C.: unpublished Ph. D. dissertation, American University, 1971).

15. Interview with George S. Sternlieb, Director, Center for Urban Policy Research, Rutgers University, in *U.S. News & World Report*, July 26, 1971, pp. 42–49.

Note: In addition to the references above, other useful treatments of suburban politics may be found in the following books: Herbert Gans, *The Levittowners* (New York: Pantheon Books, 1967); Charles E. Gilbert, *Governing the Suburbs* (Bloomington: Indiana University Press, 1967); Anwar Syed, *The Political Theory of American Local Government* (New York: Random House, 1966); and Oliver P. Williams, *et al.*, *Suburban Differences and Metropolitan Policies* (Philadelphia: University of Pennsylvania Press, 1965). On the effects of Congressional reapportionment based on the 1970 Census, see "Suburbia Emerges as Major Gainer from 1970 Census," *Congressional Quarterly*, XXVIII, 31 (July 31, 1970), pp. 1957–1963.

part four

COMMUNITY

POWER

STRUCTURES

8

Who

Has

Power?

Urban politics and politics in general is concerned with the distribution of power among competing groups. Any serious analysis of urban politics must face several questions pertaining to power. To start with, there is the problem of the nature of political power. What exactly is meant by the term "power"? Where can power be found? Is it in the hands of a small elite group which constitutes a "power structure"? Or is it dispersed among rival and competing groups? Are there any alternatives to an elitist explanation of the location of power on the one hand and the pluralist explanation on the other? In this connection, what is the role of community organizations, which are gaining new prominence in local affairs? Another kind of question deals with the dispersal of power in a given community—which groups and which individuals are the most powerful? These general questions form the framework of the discussion which follows.

THE STUDY OF POWER

The general nature of political power has been sketched in recent years by Bertrand Russell and by de Jouvenel.[1] What emerges from their studies is an appreciation of the social role of power. Power appears to be as much a necessity in human relations as food and drink. It occurs not because of any plot against humanity but because humanity—as Aristotle pointed out—cannot function adequately without it. Power relationships are interwoven into all other human relationships.

In the writings of Harold D. Lasswell, the emphasis has been on the "psychology of power." Lasswell correlated power situations with personality types in his seminal work, *Psychopathology and Politics*.[2] In subsequent works Lasswell has dealt with other aspects of power, but his fascination with its psychological content has continued.[3]

One of the most widespread general theories of political power is that developed by Karl Marx. In essence, the Marxists' contention is that economic power is the basis of all other kinds of power. Political power is held to be a derivative of economic power. As applied to the state, therefore, the Marxists maintain that the state is really nothing more than a kind of executive committee of the bourgeoisie, the top economic elite. Political decisions, while they may appear to be independent, are in fact said to be dependent upon the will of the industrial directorate. Democracy, as understood in the western world, is considered to be an elaborate sham —an effort to mask from the bulk of the people the realities of bourgeois rule.[4]

Non-Marxist political theorists, while recognizing the close interrelationships between political and economic power, reject the Marxist assertion that political power is derivative. Citing examples from recent German, American, and even Soviet history, the non-Marxists argue that political power has an existence of its own. As an example, the Nazi party, once in control of Germany, bent the great industrialists to the party's will. The Third Reich served the purposes of the party, not those of the Ruhr manufacturers and their financial allies.

Taking his cue from Machiavelli's *The Prince*, the Italian political theorist Vilfredo Pareto (1848–1923) identified political power with a political elite. An economist and a sociologist, Pareto divided mankind into two principal types. The first type consists of the "foxes," who flourish because of their cleverness and their ruthlessness. In the case of the second type, the "lions," there is a devotion to conservatism, patriotism, and the church. In their operations, the lions stress force rather than intelligence.

Pareto further divided all of society into two classes—the elite, or upper classes, and the non-elite, or lower classes. Inside the elite there is a governing group which exercises real control. This occurs regardless of the constitutional character of the society. In all societies, there may be found the "circulation of the elite." What this means is that there is a continuing movement from the lower to the upper classes. Every existing elite is, sooner or later, doomed to extinction. From these arguments Pareto drew gloomy conclusions as to the future of the western democracies.[5]

A final, general approach to the subject of power comes from Max Weber. By stressing the importance of bureaucracies in the governmental and corporate areas of contemporary life, Weber tended to locate power in a hierarchical structure. The inference, of course, is that the greatest concentration of power is to be found at the apex of the pyramid. The strata in the hierarchy would possess diminishing power as one descended from the high to the lower levels.[6] In both Marx and Weber, power is identified with positions in society. But Marx identifies power with the uppermost economic class, whereas Weber associates power with the top strata of bureaucracies. Although there may be overlapping areas in these two definitions regarding the allocation of power, it is evident that the concepts are easily distinguishable from each other.

In all of the studies cited to this point, the efforts to define or to locate power have been approached in a general way. A group or a class has been the locus of investigation. Recently, a good deal of attention has been given to the specifics of power relationships. Since this approach is now dominant, this chapter will attempt to illustrate it in some detail.

A familiar method in the examination of power is to imagine that power concerns the relationship among actors. If A has no influence, let us assume that B does x. But if A has influence, let us assume that B does not do x but does y. In other words, A has influenced B to do something that B would not otherwise have done. This accords with one's common-sense notion of what influence is.

In this illustration, both the existence and the direction of influence have been identified. But suppose, as often happens in real life, we want to determine the *relative* influence among different actors. Whether the actors are persons, groups, or nations, the problem has obviously become more complicated. As Robert A. Dahl has pointed out, it is not impossible to come to grips with a question of this type. He warns that it is easily possible to come up with only a partial approximation of the true answer.[7] In addition, there is the troublesome problem of potential influence. Ordinarily a difference exists between an actor's actual influence and his maximum potential influence. This is an important factor in real-life political calculations.

For purposes of political analysis it is important to make a distinction between the terms "influence" and "power." Dahl does this, and begins by singling out two particular kinds of influence.

One, *reliable influence,* occurs when the probability of compliance with a request is very high. The other, *coercive influence,* is based "on the threat or expectation of extremely severe penalties or great losses, particularly physical punishment, torture, imprisonment, and death."[8] If one imagines that influence runs along a continuum, one extreme of that continuum is characterized by coercion. This is the area, as noted above, of the most severe penalties. Dahl says: "This is the domain of *coercive influence,* which is sometimes called *power.*"[9]

Dahl continues in his analysis, to cite four ways in which power may be observed in order to understand its impact and distribution. They—and their respective limitations—are as follows:

1. One can assume that "an actor's power is closely correlated with his position in an official or semi-official hierarchy."[10] For example, it could be assumed that because a man is a university president he possesses considerable power. But this assumption is obviously often not warranted.

2. Or it can be assumed, as was done in Floyd Hunter's famous study of Atlanta, that well-placed judges or observers can identify those persons who possess power.[11] The problem here, of course, is that there is no way of checking on the judgment of the judges.

3. A third method is to determine who participates and how frequently in the making of decisions.[12] A drawback with this approach is that activity is not necessarily the same thing as power.

4. Then there is a fourth method, which was used by Dahl and his associates in their famous study of New Haven. Their technique was to weigh the activities of different participants in selected decisions. In this way, the pitfall of confusing mere activity with real power may be sidestepped.[13]

Dahl continues in his analysis to cite four ways in which power vantages as well as disadvantages. But in any event, the traps are plentiful for the researcher, even the most skilled, and it is common to make errors in the analysis of power relationships.[14]

The Elitist Concept

The idea that there is, or should be, a governing elite has long been attractive to political philosophers. In his *Republic,* Plato argued that the ideal form of government would be rule by philosopher-kings, that is, a highly trained and selected elite. Plato's disciple, Aristotle, found many examples of ruling elites in his pioneering studies of what we today call comparative politics.

In our time the interest has shifted from whether there should be such an elite to the more empirical question of whether one in fact exists. Regimes founded on the elitist principle, such as modern totalitarian societies, present no problem in this respect, at least for theorists of the western democracies. What does present a problem is whether the assumptions of the modern democratic states are borne out in actual fact. Does a country based on the idea of competitive parties and universal suffrage necessarily make the concept of a ruling elite irrelevant? Does the problem of a small ruling group disappear when a nation adopts a parliamentary or a presidential form of popular government?

Many prominent political philosophers have contended that ruling elites not only exist but have flourished in the modern democracies. This is a common argument with the ideological enemies of democracy, such as the Marxists and the Fascists. It is therefore usual to dismiss the findings of these critics on the ground of bias and deliberate distortion. It is held that the assumptions of apologists for totalitarian states necessarily result in an indictment of democratic beliefs.

But the assertions of western social scientists to the effect that their empirical studies have unveiled ruling elites behind a democratic façade have been taken much more seriously. Especially in America the critiques of well-known social scientists have had a profound impact. Sticking only to the contemporary era, the late C. Wright Mills, Ferdinand Lundberg, and G. William Domhoff have all concluded that an upper class elite really controls the United States. The position of Mills has already been outlined. Since Lundberg and Domhoff employ roughly the same procedure, a brief sketch of Domhoff's book, *Who Rules America?*, will illustrate the approach of both writers.[15]

The thesis of Domhoff is that the American upper class is a governing class.[16] As a starting point, it is therefore necessary to demonstrate the existence of an upper class. Using the *Social Register* of 12 major American cities as his leading index, Domhoff asserts that the listing of a person in one of these volumes demonstrates his upper class membership. Other criteria for such membership include social institutions such as private schools and exclusive clubs. On the basis of such indices, Domhoff concludes that the American upper class consists of less than one percent of the total population.[17]

The relationship between a "governing class" and a "power elite" is said to be straightforward.[18] A "governing class" is "a social upper class which owns a disproportionate amount of the country's wealth, receives a disproportionate amount of the country's yearly income, and contributes a disproportionate number of its members to positions of leadership."[19] But not all members of this top social group concern themselves with power. Some may while away their lives riding to the hounds, or entertaining mistresses, or drinking with members of the international jet set. Other members of the upper class will, of course, busy themselves with governmental or corporate affairs.

The "power elite," on the other hand, is defined as those who are "in command positions in institutions controlled by members of the upper [governing] class."[20] "Any given member of the power elite may or may not be a member of the upper class. The important thing is whether or not the institution he serves is controlled by members of the upper class."[21]

From here on, Domhoff's objective is to show that members of the upper class control or dominate major corporations, foundations, universities, and the Executive branch of the federal government.[22] In contrast, the power elite (members of the American upper class and their high-level employees) does not control but merely influences Congress, most state governments, and local governments.[23] Why this aspect of American political life escapes control of the upper class is not clear from Domhoff's account. Presumably, such dominance may not be worth the effort.[24]

While Domhoff relied on the *Social Register* as his first step in identifying the upper class, it is possible to use other indices which give similar results. Lundberg, for instance, stresses directorates in key corporations. From membership lists he then creates tables of interlocking directorships. Certain key individuals then begin to appear with regularity in powerful non-corporate institutions, such as the prestige universities, the great foundations, and important church and charitable organizations. As with Domhoff, Lundberg uses the position of an individual in society as the starting point in the search for who has power. The lists of those who are powerful, while not identical, are largely overlapping.

Even though their published works enjoyed wide circulation and drew an enthusiastic readership, Mills, Lundberg, and Domhoff ran into pointed shoals of scholarly criticism. For example, the thesis of a national governing elite was held to be so nebulous as to be virtually unresearchable. Many said that there was no way of proving or of disproving the conclusions which were stated. All three authors were charged with confusing position with power, and it was stressed that many persons with a high social position are virtually without influence or power. A third general criticism was that the national elitist school failed to distinguish between the possibility that there might be several competing elites. If there were several such groups, might not the competition really serve popular and democratic purposes after all? Finally, critics pointed out that even if there were a national elite, most people are more concerned with the question of power in their own communities. From this perspective, the problem developed: Is it possible for there to be competing elites in the cities even if there is no competition at the national level?

Interest in this question was not new, for community power studies predate the national studies by a decade. But the writings of men like Mills served to spur on the search to locate power at all levels of American life, including the local community. Research in this field obviously held advantages over research at the national level, for it was possible to observe personal behavior at first hand. Often, the researcher himself could be a participant-observer. Meetings of officials were more frequent and more accessible. Interviews and polls were more feasible on a local than on a national basis. And, of course, in terms of expense, a locally conducted scientific inquiry offered more for one's money than one on a national scale. For these reasons, the emphasis of the elitists tended to shift from national to community investigations. The result has been the proliferation of a large and important group of studies dealing with community power.

Community studies as formal, systematic investigations received their first widespread recognition in 1929. In that year Robert S. and Helen M. Lynd published *Middletown*, their study of Muncie, Indiana. Some eight years later they brought out the results of a further investigation of the same city.[25] The most general finding of the Lynds, in both studies, was that Middletown was controlled, in all important respects, by the "X Family." Using a social anthropological approach, the Lynds found that the city's most important family dominated the business class of Middletown, and through that class maintained its influence in education, housing, religion, and government. In other words, a business elite ran the community, but the X family dominated that elite.

In the years following the appearance of the Lynds' studies, scores of books on American communities have been written. Of such works, the most influential study to arrive at elitist conclusions has unquestionably been *Community Power Structure*, Floyd

Hunter's famous analysis of decision-makers in Atlanta.[26] Published in 1953, the Hunter investigation has served as the archetype for a whole school of community studies. Its methodology has been widely imitated, and its findings have been replicated in numerous instances. Because of the overriding importance of the Atlanta study, its main findings warrant summarization.

Hunter tells us that his project grew out of an intense feeling of dissatisfaction with the existing knowledge as to how the governors and the governed communicated with each other.[27] In the belief that a case-study of leadership and power relationships in an actual city would help clarify the communication process, he decided to study the situation in Atlanta, which he referred to as Regional City.

It was Hunter's first task to find out who in Atlanta held power. In order to pursue this question, he employed a reputational method. "In Regional City," he says, "the men of power were located by finding persons in prominent positions in four groups that may be assumed to have power connections."[28] The groups were identified with business, government, civic associations, and "society." "From the recognized, or nominal, leaders of the groups mentioned, lists of persons presumed to have power in community affairs were obtained."[29] Using a process of "judges" to determine leadership rank, and also a system of self-selection, some 40 persons in the top levels of power in Regional City were selected from more than 175 names.[30]

What people do for a living locates them in a community. On this basis, the occupational breakdown of the 40 leaders fell into certain clusters. Eleven of the 40 were directly associated with the activities of large commercial enterprises. Seven persons were in banking and investment operations, the second largest category. In the "service" category were five lawyers and one dentist. Five persons had major industrial responsibilities. Government personnel were represented by four persons. Two labor leaders, representing very large unions, made the listing. The five remaining persons were classified by Hunter as "leisure personnel," persons with social or civic organization responsibilities but no day-to-day professional concerns. Of these persons, one was a woman who spent little time in Regional City but who contributed annually $100,000 to charitable purposes in the community.[31]

Though the very top policy-makers differ in many respects, they have certain common characteristics. For example, Hunter indicates that they tend to have expensive offices, they frequent similar social clubs, and they reside in the best residential district of the city.[32] The professional men, used as a contrasting group in the study, cluster in a different residential district.[33] Comparisons of this type are made among the other segments of the 40 leaders.

But above all else, the leaders are persons of power status. "They are persons of dominance, prestige, and influence. They are, in part, the decision-makers for the total community."[34] Further, "They are able to enforce their decisions by persuasion, intimidation, coercion, and, if necessary, force."[35]

It would be an error to assume that the power personnel represent a "true pyramid of political power." Though they are dominant economically, and influential politically when they want to be, they have no continuing and permanent mechanism for transmitting their views to the various legislative bodies of the area. On some political issues the power group is simply not interested in the outcome.

In Regional City there is a large Black community which is next to the heart of the business and commercial districts. It is a substandard community and it is segregated, but it is functional. It provides a substantial labor force for the total community, and it is organized. In terms of power, "The Negro community represents a sub-structure of power as well as a sub-community."[36]

Yet the relationship between the Black leaders and the men of top decision in the larger community is "superficial."[37] As a result, communication between the smaller and the larger community was incomplete and sporadic.

Certain other aspects of community power were underscored in the Regional City study.[38] Contrary to popular belief, the men of power did not operate clandestinely and behind the cloak of nightfall. In real life, "The men of power usually operate openly with one another and on equal terms."[39] Another important consideration is the process of selection. On this, Hunter comments: "As it presently stands, leaders are for the most part self-selected."[40] When it comes to planning which relates to government activity, the policy-making group is suspicious. It shows this suspicion by accepting reports of planning experts but by making sure that the reports gather dust in the agency files. In short, the recommended programs are stopped before any implementation can be undertaken.[41]

Even though many of the top leaders of Atlanta are fearful regarding the directions of social change, their fears to date have been more imaginary than real. On most of the important issues, the policy-makers are united, and this is a reason for their collective strength. So far as their own basic value-systems are concerned, the leaders are in nearly total agreement.[42]

In his concluding essay, Hunter returns to the role of government in a community controlled by a business elite. Only government, he contends, is big enough to provide for social planning which will take into account the interests of both the upper and lower structures of power. Expressing his faith in the democratic process, Hunter sees the possibility of reform of structural arrangements through changes in the process of selecting leaders. He would like the citizen, in relation to community participation on the level of policy decision, to have a "voice in determining who would be at the top."[43]

The Pluralist Concept

Long the dominant model for community studies, the elitist concept has come under continuous attack during the last decade. As a result, its former dominance has been lost, and it now shares the limelight with the pluralist model. Of the many community studies which support the pluralists' conclusions, the most influential has been Robert Dahl's 1961 study of New Haven, Connecticut.[44] Because of the importance of this work in subsequent community power studies, some familiarity with its methodology and its findings is essential.

Dahl begins by noting that in any American democratic political system—including New Haven—knowledge, wealth, social position, and other resources are unequally distributed. This being so, the general question arises as to whether it is even remotely likely that the "people" can rule. But if the people, even in popular government, do not seem to be in a position to make decisions, who does make them? In order to reduce this broad query to manageable proportions, Dahl proposes to launch more specific inquiries relating to the distribution and patterns of influence and to the activities and characteristics of leaders.[45] He is also interested in learning whether his approach to community power will throw light upon the problem of change and stability in a democratic system generally.

In the New Haven investigation, the emphasis is placed upon decision-making in the community. In turn, this inquiry is focused on three specific issue-areas: urban redevelopment, public education, and political nominations. These areas were chosen because Dahl felt they were significant and that data were available for in-depth examination. Decisions in the first two of these areas "require formal assent of local government officials at many points."[46] While the third area, nominations, is only quasi-governmental, it is included because it is reasonable to assume that whoever controls nominations has influence over the elected officials.

The researchers posit several hypotheses relating to the distribution of influence in the three control areas. After studying the leaders in these areas, Dahl concludes that only a small number of people have direct influence "in the sense that they successfully initiate or veto proposals for policies."[47] On the other hand, in critical or close elections, the voters have great indirect influence on the decisions subsequently made by the elected leaders.

To know the distribution of influence does not by itself give sufficient information to answer the question, Who governs? It is also essential to know something about the patterns of influence. For analytical purposes, it is useful to imagine two situations. In the first, the leaders in every issue-area could be assumed to be substantially identical and to agree on the policies they want. It could be further assumed that they come from the same social stratum. Given these assumptions, there would, of course, be an elite with presumably ample power to make all the important community decisions if it wished. What we have here is the elitist hypothesis.

But a rival supposition is also logical. If the various leaders differ from issue-area to issue-area and also among themselves, power is not held by a united elite. The power of one leader would be off-set or checked by the power of another. In terms of supporting their leaders, the citizens would have choices not available under elitist rule. So the inquiry next turns to the questions of what strata furnish the leaders and the extent of their agreement or disagreement.[48]

At this point in the New Haven study the strength of the pluralist position emerges. Of the 50 different persons identified as leaders in the three issue-areas, only three "initiated or vetoed policies in more than one issue-area."[49] These were Celentano and Lee—two mayors—and Logue, one of the top leaders in redevelopment. The same specialization of influence was found to exist among the sub-leaders. So far as background was concerned, the leaders did *not* come from a single homogeneous stratum of the community. On the contrary, they manifested considerable ethnic, religious, and economic diversity.[50]

The two conclusions regarding patterns of influence were these:

First, a leader in one issue-area is not likely to be influential in another. If he is, he is probably a public official and most likely the mayor.

Second, leaders in different issue-areas do not seem to be drawn from a single homogeneous stratum of the community.[51]

These findings add up to a rejection of the Hunter elitist thesis. However power is exercised in New Haven, it is not managed by a covert elite of the top economic stratum.[52] Other aspects of the study have important implications for political theorists, but the central thesis is that power is located not in one but in several groups, depending on the issue. New Haven, Dahl concludes, is a "pluralistic democracy."[53]

In carrying out his study, Dahl was aided by several gifted research assistants. One of them—Nelson W. Polsby—wrote an important companion volume to *Who Governs?* Entitled *Community Power and Political Theory*, Polsby's volume argued the pluralist case with skill and tenacity.[54] Polsby's technique was to review critically the principal studies which tended to find a stratified socio-economic elite in control of American communities. On the basis of the evidence in the studies themselves, Polsby contended that they contradicted rather than supported stratification theory. He also insisted that the findings in New Haven furnished no support for such a theory.

There developed from the Polsby and other hostile analyses of stratification theory one of the more captivating scholarly battles of our time. Generally, the sociologists supported the elitist position, while the political scientists endorsed the pluralist concept. Methodological sharpshooters, who had hitherto held their fire, emerged from their fastnesses to take careful shots at each other. But by all odds the keenest of the marksmen was Nelson Polsby, whose book must be read in toto to obtain a proper appreciation of his analytical skill.

The Elitist-Pluralist Continuum

As the scholarly debate escalated, analysts of community power tended to fall into two rather sharply divided camps—the elitists and the pluralists. In turn this division appeared to coincide with an interdisciplinary distinction, with the sociologists on the side of Hunter and the elitists, and the political scientists in support of Dahl and the pluralists. Each school continued to produce further studies which were cited as additional proof of that group's earlier findings.[55]

A significant effort to resolve the dispute was made by Robert V. Presthus in *Men at the Top*, published in 1964.[56] In his effort to find leaders in two small cities, he employed and then compared different research techniques. This method permitted him to arrive at some findings on reputational as against decision-making approaches to community power. He also considered the relationship of his specific findings to the subject of pluralism. On this point, he speculated: "To some extent, where the sociologists found monopoly and called it elitism, political scientists found oligopoly but defined it in more honorific terms as pluralism."[57]

One of the most detailed inquiries into the validity of the elitist thesis was that undertaken by Arnold M. Rose, a distinguished sociologist at the University of Minnesota. In *The Power Structure*, published in 1967, Rose subjected the views of Hunter to a microscopic examination.[58] In the same work he critically scrutinized— from a macroscopic perspective—the thesis of C. Wright Mills. On the basis both of this intensive review and also of his own independent studies, Rose opted for the "multi-influence" or pluralist view of power in America. In Rose's words,

In sharper summary, the conclusions of this book—in contrast with those of Mills and Hunter—are that [the] power structure of the United States is highly complex and diversified (rather than unitary and monolithic), that the political system is more or less democratic (with the glaring exception of the Negro's position until the 1960's), that in political processes the political elite is ascendant over and not subordinate to the economic elite, and that the political elite influences or controls the economic elite at least as much as the economic elite controls the political elite.[59]

Acknowledging that the economic-elite thesis had been criticized by earlier writers, Rose pointed out that the bulk of the scholarly analysis had come from the pens of political scientists and philosophers. He thought there might be "special merit in a criticism by an empirically based sociologist" such as himself.[60]

But like other serious social scientists, Rose was both baffled and intrigued by the social science mystery surrounding the various community studies. How was it possible for reputable and careful researchers to arrive at such contradictory findings? After mulling the problem over, Rose concluded that there is a growing feeling on the part of the investigators "that the power structure varies with the type of community."[61] By comparing several communities, he noted, it is possible to rank them along an "elitist-pluralist continuum."[62] As more and more studies became available, he predicted that this practice would become more common.

After a full decade of the debate between elitists and pluralists, and after contributions by various revisionists, where does the situation stand now? Three general statements can be made with some assurance that they will hold up.

First, the methods used in a community study go a long way toward determining what will be found. It can hardly be a coincidence that researchers who use the reputational approach always discover that an economic elite is dominant. Nor can it be a coincidence that investigators who employ the decision-making approach always arrive at the conclusion that power is dispersed among several groups, generally with little overlap on the part of the group leaders. Quite clearly, there is a very high relationship between methodology and findings in the area of community power studies.

Secondly, the communities themselves—as Rose suggested—may be placed at appropriate positions along an elitist-pluralist continuum. This is to say that the question of elite dominance or of the dominance by a number of different groups is really a question of degree. Evident though this statement may be in retrospect, it was much less so when the elitist-pluralist debate was at its highest decibel. On both sides partisans tended to confuse the elitist or pluralist *models* with a static, unmoving *typology* of opposites. By not allowing for in-between situations, these partisans failed to do justice to their own efforts.

Thirdly, communities change over time, and the changes bear directly on the question of which group or groups control a particular community. In the New Haven study, for instance, we are told that the city in colonial times was dominated by a small, educated, well-to-do patrician elite. After several changes in the ruling structure, the present "pluralistic democracy" came into being. The inference is that the changes in political structure were brought about by massive factors of social change: economic, demographic, and political.

It also appears likely that a particular community will evolve from elitist to pluralist rule as its economy proceeds from a one-industry to a multi-industry basis. In other words, economic diversity and competition are likely to result in competition in other areas, political as well as social. A true test of this thesis will be its relevance to studies carried on, over a period of time, of cities such as Dallas, which is commonly believed to approximate the Hunter model. But even if Dallas proves to be an exception, there is reason to believe that, in general, industrial and business diversification, especially in heterogeneous communities, will work in the direction of a multi-influence society.

Community Organizations

In their search for who holds power, investigators have sometimes found power concentrated in a dominant economic elite and at other times scattered among various competing groups. But there remains a third possibility that is worth investigating. It is possible that power in a particular urban area could also reside in territorially organized neighborhood groups. If this should prove to be the case, then local community power could be envisaged as a counterbalance to the power of a dominant elite or of a multiplicity of elite groups. It is also possible that local neighborhood organizations, if federalized, might serve as a countervailing power both to an area-wide political organization and also to the most influential interest groups.

That this third approach toward community power is more than a Utopian dream has been demonstrated in a number of American cities. The experience of one organization—the East Central Citizens Organization (ECCO) in Columbus, Ohio—is illustrative. Milton Kotler, who studied ECCO at length, notes that it is the oldest of some seventy neighborhood corporations around the country, and one of the most successful.[63]

Founded in 1965, ECCO is a neighborhood corporation. Its neighborhood consists of approximately one square mile containing 6,500 people, mostly Black. By all usual statistical tests, the area is poor. ECCO was formed when a neighborhood church, The First English Lutheran Church, agreed to transfer its settlement house to neighborhood control. The transfer was substantial, in that it involved a large number of services. These services included a nursery school for retarded children, tutoring, dances, psychological guidance, clubs for the young and the elderly, and emergency welfare services.[64]

With the neighborhood people who had been involved in the settlement house serving as the nucleus, local leadership drafted a charter and the bylaws necessary to establish a corporation. The Office of Economic Opportunity came forth with a grant of $180,000. In January, 1966, the church agency was formally transferred to the new tax-exempt corporation.[65] In the spring of the same year the neighborhood met as a general assembly and chose its first Executive Council of twenty-one. The Council then proceeded to hire an executive staff.

Under the bylaws, "any resident at least sixteen years old who lives within the boundaries of the corporate territory can sign the roster and become a member."[66] By being a member, a resident can vote in the assembly, which serves as the legislative arm of ECCO. The Executive Council (which now has 30 members) is elected from four neighborhood clubs (which existed before ECCO and became four ECCO districts) and at-large in an annual assembly. In 1968 the annual budget of ECCO stood at approximately $203,000, which came mainly from the OEO.[67]

Among the many programs of ECCO are the following: operation of the Youth Civic Center, various educational projects, housing responsibilities in cooperation with the city government, employment activities, operation of a health program with the Public Health Service, economic development, social service programs, and many recreational activities. Clearly, such a wide range of endeavors brings ECCO, actually or potentially, into conflict with other agencies in the city. Despite this, ". . . it is enough to say here that ECCO grows stronger and continues to thrive."[68]

So far as strategy is concerned, ECCO strives to develop new programs and to reach agreement with the city of Columbus "for territorial jurisdiction over these public activities."[69] According to Kotler, the long-range objective is for ECCO to become in law a "political entity of the municipal government."[70] The type of self-rule which ECCO is trying to obtain would appear to be analogous to the kind of self-rule which exists in a typical small town. In order to achieve this objective of a self-governing neighborhood, certain powers exercised by the city would have to be transferred to the neighborhood corporation.[71]

From Kotler's point of view, separatism along racial lines is as objectionable as bureaucratic centralization operating under City Hall. Rejecting the notion that Black communities should sever all relations with white society, he asserts: "Neighborhood government challenges this separatism, and instead seeks the inclusion of localities, Black and white, into the general government."[72] What is ultimately envisaged is a constitutional arrangement whereby power is distributed among the various neighborhood governments, which, in turn, are federated to form a common city government. ECCO has not remotely approached the realization of this goal, but its supporters—we are told—view its attainment as both possible and desirable.

For reasons very different from Kotler's, Black power theorists have also viewed community-controlled governmental institutions with considerable favor. Two of the leading theoreticians whom we have already mentioned—Charles V. Hamilton and Stokely Carmichael—have stressed Black control over institutions in Black neighborhoods as a primary goal.[73] Such control is seen as contributing to a new sense of community among Black people. It is also held to create both a psychological feeling of self-reliance and a physical condition of self-sufficiency.

But the Black cohesiveness and exclusivity implied by the term "Black power" has been severely criticized by Bayard Rustin, a distinguished Black labor and civil rights leader.[74] Rustin has maintained that "Black power" is harmful to the civil rights movement because it diverts the movement from a meaningful debate over tactics and isolates the Black community. Generally, in place of "Black power," Rustin advocates the maintenance and extension of the liberal-labor-civil rights coalition. His objective is to fight effectively for a more equal and just society for Black and white alike.

The Local Neighborhood and Power in the Metropolis

The Columbus, Ohio and similar studies suggest that the simple dichotomy of elitist versus pluralist power is somewhat misleading. Even when modified to take into account such factors as historical development and population changes, the most distinguished community studies often appear to be marginal to the real world of urban politics.

This marginality may be due to various causes, including the virtual neglect of the masses of ordinary men and women who live and work in the metropolis. The pages of the community studies are crowded with Economic and Social Notables, with mayors and political leaders, with financial tycoons and labor barons. But this is a highly select population—a tiny fraction of the total community. Absent are the great masses of people who work in factories or in assembly-line offices, raise and educate children, attend church and fraternal meetings, watch TV in the evenings, and dutifully turn out at election times. In short, the world of the community studies is underpopulated and is, to this extent, unreal.

It is at this point that the analyses of community organizations —neighborhood corporations like ECCO—are useful. They tend to fill the population void found in the usual community studies. No doubt neighborhood organizations may be either elitist or pluralist—or somewhere in between. This does not especially matter. What is evident is that these associations offer at least the theoretical possibility of mass-participation by ordinary people in important aspects of decision-making in the local neighborhood. In doing so these associations offer the opportunity for a dispersal of power quite unlike that discovered in the elitist or pluralist community studies.

Whether such dispersal actually occurs, and how often, is, of course, a matter to be determined empirically. But there is reason to believe that there is an increasing willingness to deal into the decision-making arenas of the large cities various hitherto excluded local groups and organizations.[75] Both the expansion of the political arenas and the development of new channels to them are in large measure responses to the neighborhood-based organizations. The creation of such organizations in the last decade has resulted in a new emphasis on localism inside the great metropolitan areas. As a result, localism as a political factor in urban politics is undergoing a great revival.

From a theoretical perspective, the recent experience with neighborhood organizations suggests that they may constitute an alternative power model to those of the elitists and the pluralists. Or, if not precisely an alternative model, the neighborhood concept may be envisaged as a supplementary model to the other two.

To return to the original question—Who has power?—it is clear that power in the metropolitan area continues to be elusive. Yet the development—and potential proliferation—of neighborhood organizations may make both observation of the phenomenon of power and its practical management more feasible than in the past. Local community control through these associations in such areas of vital popular concern as education, housing, and the police would obviously affect the course of urban politics. Not only would there be important new actors, but the rules of the "game" would be seriously altered.

It is possible that such local control would fill the gaps in governance brought about by the observable decay of the traditional brokerage politics of the metropolis. In any case, any new or revised model of urban politics must take into account the potential and real roles of neighborhood organizations.

CHAPTER
NOTES

1. See Bertrand Russell, *Power* (New York: W. W. Norton, 1938), and Bertrand de Jouvenel, *On Power* (New York: Viking Press, 1949).

2. Harold D. Lasswell, *Psychopathology and Politics* (New York: Viking Press, 1960).

3. See, especially, Harold D. Lasswell, *Politics: Who Gets What, When, How* (New York: Whittlesey House, 1936), and Harold D. Lasswell and Abraham Kaplan, *Power and Society* (New Haven: Yale University Press, 1950).

4. A recent and highly useful commentary on Marx is found in Henri Lefebvre, *The Sociology of Marx* (New York: Pantheon Books, 1968).

5. See Vilfredo Pareto, *The Mind and Society* (New York: Harcourt, Brace, 1935, 4 vols.). This work was first published in 1915–1916 under the title *Tratto di sociologia generale*.

6. Generally on Weber, see Hans Gerth and C. Wright Mills, *From Max Weber: Essays in Sociology* (New York: Oxford University Press, 1946). Weber's famous definition of power is "the chance of a man or of a number of men to realize their own will in a communal action even against the resistance of others who are participating in the action." Citation at p. 180.

7. Robert A. Dahl, *Modern Political Analysis* (Englewood Cliffs, New Jersey: Prentice-Hall, 1963), pp. 41–47.

8. *Ibid.*, p. 50.

9. *Ibid.*, p. 50.

10. *Ibid.*, p. 52.

11. *Ibid.*, p. 52.

12. *Ibid.*, p. 53.

13. *Ibid.*, p. 53.

14. *Ibid.*, pp. 53–54.

15. Ferdinand Lundberg, *America's 60 Families* (New York: Vanguard Press, 1937); G. William Domhoff, *Who Rules America?* (Englewood Cliffs, New Jersey: Prentice-Hall, 1967).

16. Domhoff, *op. cit.*, p. 3.

17. *Ibid.*, p. 7.

18. *Ibid.*, p. 9.

19. *Ibid.*, p. 9.

20. *Ibid.*, p. 10.

21. *Ibid.*, p. 10.

22. *Ibid.*, p. 11.

23. *Ibid.*, p. 11.

24. *Ibid.*, pp. 132–137.

25. Robert S. and Helen M. Lynd, *Middletown* (New York: Harcourt, Brace, 1929); and, by the same authors, *Middletown in Transition* (New York: Harcourt, Brace, 1937).

26. Floyd Hunter, *Community Power Structure* (Garden City, New York: Anchor Books edition, 1963). The book was originally published in 1953.

27. *Ibid.*, Anchor Books edition, p. 1.

28. *Ibid.*, p. 11.

29. *Ibid.*, pp. 11–12.

30. *Ibid.*, p. 12.

31. *Ibid.*, p. 13.

32. *Ibid.*, pp. 14–19.

33. *Ibid.*, p. 22.

34. *Ibid.*, p. 24.

35. *Ibid.*, p. 24.

36. *Ibid.*, p. 110.

37. *Ibid.*, p. 139.

38. *Ibid.*, p. 139.

39. *Ibid.*, p. 178.

40. *Ibid.*, p. 227.

41. *Ibid.*, p. 234.

42. *Ibid.*, p. 241.

43. *Ibid.*, p. 253.

44. Robert A. Dahl, *Who Governs?* (New Haven: Yale University Press, 1961).

45. *Ibid.*, pp. 7–8.

46. *Ibid.*, p. 103.

47. *Ibid.*, p. 163.

48. *Ibid.*, p. 165.

49. *Ibid.*, p. 181.

50. *Ibid.*, p. 183.

51. *Ibid.*, p. 183.

52. *Ibid.*, p. 185.

53. *Ibid.*, p. 305.

54. Nelson W. Polsby, *Community Power and Political Theory* (New Haven: Yale University Press, 1963).

55. A bibliography of even the most famous community studies is impressive. For a listing of 240 relevant books and articles, see Willis D. Hawley and Frederick M. Wirt, eds., *The Search for Community Power* (Englewood Cliffs, New Jersey: Prentice-Hall, 1968), pp. 367–379.

56. Robert V. Presthus, *Men at the Top: A Study in Community Power* (New York: Oxford University Press, 1964).

57. Quoted in Hawley and Wirt, *op. cit.*, p. 209.

58. Arnold M. Rose, *The Power Structure* (New York: Oxford University Press, 1967).

59. *Ibid.*, p. 492.

60. *Ibid.*, p. 39.

61. *Ibid.*, p. 297.

62. *Ibid.*, p. 297.

63. See Milton Kotler, *Neighborhood Government* (Indianapolis: Bobbs-Merrill, 1969). The account of ECCO is taken from this work.

64. *Ibid.*, p. 45.

65. *Ibid.*, p. 45.

66. *Ibid.*, p. 46.

67. *Ibid.*, p. 46.

68. *Ibid.*, p. 48.

69. *Ibid.*, p. 49.

70. *Ibid.*, p. 49.

71. *Ibid.*, p. 69.

72. *Ibid.*, p. 89.

73. Stokely Carmichael and Charles V. Hamilton, *Black Power: The Politics of Liberation in America* (New York: Random House, 1967). They define "Black power" as "a call for Black people in this country to unite, to recognize their heritage, to build a sense of community." P. 44.

74. See Bayard Rustin, " 'Black Power' and Coalition Politics," *Commentary*, Vol. 42, No. 3 (Sept., 1966), pp. 35–40.

75. The experience in Baltimore with regard to the anti-poverty effort is instructive on this point. See Peter Bachrach and Morton S. Baratz, *Power and Poverty* (New York: Oxford University Press, 1970).

part five

POLICY

POLITICS

9

The Politics

of Education

We have stressed that the pluralistic model of urban politics has two basic components—group theory, which is, as the name suggests, taken from the work of sociologists, group psychologists, and political behaviorists, and the community/state dichotomy. The relevance of the group theory component of the model has been analyzed in some detail in Parts Two and Three. It is the other component of the model—the community/state dichotomy—which forms the basis of our examination in Part Five. It will be recalled that this component, which stresses limited government, was given its modern definition by Robert M. MacIver in 1947.

From the community/state separation flow two deductions which have operational implications for our analysis. A first is that the *area* of political activity is both confined and clearly delineated. A second and equally important deduction is that the *level* of political activity is low. The overall strategy of Part Five is to employ the community/state dichotomy and its implications in an analysis of urban politics in three important areas of urban American life— education, housing and urban renewal, and public safety or "law and order." Each of these areas is treated in a separate succeeding chapter. Much as we have done with our analysis of the group theory model, our analysis will be within the framework of the community/state dichotomy of the pluralistic model. In this fashion the model can be tested in the real world of urban politics.

If we find that the area of political activity remains roughly constant, and if we further find that the level of such activity remains low, then we can say that the model retains its effectiveness in helping to explain and to understand the urban political process. If, on the contrary, we find that the area of political activity is expanding, and that the intensity of conflict is rising, then we will have to conclude that the urban model has lost a good deal of its applicability to the present-day urban situation. Should we judge the model to be irrelevant, this will not be a unique finding; many earlier prominent social models have suffered a similar eclipse.

A primary goal of Part Five is to test the pluralistic model against the real world of our time. But another goal is to analyze the factors working for social and political change in three of the areas of most direct concern to persons living in the great metropolitan complexes. We begin with a consideration of public education in the years since 1945.

PUBLIC EDUCATION:
AN OVERVIEW

At its annual meeting held in July, 1970, in San Francisco, the National Education Association released a flood of statistics concerning the public school systems in the United States.[1] The following information is worthy of note:

1. The average American teacher is a woman, is 39 years old, and earns $8,900 per year on a ten-month basis.

2. There are 2.2 million teachers in the public schools, of whom 32.4 percent are men. Ninety-five percent hold a bachelor's degree, and more than 30 percent a master's degree.

3. Enrollment in elementary and secondary schools now stands at 47.2 million. Of this total, 62 percent of the students are in elementary schools.

4. During the 1950–60 decade, the school-age population increased 47 percent. In the next decade, it increased 20.3 percent.

5. More people are in school and they are staying longer. The number of school years completed by adults over 25 stood at 8.6 years in 1940; 9.3 years in 1950; 10.5 years in 1960; and reached 12.1 years in 1969.

6. In all, some 52.6 percent of the population has finished high school and 10.5 percent has attended college for four or more years.

7. Americans are spending at the rate of $32.2 billion per year on education. This comes to $766 per pupil. Ten years earlier the national expenditure for each student averaged $375.

8. The NEA convention was told that local taxes provide 52.5 percent of school revenue, while the states provide 40.8 percent and the federal government the remaining 6.7 percent.

By any standards, these figures are impressive. Yet the NEA delegates were apparently not overly cheered by them. In his address to the 7,000 members present in the convention hall, outgoing NEA president George Fischer asserted that the Nixon administration "had declared war on public education."[2] He said that some contemporary "experts are predicting that public education cannot survive the onslaughts leveled against it in 1970." In connection with the alleged "retreat" on the part of the federal government, Fischer declared: "It's tragic that the federal government should be more interested in supersonic aircraft, public highways and new airports than giving 50 million young people the better educational tools to in turn develop the economy." Despite all of this, Fischer concluded on a positive note: "I believe," he said, "that our schools are succeeding."

However, the NEA president's guarded optimism was not supported by a report the NEA released earlier in the day showing the results of a national study of reading. The study indicates that there are three million adult illiterates in the United States; that one in four students now in school is not learning how to read, and that half of the nation's unemployed young people, aged 16 to 21, are illiterate. To correct this situation, the report offered various recommendations. But the overall picture was one of monumental failure in the area of literacy education.

This and other deficiencies are even more appalling in light of the vast expenditures which are made for the public schools. After national defense, public education is the single largest public undertaking in the country. It is the costliest of all the functions financed by state government. It is not surprising that there is increasing public resistance to the demand of boards of education for ever-higher annual budgets. In the process, the educational preserves, once the exclusive territory of the professional educational guides and their camp followers, have been invaded by a vast army of nonprofessional but concerned parents and taxpayers.

This invasion has seriously challenged the official theory of the American school system. We have seen that the American school system historically has been characterized by a localism that sets it sharply apart from European systems. The primary unit of the system has been and in most states remains the local district with its local school board. In most places the board is elected, but in some of the larger cities the boards are appointed. Where a board is elected, it usually possesses independent taxing power. Where it is appointed, it normally must submit its budget to the city council for approval and for implementation. In either case the emphasis is on the local school board, regardless of the size of the municipality.

But the official doctrine goes beyond the proposition that schools should be locally governed. It also holds that the government of the schools should be as independent as possible from the government of the municipality. In other words, politics and education should be separated into different worlds. The objective, of course, is to prevent "the politicians" from contaminating the educational process.[3] School Board members tend to be upstanding citizens and, in actual fact, *do* tend to be found on the directorates of civic associations, especially in the smaller and medium-sized communities.

It is a matter of debate as to how well this highly decentralized system has served the nation. But it became absolutely clear after World War II that the forces of change were strengthening. Generally, the advocates of reform argued that that state aid to local districts should be increased, and proposed various formulae for increasing it. In their 1962 study of state aid in eight northeastern states, Stephen K. Bailey and his associates traced the evolution of this movement in some detail.[4]

In building up support for reform, this study found, the schoolmen were able to count on certain allies: professional educators, governors, legislators, party leaders, teachers and their lay disciples, and particular business interests.[5] At the same time, there were certain depressants which worked against increased general state aid to education in the northeast following World War II. The Bailey study identified these forces as tax-minded business groups, the tradition of localism, the conservatism of certain politicians, and the disorder and naïveté of the educators themselves.[6]

Interestingly enough, the Roman Catholic Church, often thought of as a strongly negative force, was not found to be so in fact. The four investigators concluded: "Whatever may be true of the Church as a depressant upon local and federal public school spending—and even here the story is mixed—the Church cannot be reasonably accused of being a depressant at the level of state aid."[7]

When all the factors had been assessed, it was found that the most profound and persistent of the depressants on state school subsidies was "rural localism, whose proponents are typically over-represented in state legislatures throughout most of the northeast."[8]

Even though, in the northeast and elsewhere, the reformers were able to increase the level of state aid, they were not able to resolve one of the basic problems, namely, the local school board itself. The essential difficulty was this: The school board had to enter more and more into active political alliances to get more money. Yet at the same time local boards continued to insist on their historic autonomy. Thus, the boards often became paralyzed with indecision and ineffectiveness.

This development is chronicled in depth by Robert Bendiner, a skilled journalist who specializes in educational affairs. In *The Politics of Schools*, Bendiner commented on the role and status of school boards.[9] His analysis was based on wide travel and detailed interviews, and his conclusions were not sanguine regarding the future of local boards. At one time, he noted, the problem closest to the heart of public education was the relationship between the superintendent and the board, but this has ceased to be the most important question. The basic question today is whether the boards themselves are suitable instruments for dealing with the great current problems facing public education: such as finance, unionization of teachers, and the racial balance of student populations.

Bendiner concluded, from his evidence that: "It must be plain from all that has gone before that in three major aspects [those above] all vital to public education, the American school board has reached a point where what was mere inadequacy has come close to total helplessness, where decline and fall are no longer easily distinguished."[10]

Whether one agrees in toto with Bendiner's assessment is not important. What is significant is the large measure of agreement by educational observers to the effect that public education is in serious trouble. This is so, they believe, despite able and sometimes Herculean efforts by educational officials to aid the schools. And, as has been widely reported, public opinion polls have shown that parents' satisfaction with their children's education has been decreasing.

In view of the energy and concern that have since 1945 been poured into the public educational system, the returns have been disappointing. One can only conclude that the failures of the system must largely be attributable to some basic flaw in the system itself. Simply adding "more of the same" has not achieved the desired educational objectives.

It is not always easy to identify fundamental defects in the structures of great social institutions, for the foundations, as it were, are often out of sight. But in the case of the American educational system this is no longer so. On the basis of numerous intensive studies made during the last quarter of a century, it is evident that one of the basic building blocks of the educational structure has crumbled—the supporting block for the concept that governments which manage education should be independent of other governments. The idea that education should be autonomous and outside "politics" has now become not only obsolete; in so far as it still commands a following, the concept constitutes an obstacle to educational advancement.

As this condition has increasingly been appreciated, schoolmen have tended to abandon the concept of autonomy and have substituted for it the idea of cooperation with the political branches of government, that is, the urban mayors and councils and the state governors and legislatures. This has meant, of course, a change in the basic rules of the game, but the outlook is promising. The shift in the policies of schoolmen from rugged independence to cooperation took place over a considerable period of time, and it is by no means complete. But the principal factors working in the direction of politicization are clear. Of them, the most obvious, and the first chronologically, was money, and we shall begin with that.

MONEY AS A FACTOR IN POLITICIZING EDUCATION

Traditionally, American school districts were financed primarily through local property taxes. Yet in recent decades local educational systems have increasingly appealed to the state governments for assistance. General state aid—or "foundation programs," as they are usually called—are designed to establish an acceptable minimum program for all parts of the state.

The end of World War II brought a sharp increase in requests by local districts for more substantial general state aid. The reason was quite clear. During the war, school construction was almost completely halted. Some districts had budgetary surpluses which could be applied to new schools, but others did not. Where the local need was high and the money non-existent, the stage was set for pushing demands for state assistance.

In addition, salaries of teachers lagged behind the wages paid in various other fields, and local districts therefore ran into teacher recruiting difficulties. This situation was aggravated by the postwar baby boom, which began to hit the schools in the early 1950's.

How eight northeastern states responded to demands for greater state assistance was documented in the Bailey study.[11] Some figures from two states illustrate what happened throughout the area. In 1946, for example, Connecticut appropriated $5.7 million for aid to public elementary and secondary education. For 1951 the figure was $17.6 million and for 1961 it was $56.5 million.[12] A similar spectacular increase was shown in the case of New York, where the state aid stood at $128 million in 1946; $281 million in 1951; and $750 million in 1961. All of the other states in the study—Maine, Massachusetts, New Hampshire, New Jersey, Rhode Island, and Vermont—also dramatically increased the amount of state aid to public schools.

To discover how and why the increases were made by the particular states, the researchers analyzed the legislative history of state aid in the respective state capitols. In every case, the increases came from the successful building of coalitions and the application of political pressures. The basic theorem of the investigation, then, was this: ". . . the amount of money state governments make available for general aid to public schools is determined politically."[13] And the future level of support will depend on the continued use of political skills: "If state aid to education is to continue at its present rate, or is to expand, it will be because politically active schoolmen have the knowledge and skill to marshal effective political power."[14]

The politics of school finance was also dealt with in a 1964 analysis of public school systems in Michigan, Illinois, and Missouri.[15] Again, the conclusion of the investigators is that local control of public schools is more a myth than a fact. Nowhere is this better illustrated than in the dependence of local districts upon the states for revenues. As a result, in Michigan, for example, school politics at the state level is mostly a battle over who gets and who contributes how much money.[16]

The increasing dependence of local districts on state aid has, of course, created a shift in battlegrounds from the local level to the state level; a move which has also added to the number of actors who participate in the financial struggles in education. It has also increased the intensity of the conflict. To refer to Michigan again, the added appropriations by the state resulted in heavy and successful pressures for state appropriations to church schools. However, the practice of appropriating state funds for church schools in Michigan proved to be short-lived. In 1970, the legislature had authorized a $22 million program of subsidies to non-public schools to help pay salaries of lay teachers of secular subjects. Later in the same year the voters approved an amendment to the state's constitution which outlawed the spending of public funds for such purposes. In April, 1971, the Michigan Supreme Court upheld the amendment and applied it to the non-public school program. The result was the invalidation of the program.

Another consequence of the increasing reliance on state assistance is a demand for equalization of revenues between suburban and urban districts. As of 1965, it was estimated that for the 37 largest metropolitan areas in the country taken as a whole, some $449 was spent for each pupil in the central cities. At the same time, some $573 was being spent for each student in the suburbs, or a differential in favor of the suburban student of $124.[17]

But for specific areas, the differences were even greater: St. Louis —$183; San Francisco-Oakland—$193; Los Angeles-Long Beach —$230; Dallas—$263; Buffalo—$270; Houston—$483.[18] Differences of these magnitudes inevitably result in demands by central city educational groups that the state increase its payments to central city school boards. In this way, too, the financial battle shifts from the level of the municipality to the state level.

Even though the state's share of school expenses had climbed to 40.8 percent by the end of the 1960–70 decade, the fact remained that more than half of the funds—52.5 percent—still came from local taxes. During the same period the actual amount of state and local taxes increased sharply as government expenses soared. As we have seen, higher taxes generally, coupled with inflation and a fairly high level of unemployment, resulted in understandable taxpayer resentment.

There is not much a taxpayer can effectively do to protest high taxes, yet one thing he can do is to vote down school bond issues. At the end of the decade of the 1960's, in what looked like a full-scale taxpayers' "revolt," school financial measures were being voted down in record numbers by voters in school districts in every section of the country. Table 9.1 taken from United States Office of Education sources, gives a comparison for the years 1957–58 and 1968–69 respectively.

A later study, made of the spring, 1970 school bond elections by the Investment Bankers Association of America, showed that only

TABLE 9.1
Results of U.S. Public School Bond
Elections: 1957–58 to 1968–69

	Number of Elections		Percent Approved Based on Number	Par Value of Issues Voted on (in Millions)		Percent Approved Based on Dollar Value
	Total	Approved		Total	Approved	
1957–58	*	*	*	$1,542	$1,123	72.8
1958–59	*	*	*	1,801	1,433	79.6
1959–60	*	*	*	2,672	1,792	67.1
1960–61	*	*	*	1,605	1,218	75.9
1961–62	1,432	1,034	72.2	1,849	1,273	68.9
1962–63	2,048	1,482	72.4	2,659	1,851	69.6
1963–64	2,071	1,501	72.5	2,672	1,900	71.1
1964–65	2,041	1,525	74.7	3,129	2,485	79.4
1965–66	1,745	1,265	72.5	3,560	2,652	74.5
1966–67	1,625	1,082	66.6	3,063	2,119	69.2
1967–68	1,750	1,183	67.6	3,740	2,338	62.5
1968–69	1,341	762	56.8	3,913	1,707	43.6

* Data not available.
SOURCE: U.S. Dept. of Health, Education, and Welfare, Office of Education, circulars on "Bond Sales for Public School Purposes," reprinted in The New York Times, Jan. 12, 1970.

32.6 percent of the school bonding proposals, in dollar value, were approved at the polls.[19] At the same time numerous measures to increase property taxes for the support of school districts were defeated in referenda.

Pessimists viewed these fiscal developments as a harbinger of total disaster. The optimists, however, viewed the interpretation more positively. They agreed with Dr. R. L. Johns, director of the National Educational Finance project, who said, with apparent satisfaction: "I think we're on the verge of a major revolution in school financing."[20] What Dr. Johns expected was a new system for financing the public schools, with reliance shifted to more federal aid plus state and local income taxes. By 1980, Dr. Johns predicted, state and federal sources would be paying 80 percent of local education costs. "It won't be a revolution like a clap of thunder," he said. "It may take 10 years, but it will come."[21]

The specifics of educational finance may be left to the experts in the field. But the odds are one out of one that the future of school financing in this country will be decided politically. Consequently, educators are having to learn how to play the "game" with the greatest possible skill.

UNIONIZATION AS A FACTOR IN POLITICIZING EDUCATION

Half a century ago Walter Lippmann noted that most people perceive of other people in terms of stereotypes.[22] Nowhere has this principle been better illustrated than with the American school teacher. According to the stereotype the typical teacher is an embittered, eccentric spinster, who has little love for children and little teaching skill. In view of this deeply embedded stereotype, it often was difficult for teachers' associations to be taken seriously either by school boards or by parents. That such associations are now considered models of militancy by other public employees is a pointed indication as to how completely the "image" of teachers has changed.

The reasons for this shift in public attitude are many, but the role of the National Education Association (NEA) was one of the more important factors. The largest of the teachers' organizations, the NEA, now claims 1.1 million of the nation's two million public school teachers. Until the 1960's, the NEA stressed professionalization and vigorously opposed the organization of teachers into trade unions. The NEA took a very strong position against teachers' strikes.

What shook the NEA out of its relative lethargy, and brought about a dramatic reversal of its general outlook, was the quick victory won by its chief rival in New York City in 1962. For many years labor organizations had tried to unionize teachers in New York and elsewhere. Generally, their successes were infrequent, and the results were meager. Of the unions the best-known was the American Federation of Teachers (AFT), an affiliate of the AFL-CIO. In New York City the local branch of the AFT is known as the United Federation of Teachers (UFT).

From its inception in 1916 until the early 1960's the AFT, like the NEA, opposed strikes by teachers. But events in 1960–62 in New York City brought about drastic changes. In that time the UFT held two strikes, won a collective bargaining election, and secured substantial salary increases. As a result of these victories, UFT membership climbed from about 60,000 in 1960 to 112,000 in 1965. Half of the increase was in New York City.[23]

Even so, the AFT represented in 1965 only 6.4 percent of all teachers.[24] But the UFT victory in New York City had, according to Bendiner, an "electric effect" on teachers throughout the country.[25] Within a few years the AFT was chosen as collective bargaining agent in Chicago, Detroit, Cleveland, Philadelphia, and Washington.[26]

The effect on the huge NEA of victories in New York City and elsewhere by affiliates of the AFT has been tremendous. The larger organization changed its policy toward collective bargaining, which it now favors. The NEA also backs strikes when it initiates them.[27]

How is one to account for the rise of militant unionism in the teaching profession? Stephen Cole, in his study of unionization in New York City, offers a convincing explanation.[28] The key factor in determining the willingness of teachers to join a union and to become militant, he found, is the percentage of male teachers in a school system. In New York City, the percentage of men nearly doubled between 1924 and 1960, rising from 11 to 20 percent of the total.[29]

Cole took two samples of teachers—one in New York City and the other in Perth Amboy, New Jersey—in an effort to see whether militancy and sex were correlated. He found that they were. "In the New York sample, 70 percent of male teachers and 42 percent of female teachers were militant."[30] The same degree of correlation was found to exist in the Perth Amboy sample.[31]

In his investigation Cole discovered a high correlation between the religion of New York City teachers and their militancy. He found that "In New York, Jewish teachers were more favorably predisposed [than non-Jews] to accept the union and the programs of its leadership."[32] On the basis of historical statistics which he was able to develop, Cole concluded that the percentage of Jewish teachers had increased from 22 percent in 1914 to 59 percent in 1960.[33] Thus, the increase in the percentage of Jewish teachers may be viewed as a positive factor in the unionization process in New York City.

Whether religious affiliation, including Judaism, is a factor in unionization in other school systems than New York's is anybody's guess. But there is no doubt that New York's steady increase in the percentage of male teachers has been typical of other cities as well. In 1910, only 10.5 percent of American teachers were men. By 1967, the proportion of male classroom teachers had risen to 31.7 percent.[34] All of this has increased the likelihood both of militancy and of unionization by teachers, according to Cole's analysis.

Teacher militancy, whether expressed through the NEA, the AFT, or some other organization, tends to take the teachers from the periphery of political combat and put them in the center of the struggle. An important illustration is supplied by the confrontation of a strong teachers' organization with the ordinary school board. When questions involve hard bargaining between the board and the teachers' organization, the odds are all in favor of the teachers. This is because they can and do employ expert negotiators to represent them in the bargaining sessions. These negotiators may be backstopped by a strong state-wide organization which can command expertise, experience, and research resources totally beyond the capacity of the local board. Furthermore, if the teachers' organization is rebuffed at the local level, it is always in a position to renew the battle at the state level. It is, in short, not a very fair contest when a really strong teachers' group confronts an isolated board of willing but inexperienced amateurs.

In a way, of course, all this may be of some value to the local boards. Bendiner contends that unionization has, in a sense, tended to revitalize the boards since collective bargaining involves both parties in the most minute aspects of the school day.[35] Still, as the United Federation of Teachers has repeatedly shown in New York City, a skilled union can successfully compete with a board as powerful as New York's.

Both the NEA and the AFT envisage an increasingly active political future. In a review of labor relations in education for the 1960–70 decade, Albert Shanker, the president of the United Federation of Teachers, predicted a bigger role for the unions in the years ahead.[36] The new strength of the teachers, he said, would be used in two major areas: economic and professional. The teachers also expect to achieve a good deal of power in the decision-making of the educational system.

Coming from the president of the UFT, such thoughts may not appear startling. But the inaugural address of the NEA president for 1970–71, Helen Bain, must have aroused some apprehension on the part of many school board members. At the July, 1970, San Francisco convention, Mrs. Bain declared: "Whether we like it or not, education is in the political arena. It is imperative that we tool up our political might to defend the right of every child to be given an equal chance to grow."[37]

The Nashville teacher asserted that the NEA had learned that sometimes teachers' strikes are necessary. "And the NEA will be 100 percent behind them," she added. Not only should the NEA increase its own lobbying efforts, but teachers themselves should as individuals become more prominent in politics. "Every teacher," she counselled, "not only should belong to a political party, but some of you have to run for committeeman or committee-woman."

Mrs. Bain's speech pointed out how obsolete the old stereotype of teachers and their organizations had become. At the same time her speech indicated that teachers' groups may be much more politically militant in the future.

THE DRIVE FOR EQUALITY
OF OPPORTUNITY

A third and final factor in the politicization of education has been the continuing drive for equal educational opportunity regardless of race or income. The general contour of the situation is well-known, and there is no need to retrace the familiar terrain here. The focus of our immediate attention is, rather, on education in the largest cities.

Social Change

The massive post-World War II Black and Puerto Rican migration from rural areas to metropolitan centers seriously challenged established educational patterns. So did the concomitant large-scale movement of whites from the cities to the suburbs. As the racial and ethnic compositions of neighborhoods changed, the schools which served them also changed. Some entire school systems—Washington, D.C., is an example—shifted from a majority of white students to a majority of Blacks.

The extent of the changes is illustrated by a few statistics from the Philadelphia school system. In 1969–70 total enrollment was about 290,000 students.[38] Between October, 1968, and January, 1970, Black enrollment in the public schools increased by 3,408 pupils. During the same period white enrollment declined by 3,795. The increase brought Black enrollment to 169,490, or 59.8 percent of total enrollment. White enrollment constituted about 38 percent of the total, the balance consisting of Puerto Ricans and others.

In Philadelphia there is also an extensive system of Roman Catholic schools. Total enrollment for the school year 1969–70 was 139,620.[39] Since the overwhelming majority of students enrolled in schools under the Archdiocesan Board of Education are white, it is evident that in Philadelphia a good deal of voluntary racial segregation occurs along religious lines.

In New York City, Black enrollment in the public schools for the same period stood at 32.2 percent of the total, while the Puerto Rican percentage was 21.5 percent.[40] The Black percentage in Baltimore was 65.1 percent. The Detroit school system was 63 percent non-white. For Washington, D.C., the 1969–70 statistics indicated that 93.5 percent of all students were Black.[41]

Social change of this magnitude is bound to have repercussions in the worlds of education and politics. Even where the changes in racial composition of school populations have been less dramatic than in those cities mentioned, the tendency for population change to affect political action has been marked. In Boston, for example, Mrs. Louise Day Hicks was able to achieve prominence as a mayoralty candidate by using the busing of public school students —which she opposed—as her leading issue.

In the face of serious racial problems, most local school boards are helpless. The Evanston, Illinois, and Berkeley, California, boards were able successfully—through a combination of skill and luck—to meet the issue of de facto segregation. Yet their success has proved to be atypical. The average school board, as Bendiner notes, makes a good "whipping boy" but is a very poor instrument of social justice.[42] It has neither the authority nor the know-how to cope with racially-related problems. Meanwhile, the problems are getting worse.

Race vs. Class Divisions

In analyzing the ills of urban education, attention has quite understandably been directed to the highly visible question of divisions along racial lines. But it also is possible to consider racial divisions as secondary to class divisions. In a widely quoted article, Patricia Cayo Sexton contended that the basic conflicts within city school systems arise from a conflict of interests between haves and have-nots.[43] She considers race a subdimension of the larger problem. Acknowledging that there is ethnic and other conflict in city schools, she adds: "But, usually, when the chaff and wheat are separated, what is left is the 'haves' in one pile and the 'have-nots' in another, with some impurities in each—middle-class white 'liberals,' for example, who support some Negro demands and white have-nots who oppose them."[44]

Sexton identified the principal actors within the city as follows: "1) Negroes; 2) labor unions; 3) white have-nots; 4) white liberals;

5) the Jewish community; 6) the Catholic community; 7) business organizations and their allies in city silk-stocking areas."[45] While these elements often overlap, they have separate identities.

When applied to the history of educational conflict in New York City, the Sexton method of class analysis brings new insight into the problems. But it does not, of course, necessarily point to clear-cut solutions of the difficulties. On the national level, President Nixon's excounselor on urban affairs, Daniel P. Moynihan, has employed a similar technique. He has consistently approached urban racial problems on the basis of class. He has maintained, for example, that the best way to proceed is to create a large and stable Black working class and to enlarge the Black middle class. In pursuing this objective, Moynihan necessarily gives a priority to economic reforms and measures. It is implied in this approach that a prosperous community would not tolerate schools of the kind that dot the urban ghettos.

School Integration

The politics of school integration, as played in large northern cities, has taken some unexpected turns. In Detroit, the school board voted in April, 1970, to decentralize the schools. The plan called for the creation of seven districts, each with its own school board, as well as one central board of education. The board also voted to change the feeder pattern for some Detroit high schools in an effort to prevent increased segregation. Under this scheme Black students would have been sent to the nearly all-white high schools on the city's outer edges. More white students would have been channeled into the racially mixed schools. Though the plan called for no formal busing, some students would have had to travel five miles to reach their high schools.[46]

The unveiling of the school board's plan for integration touched off a furor of classic proportions, including demands for the recall of the four school board members out of seven who had supported the plan. Action to nullify the proposal was instantly begun in the state legislature. Though the details of the Detroit battle make interesting and sometimes depressing reading, the attention of political analysts was centered not on these details but on the new political alliance which developed. "Conservative" whites and "liberal" Blacks came together to seek a political trade-off: less integration for more community control over the schools. It is probable that the kind of anti-integration coalition which developed in Detroit will occur wherever the strength of white conservatives and community-control-minded Blacks is great enough to make a trade-off attractive to each party.

DECENTRALIZATION AS A
POLITICAL ISSUE: THE CASE
OF OCEAN HILL-BROWNSVILLE

We have already noted the power of the UFT in New York. An illustration of this power is provided by the case of Ocean Hill-Brownsville. In the fall of 1968 the United Federation of Teachers struck three times against the New York City Board of Education. Beginning as a dispute over whether the central board or the local board should have control of teachers in one experimental school district, the controversy mushroomed into one of the most intensive and widespread confrontations in American educational history. Since what happened in New York could also happen in other large cities, a brief review of the events which occurred there may serve as a preview of developments elsewhere, especially in Chicago, Detroit, Philadelphia, and Los Angeles.

The New York public school system is gargantuan; in the 1969-70 school year it had an enrollment of 1,121,922 students. Other statistics are scaled proportionately: in the same year, there were about 60,000 teachers; there were 900 schools; the whole enterprise cost $1 billion a year to operate. The entire apparatus is under the supervision of a Board of Education, which now shares power with local community school boards. Until 1961, the Board was selected by the mayor. Since then, a screening-panel procedure has been in operation. Under this plan, Board members are nominated by civic groups, and appointed by the mayor, the net effect of which is to strengthen the role of the civic groups and weaken the influence of the mayor.[47]

For some years there have existed local school boards. In 1961 the Board of Education was empowered to appoint local school board members for 25 new districts, a number which increased in 1965 to 31.[48] The local boards were given no real authority to make school policy. Their chief function was to act as community buffers. Actual authority resided in the Board, the superintendent appointed by the Board, the educational bureaucracy, and special interest groups.[49] This was the general distribution of power at the time of the 1968 strikes.

Under a state-mandated reform program which went into effect on July 1, 1970, this relationship was substantially altered. On that date the old local boards legally ceased to exist, and were replaced by 31 community school boards. Elected by residents of the neighborhoods where the schools were located, the new boards took over some of the management functions formerly exercised by the Board of Education.

The April, 1969, state law—a compromise of many proposals considered in Albany—gave the local boards considerable control over elementary, intermediate, and junior high schools by decentralizing their administration from the central Board of Education. The central board, however, continued to administer the city's high schools. Under the decentralization statute, the community boards were given the following powers: to employ a district superintendent and define his duties; to hire, promote, and dismiss school employees within bounds determined by the Board of Education and the United Federation of Teachers; to select instructional materials; to operate community centers and cafeterias and to maintain school buildings. As part of the overall reform, the Board of Education was reorganized and its membership was reduced from nine to five members.[50]

Two aspects of the New York City school system are especially noteworthy. One—the militancy of the teachers under the leadership of the United Federation of Teachers—has already been commented on. The second outstanding feature is the strength of the educational bureaucracy. Sizeable, centralized, cautious, it has developed a reputation for opposing innovation and experimentation.[51] Indeed, its headquarters—110 Livingston Street—has become synonymous with educational standpatism.

Marilyn Gittell, in her careful analysis of school policy-making in New York City, found that the general public had accepted the claim of the educational professionals that only they had the competence to make educational policy. Because of this, the educators were largely left to themselves. "The most significant trend in education in New York City over the past two decades," she wrote in 1967, "has been the isolation of school administration from the city government."[52]

In his monumental study, *110 Livingston Street*, sociologist David Rogers referred to the New York City school system as "a model of bureaucratic pathology," and placed much of the blame on the heads of the professional bureaucrats.[53] He specifically charged them with virtual sabotage of desegregation efforts.[54] In a general judgment, he declared: "The New York City schools have failed in ghetto areas, in most desegregated communities, and in many white ones as well."[55]

Efforts to arrest the decline of the school system and to improve the capacities of students were, of course, undertaken. In particular, compensatory education programs and desegregation were adopted as reform strategies. But they were not able to reverse the general trend.[56]

Several much more far-reaching proposals have been advanced in New York and elsewhere for revitalizing the schools. One calls for setting up alternative and competing forms of public and private education. A second would set up a single metropolitan school system which would embrace the central city and adjacent suburbs. A third major proposal would drastically decentralize the school systems in the large cities. It was the third of these propositions which gained maximum support among educational reformers in New York.

Mayor Lindsay supplied the impetus for widespread discussion of decentralization when he appointed a Decentralization Panel on April 30, 1967. It was charged with developing a plan which would, among other things, ". . . foster greater community initiative and participation in the development of educational policy. . . ."[57] Chaired by McGeorge Bundy, president of the Ford Foundation, the panel made its own investigation of the school system. It also took pains to build up support for its recommendations from civic, community, and professional groups before making the report public.[58]

The report called for drastic decentralization of the system into from 30 to 60 relatively autonomous local community school boards. These boards were to be chosen by the parents, the mayor, and a central agency. Under this plan, the Board of Education would lose many of its powers, becoming essentially a support and planning organization.

The reaction of the Board of Education to the Bundy report was uncharacteristically swift: it issued its rebuttal one day after the release of the report! In its rebuttal the Board made it clear that it stood by an earlier plan of its own, which called for the retention of a central board with real powers. The United Federation of Teachers, certain white civic groups, and a few pro-integration national civil rights leaders joined in a mounting attack on various features of the Bundy report.[59]

In the ensuing fracas, Mayor Lindsay was very much in the middle. Lindsay at this time proposed to the governor, the State legislature, and the Board of Regents the restoring of certain powers to a central board of education. As finally enacted by the legislature, the decentralization statute followed the mayor's advice. An overall Board of Education for the system was retained, but the elected community school boards were given considerable managerial authority.

The dramatic events of Ocean Hill-Brownsville unfolded against this background. The decentralization movement had begun during the winter of 1966–67. Its most vigorous support had come from militant leaders in New York's Black ghettos. In response to their demands, the Board of Education established three experimental school districts in slum areas. These were known as IS 201 in Harlem, Two Bridges on Manhattan's Lower East Side, and Ocean Hill-Brownsville in Brooklyn. The three teachers' strikes which occurred in the fall of 1968 arose because of difficulties in the last district.[60]

Ocean Hill-Brownsville is not, either in an historic or in a sociological sense, a true community. It is deficient in terms of stability, communal institutions, and a sense of identity. It is a run-down section of Brooklyn now populated by Blacks and Puerto Ricans. The lines of the district had been drawn by the Board of Education to artificially create a "community." That any considerable sense of community at all developed is a tribute to the skill and savoir-faire of Rhody A. McCoy, a Black educator who was appointed unit administrator of the experiment.

McCoy found that his district had about 9,000 pupils, whose families were 80 percent Black, 18 percent Puerto Rican, and two percent "other."[61]

The district included six elementary and two intermediate schools. The teaching staff was 80 percent white with about 85 percent of them of Jewish background. Under the terms of the demonstration district plan, Ocean Hill-Brownsville was to elect a "governing" board with advisory powers. An election was duly held, and a board was created consisting of seven parents, five community representatives, two supervisors, two teachers, and one college representative.

Serious friction between the local board and the UFT broke out almost immediately when, in September, 1967, the board refused to support a city-wide teachers' strike over contract terms that lasted 14 days. From that point on the relationship between UFT and the local board deteriorated rapidly. According to the union, the UFT at first gave support to the experiment in Ocean Hill. But when discipline broke down in the district schools, ". . . many UFT teachers became disillusioned with the experiment and began to oppose it actively."[62]

The local board had a different version. According to this account, union opposition to the local board existed from the start. Any lapses in student discipline, it was charged, had been instigated by the union to discredit the local board.[63] Matters came to a head when in May, 1968, the board sought to transfer about 20 teachers and supervisors in—as McCoy subsequently put it—"the interest of improved education."[64]

The principal developments in the escalation of the dispute were these:[65]

1) May 8, 1968. The local board ordered the involuntary transfer of 13 teachers, five assistant principals, and one principal to central headquarters for reassignment. The UFT protested, claiming the transfers were in fact firings and violated "due process." The UFT struck the district and 350 teachers walked out.

2) The Ocean Hill-Brownsville governing board insisted on the transfers and sought to establish in addition its right to hire and fire teachers—a right it did not clearly possess in the law.[66]

3) The district's schools were closed for the last few weeks of the 1967–68 school year.

4) During the summer of 1968, the local board hired many young, nonunion teachers, explaining that these teachers were innovative and open-minded. The UFT implied that the new male teachers were merely opportunists trying to avoid the draft.

5) When schools opened in the fall, the UFT teachers working in Ocean Hill-Brownsville found that they had been replaced. The UFT charged a "lock out," and called a city-wide strike on September 9, 1968.

6) Most of the city schools were shut down, but the three demonstration school districts were staffed and remained open.

7) September 10, 1968. The UFT reached an agreement with the Board of Education to reinstate the UFT teachers transferred from Ocean Hill-Brownsville and the 350 supporting strikers.

8) September 13, 1968. The teachers struck again, on the ground that the September 10 agreement had been violated.

9) September 30, 1968. The second strike ended.

10) October 1–9, 1968. The disputed teachers returned to classrooms in Ocean Hill-Brownsville. Nonstriking teachers shut down JHS 271 in the district. McCoy and seven of his eight principals were relieved of their duties and reassigned to central headquarters. McCoy refused reassignment and remained in Ocean Hill. Disorders resulted in closing down JHS 271.

11) October 11–13, 1968. Seven principals were reinstated, and JHS 271 reopened. The UFT issued an ultimatum to meet its demands or face another strike. The demands were to keep JHS 271 closed; to return only principals who promised to abide by earlier agreements reached between the Board of Education and UFT; to declare Ocean Hill-Brownsville to have been a failure; to remove permanently any officials of the district who had engaged in tactics of harassment or intimidation; to return the schools of the district to the central school system.

12) October 14, 1968. Claiming that UFT members at JHS 271 were threatened with death, the UFT struck the city's schools for the third time.

13) November 17, 1968. The third strike ended. The Board of Education and the UFT agreed to a plan to place the Ocean Hill-Brownsville district under state trusteeship. The local board did not participate in the decision and did not concur with it. The local board and McCoy were suspended, and were to remain so until the State Education Commissioner James E. Allen lifted the suspensions. Involuntary transfers of teachers were to be adjudicated through the use of arbitration machinery.

Placing Ocean Hill-Brownsville under state trusteeship placated the UFT, but it did not bring peace and understanding to the UFT-local board relationship. However, some weeks after the settlement, McCoy was reinstated as unit administrator, and eventually state trusteeship was terminated. Under the state-ordered decentralization program which went into effect on July 1, 1970, Ocean Hill-Brownsville and the other two experimental districts lost their special status. Ocean Hill-Brownsville on that date became part of Community School District 23 in Brooklyn.

The process of absorption was characteristically controversial. The chairman of the new community school board, Assemblyman Samuel D. Wright, a Black and a Democrat, declared that the eight schools formerly in the Ocean Hill-Brownsville district would be treated in the same manner as the rest of District 23's schools. But the Rev. C. Herbert Oliver, chairman of the smaller board and leader of a boycott of the March 19, 1970 community school board elections, vowed to continue the fight for autonomy.[67] The extent of hard feeling was revealed in a letter on Ocean Hill-Brownsville stationery dated July 13 and addressed to Mayor Lindsay.[68] The letter, which was signed merely "Community of Ocean Hill-Brownsville," warned the mayor that Ocean Hill-Brownsville would be burned down unless Assemblyman Wright were removed from his chairmanship. The assemblyman made no public comment regarding the letter, nor did the mayor. The incident—minor in itself—suggested that the hostilities might continue.

On the surface, the 1968 school teachers' strikes occurred over the issue of the rights of about 20 teachers. This was the position officially taken by the UFT. But every close observer knew that the stakes were much larger. In conversations with Stephen Cole, union officials admitted as much.[69] What they feared were the possible adverse results of decentralization on a city-wide scale. If local boards were actually given the right to hire and fire teachers, the officials reasoned that the power of the union would be weakened in various ways. Collective bargaining for example, is easier for a union to handle on a city-wide basis than on a district-by-district system. Furthermore, the power of union officials within the union, and within the labor movement generally, might be seriously weakened.

Rhody A. McCoy and the Ocean Hill-Brownsville Board denied that their intention was to destroy the union. Rather, they said, they were pursuing a program of educational reform through community control. They reasoned that various other plans had been tried and had failed. Local self-determination of school policy was held to be the only positive means for solving the problems of ghetto schools. In the context of Ocean Hill-Brownsville, this meant control of the local system by resident Blacks, operating through their elected representatives.

As the dispute continued, new issues were added to those of union security and local control. Questions were raised as to whether the school system contained an over-representation of whites, especially Jews, and an under-representation of Blacks and Puerto Ricans. Specifically, it was asked whether the teaching staff in the system, the principals of the schools, and the members of the various boards were proportionately Black and Puerto Rican. Starting as demands for educational change, the demands tended to become general calls for racial and social justice.

Just as the issues were enlarged, so was the cast of actors. The UFT attempted to enlist, with some success, the combined labor movement of New York City as an active ally. It also tried to mobilize Jewish civic groups to meet what it considered the anti-Semitism inherent in the Ocean Hill-Brownsville effort to transfer teachers and defy the UFT. It called on New Yorkers generally to repel what it viewed as an attempted return to the pre-union era. Some Socialists such as Michael Harrington fervently backed the union. Ocean Hill-Brownsville also had its own allies in increasing numbers: several militant Black groups; some white as well as Negro church organizations; Black members of labor unions who repudiated the UFT position on decentralization; independent commentators such as Dwight Macdonald; the New York Civil Liberties Union; the Ford Foundation.

The ever-broadening circle of conflict rapidly drew into its vortex political figures who understandably did not want to become personally involved, for instance Mayor Lindsay, Governor Nelson Rockefeller, Education Commissioner James Allen, and the state legislators. With great energy UFT's Albert Shanker and his rival administrator Rhody McCoy sought support from labor, civic, and religious organizations in the city and around the state. What had started as a local labor conflict in Brooklyn developed rapidly into a social donnybrook of monumental proportions.

THE DECLINE OF THE UNITARY COMMUNITY IDEAL

The current drive for greater community control over urban schools is a by-product of the more general movement for equality of educational opportunity. This drive holds true whether a particular neighborhood desires to advance or to abort school integration. In either case it is usually the demand for equality of opportunity that has triggered the neighborhood response.

In challenging the control of the central educational authorities, local community groups have also questioned the basic theory which has served as the infrastructure of educational orthodoxy. Robert H. Salisbury has termed this theory "the myth of the unitary community."[70] This means that the city ". . . is a unity for the purposes of the school program."[71] While racial, religious, economic, and other differences are recognized in other areas of urban life, the doctrine holds that education need not and should not recognize or legitimize these differences. The learning and teaching processes should be the same regardless of the neighborhood. In order that the poor and the underprivileged should receive equal treatment with the children of the well-to-do, the same standards were to be applied to all schools within the city system. In addition, the doctrine jibed neatly with the melting pot philosophy of American life. To "Americanize" the children of newly arrived immigrants was viewed as an important function of the public schools.

That the myth of the unitary community was useful in other ways is beyond question. It justified the existence of an independent school system. It provided a rationale for a school board elected at-large, instead of (as was at one time the usual custom) by wards. It also, probably unintentionally, validated middle-class control of the schools by encouraging some groups to serve on school boards and by discouraging others.[72]

Reflecting on the causes for the decline of the myth, Salisbury found three principal reasons. In the first place, the prevailing educational theory made it difficult to launch differentiated programs in order to meet differing needs. (Head-start programs for the urban poor did not begin on a large scale until 1965). Secondly, because of their isolation, schoolmen were unable to build up the kind of support from groups and interests necessary for voter and legislative appeal. (They were not able to give and hence not able to ask for favors, in the manner, for example, of a public works department.) And lastly, various urban groups, especially Blacks, have come to distrust the unitary-community myth. As a consequence, Salisbury noted, the belief has largely lost its usefulness.[73]

The loss of public confidence in the unitary-community myth coincides with increasing acceptance of community control of schools. To put the matter differently, the collapse of the unitary-community myth has meant its replacement, in part at least, by a new multi-community ideology. The new two-tier educational governing system in New York City reflects a substantial gain in the acceptance of this latter doctrine.

Yet there is another aspect of the decline of the unitary-community myth, often overlooked, that may be of equal importance in the future. In repudiating the traditional doctrine, schoolmen and parents have tended to break down if not obliterate the historic distinction between city hall and the board of education. The "independent" school system—independent, that is to say, from the other operations of local government—may be phased out of existence as the value of "independence" is increasingly questioned.

An alternative to an independent city school board is a city department of education. Under this arrangement, the education department is considered an integral part of the entire municipal administration. As is the case with other departments, it is headed by an official responsible directly to the mayor and to the council. When budget-making time arrives, the department presents its requests to the council. After log-rolling and trading and weighing the competing claims of all the agencies, the council, and the mayor, determine which portion of the available resources will be made available to the public school enterprise.

At first glance, it may seem that a board of education has everything to lose and nothing to gain by becoming a municipal department. But this is not necessarily the case. Under the board arrangement, the schoolmen in the large cities face the prospect of an ever-declining base of popular support, as large sections of the middle class move to the suburbs. The corresponding in-migration of relatively poor Blacks and Puerto Ricans has not made up for this loss of support, because these groups generally do not value education as much as the middle class. They have therefore not shown any great enthusiasm to raise their own taxes to support the schools.

Besides a shrinking urban popular base, the independent board of education system has suffered from its inability to operate effectively at the state level. Salisbury summarizes the recent experience of the big Missouri cities—St. Louis and Kansas City—before the state legislature.[74] Both cities, to be sure, receive state funds. But the isolation of the urban schoolmen from the rest of the political system works against their interests. State legislators, including those from urban areas, are ". . . profoundly uninterested in the concerns of *any* groups which successfully keep themselves apart from the political system of the city."[75] In the absence of allies, urban schoolmen have had to shift for themselves in Missouri, and they have not done very well.

Even where the independence of an urban board of education is proudly and publicly proclaimed, that independence may be more phantasmagoric than tangible. The Board of Education of Philadelphia furnishes an illustration.[76] In the spring of 1970, plagued with rising costs of operation and pinned to an inadequate income base, the board desperately sought additional income from the only two possible sources—the state and the city. (Aside from some people in the Department of Health, Education, and Welfare in Washington, no one seriously considered large-scale federal aid more than a remote possibility.) Both approaches met with little initial acceptance, primarily because the board found itself isolated from the ordinary political process.

Then came an abrupt about-face in tactics. Under the leadership of its president, former mayor Richardson Dilworth, the board entered into a working alliance with the Roman Catholic Archdiocesan Board of Education, which had financial problems of its own. Both boards agreed to pool their efforts before the state legislature. In the future, requests by the public board for additional state funds for Philadelphia would be vigorously supported by the church board. In return, requests for large appropriations to church schools—a practice then in effect in Pennsylvania—would be publicly endorsed by the public board. Through a policy of mutual support, both boards obviously hoped to increase the state allocations for each. An analogous strategy was adopted by the two boards in confronting the city council of Philadelphia.

It will require time to determine whether any increased benefits which accrue to the two school systems as a result of their cooperative policy more than offset the liabilities which are likely to be incurred. What is more certain about the new pattern of cooperation is the great likelihood that it will be followed elsewhere. It is the hope of the proponents of this plan that both public and parochial school education in the large cities will be able to strengthen considerably their financial bases.

In so far as cooperation between public and parochial school authorities depends on the sharing of public funds, there are formidable obstacles to be surmounted. Chief among these is the constitutional issue of church and state. As we have noted, on June 28, 1971, the United States Supreme Court declared invalid the Pennsylvania statute under which that state had been providing more than $17 million a year to private schools for non-religious educational services. The vote was 8 to 0. In a related decision rendered on the same day, the Court in an 8 to 1 vote struck down a Rhode Island act which added a 15 percent supplement to the salaries of teachers of secular subjects in non-profit private schools. Both laws were held to be unconstitutional on the ground that they violated freedom of religion as defined in the First Amendment.

Nonetheless, if the cooperative approach works out the way it is intended to do, it will be because the plan broadens the *political* base which supports both school systems. It will be another way in which the American educational enterprise is entering more and more fully into the political process, and will be one more manifestation of the continually increasing politicization of education in the great urban centers.

CHAPTER
NOTES

1. The convention was covered in depth by John P. Corr, education writer of the Philadelphia *Inquirer*. The figures come from his article in the issue of July 6, 1970.

2. *Ibid.*, July 4, 1970.

3. The bibliography on politics and education is growing rapidly. A very useful listing is found in Marilyn Gittell, *Participants and Participation: A Study of School Policy in New York City* (New York: Praeger, 1967), pp. 96–100.

4. Stephen K. Bailey, Richard T. Frost, Paul E. Marsh, and Robert C. Wood, *Schoolmen and Politics: A Study of State Aid to Education in the Northeast* (Syracuse: Syracuse University Press, 1962).

5. *Ibid.*, p. 42.

6. *Ibid.*, p. 56.

7. *Ibid.*, p. 46.

8. *Ibid.*, p. 47.

9. See Robert Bendiner, *The Politics of Schools: A Crisis in Self-Government* (New York: Harper & Row, 1969).

10. *Ibid.*, p. 165.

11. Bailey *et al.*, *op. cit.*

12. *Ibid.*, p. 15.

13. *Ibid.*, p. vii.

14. *Ibid.*, p. vii.

15. See Nicholas A. Masters, Robert H. Salisbury, and Thomas H. Eliot, *State Politics and the Public Schools: An Exploratory Analysis* (New York: Knopf, 1964).

16. *Ibid.*, p. 267.

17. Bendiner, *op. cit.*, p. 155.

18. *Ibid.*, p. 156.

19. *New York Times*, May 24, 1970.

20. *Ibid.*

21. *Ibid.*

22. Walter Lippmann, *Public Opinion* (New York: Macmillan, 1922), Part III.

23. See Stephen Cole, *The Unionization of Teachers: A Case Study of the UFT* (New York: Praeger, 1969), p. 6.

24. *Ibid.*, p. 198.

25. Bendiner, *op. cit.*, p. 94.

26. *Ibid.*, p. 94.

27. Cole, *op. cit.*, p. 7.

28. Cole, *op. cit.*, gives a history of the teacher union movement in New York City, pp. 11–21. This is indispensable background for an understanding of the role eventually played by UFT.

29. Cole, *Ibid.*, p. 96.

30. *Ibid.*, p. 87.

31. *Ibid.*, p. 90.

32. *Ibid.*, p. 94.

33. *Ibid.*, p. 95, Table 5–7.

34. The figures are given in Thomas R. Dye, *Politics in States and Communities* (Englewood Cliffs, N.J.: Prentice-Hall, 1969), p. 389.

35. Bendiner, *op. cit.*, p. 86.

36. Albert Shanker, "For Teachers, Bigger Role," *New York Times,* Jan. 12, 1970, p. 53.

37. As quoted by the Associated Press, Philadelphia *Bulletin,* July 7, 1970.

38. Philadelphia Board of Education, as reported in Philadelphia *Bulletin,* June 12, 1970.

39. *Bulletin Almanac,* 1970, p. 390.

40. *New York Times,* Jan. 12, 1970.

41. Philadelphia *Bulletin,* June 12, 1970.

42. Bendiner, *op. cit.*, p. 82.

43. Patricia Cayo Sexton, "City Schools," Vol. 353, *The Annals* (March, 1964), pp. 95–106.

44. *Ibid.*, p. 96.

45. *Ibid.*, p. 103.

46. *New York Times,* June 13, 1970.

47. Gittell, *op. cit.*, pp. 4–5.

48. *Ibid.*, p. 7.

49. *Ibid.*, p. 8.

50. Major analyses of the decentralization program were presented in the *New York Times* editions of July 1 and July 27, 1970.

51. There is an expanding literature on the Board of Education, but see, especially, Gittell, *op. cit.*, and also David Rogers, *110 Livingston Street: Politics and Bureaucracy in the New York City Schools* (New York: Random House, 1968).

52. Gittell, *op. cit.*, p. 47.

53. Rogers, *op. cit.*, especially chapter VIII, "The Professional Bureaucracy," pp. 266–323.

54. *Ibid.*, p. 322.

55. *Ibid.*, p. 473.

56. *Ibid.*, p. 474.

57. *Ibid.*, p. 475.

58. *Ibid.*, p. 474.

59. *Ibid.*, p. 477.

60. See the account in Cole, *op. cit.*, pp. 194–195.

61. Rhody A. McCoy, "Ocean Hill Struggles for Identity," *New York Times*, Jan. 12, 1970, p. 69.

62. Cole, *op. cit.*, p. 195.

63. *Ibid.*, p. 195.

64. McCoy, *loc. cit.*

65. Documents and analyses relating to the Ocean Hill-Brownsville controversy were assembled according to issues and events by Maurice R. Berube and Marilyn Gittell and published under the title *Confrontation at Ocean Hill-Brownsville: The New York School Strikes of 1968* (New York: Praeger, 1969). The chronology of escalation of the dispute is taken from pp. 335–340 of this basic work. For an inquiry into the merits of community control generally, see Mario Fantini, Marilyn Gittell, and Richard Magat, *Community Control and the Urban School* (New York: Praeger, 1970).

66. Cole, *op. cit.*, p. 195.

67. *New York Times*, July 10, 1970.

68. The letter is published in the *New York Times* of July 15, 1970.

69. Cole, *op. cit.*, pp. 195–196.

70. Robert H. Salisbury, "Schools and Politics in The Big City," Vol. 37, No. 3, *Harvard Educational Review* (1967), pp. 408–429. Though the term "seminal" has been cheapened by over-use, this article has proved to be seminal in the best sense of the word. It has provoked an enormous amount of comment and discussion.

71. *Ibid.*, p. 412.

72. *Ibid.*, p. 415.

73. *Ibid.*, p. 417.

74. *Ibid.*, pp. 418–420.

75. *Ibid.*, p. 419.

76. The account has been drawn from interviews with Philadelphia schoolmen as well as from continuing stories in the Philadelphia press.

10

The Politics

of Housing

and Urban

Renewal

The housing industry has, historically, furnished a prime example of the private determination of public policy. This is to say that most of the important decisions regarding housing have been determined by private, not public, interests. Builders, contractors, and construction workers—as well as buyers and sellers—have been viewed as individual actors in a competitive, free marketplace. This industry operates with a minimum of governmental direction and controls.

Yet the housing industry has not always operated without constraints or governmental regulations. For even the most casual would-be purchaser of a house it becomes quickly apparent that housing is enmeshed in a web of legally devised restrictions. If the local zoning board has decided that the minimum lot for residential dwellings shall be one acre, for all practical purposes that is the definitive resolution of the issue. If the board's regulations provide that a particular section or a locality may be both industrial and residential, then the home buyer knows perfectly well that his protection against industrial expansion is tenuous. And so it goes— land use in urban and suburban areas is closely controlled by zoning boards and related agencies which are only indirectly responsible to the electorate, i.e., they are appointed by elected officials.

In addition to the builder, the contractor, the construction worker, the zoning commission, and the buyer, there is another actor whose role is of maximum importance—the realtor, or the broker who brings together potential buyers and sellers. Usually licensed by a local authority, the realtor performs a variety of functions. Bringing buyer and seller into a face-to-face situation is one of the more obvious of them. Beyond this relatively simple activity, the realtor plays a sociological role of great community significance. In directing potential buyers to potential sellers, the real estate broker acts as a traffic director; he very largely determines who shall live in what neighborhood and, subject to the laws, who shall be excluded.

The realtor and his colleagues play an essential part in upgrading, downgrading, or maintaining the status quo of a community. Legally recognized as private entrepreneurs, the real estate brokers —working closely with the zoning boards and allied interests— have become an important element in social control. They can determine—all other things being equal—the social composition of a community.

Taken together, it could be argued that the contractors, the builders, the unions, the realtors, and the zoning officials constitute a system of private government. Using such criteria as income, ethnicity, and religion, they rather effectively determine housing patterns and allocate housing for most Americans.

Until recent times, it was assumed that a privately controlled housing industry operating in a marketplace economy was the ideal mechanism for dealing with urban housing problems. Whatever politics took place in this area was assumed to be a politics of private housing. Central to its concerns were such questions as zoning laws, community composition, and community stability. During the Depression of the 1930's—when there were hundreds of thousands of mortgage foreclosures on private dwellings—this belief in the unilateral efficacy of private housing was shaken. Housing shortages brought about in World War II further challenged the prevailing view. Finally, the vast internal population changes between 1950 and 1970 created conditions apparently beyond the ability of the private housing industry to cope with on a traditional basis.

As a consequence, the United States government established a series of programs for the creation of public housing. Though a few states and cities also pioneered in this area, the general initiative was taken by and remains with the federal government. Growing out of the original public housing programs there developed also a related interest in urban renewal. In both cases the basic motivation was to bring about a substantial degree of urban improvement—variously defined. Such programs—federal, state, and local—have resulted in the creation of a politics of public housing. It is this aspect of the housing problem which mainly concerns us here.

In the past, where one lived in America's metropolitan areas was determined in large measure by one's social class. To be sure, there were other factors, such as convenience to work and schools. But the type of neighborhood one lived in was in most cases predetermined by one's class standing.

Today in the large cities the situation is changing dramatically. Social class is still a leading factor in the choice of neighborhoods and of housing. But in many central cities it has been displaced by race as the most salient factor. When social class and race coincide —as often happens—the effect may well be to encourage housing segregation along racial lines. When these conditions do not coincide, the effect may be to encourage housing segregation along economic lines. An example of the latter situation is the upper West Side of New York City, where racial segregation is far less important than segregation in terms of income. But this is the exception rather than the rule.

The politics of housing has increasingly reflected the racial tensions of urban society. Indeed, this whole area has become a barometer of racial relationships. Consequently, the politics of housing—both public and private—has tended to become racially oriented, and any realistic political analysis of housing must take this increasingly important element into account.

THE HOUSING PICTURE: AN OVERVIEW

President Lyndon B. Johnson on January 12, 1967, appointed a National Commission on Urban Problems to carry out a study of the nation's housing as authorized in section 301 of the Housing and Urban Development Act of 1965. In fulfilling the Congressional mandate, the Commission, chaired by former Senator Paul H. Douglas, conducted hearings on relevant subjects in the central cities and suburbs of more than 20 locations throughout the country. It received testimony from almost 350 witnesses and undertook an extensive research program covering 40 specific subjects. On December 12, 1968, Chairman Douglas transmitted the report of his Commission to the President and to Hubert H. Humphrey, President of the Senate, and to John W. McCormack, Speaker of the House of Representatives. In its review of the housing situation, the Commission reported basic data and also presented specific program recommendations. The Report contained a vast amount of information, much of it hitherto uncollected, and was quickly established as an authoritative document on the housing problems facing the country.[1]

Early in its Report, the Commission drew attention to the proliferation of local governments as one source of difficulty in dealing rationally with the housing question. "Nearly two-thirds of all Americans," it declared, "live in metropolitan areas. Slightly less than half of all metropolitan area residents live in the central metropolitan cities, but most of the increase in the SMSA [Standard Metropolitan Statistical Area] population is taking place in the outlying-ring territory—suburbia."[2]

If the metropolitan areas were coordinated through some overall governmental mechanism, this separation between city and suburb might not be a serious obstacle. But this is not the case. "In 1967," the Commission noted, "our metropolitan areas were served by 20,745 local governments, or about one-fourth of all local governments in the nation. This means 91 governments per SMSA—an average of about 48 per metropolitan county."[3] But the variations were considerable. The Chicago SMSA, for example, had 1,113 local governments, or 186 per county![4]

Nonetheless, great efforts have been announced and launched for the purpose of improving the nation's housing. What have they added up to over the years? On this question, the Commission's judgment is quite clear. "Over the years accomplishments in subsidized housing are extremely inadequate," the Report asserted. "The Nation in 30 years of public housing built fewer units than Congress, back in 1949, said were needed in the immediate next 6 years."[5] After summing up a dismal bill of particulars, the Commission concluded: "If all else fails; if the localities do not build; if the States do not expand their role and increase their funds for housing programs; if the traditional housing programs and agencies do not provide a vastly increased amount of housing; then, reluctantly, we advocate that the Federal Government become the builder of last resort."[6]

FEDERAL HOUSING PROGRAMS

It is against the foregoing economic and demographic background that the federal housing programs must be viewed in order to gain a meaningful perspective, as these efforts have evolved in response to real needs.

In 1937—during the heart of the New Deal period—Congress authorized a small public housing program. This was supplemented in 1949 with additional legislation intended to renew the cities. In commenting on the significance of these developments, the noted city planner Charles Abrams declared: "These were the first real signs of a federal responsibility for the improvement of America's urban environments . . . In terms of money, the two programs were of minor significance. But in political terms, they were revolutionary . . ."[7]

Three major programs have dominated the federal government's approach to housing.[8] The first of these is the mortgage insurance program of the Federal Housing Administration. After World War II, a counterpart for veterans was established through the loan guarantee program of the Veterans Administration. Both of these programs were focused on the so-called "modal" family, that is, one which was young, employed, and with growing children. Typically, such a family desired a detached house surrounded by a small plot of land. For the young couple desirous of settling down in a home of their own with an ambition to raise children the arrangements provided by the FHA and VA were nearly ideal.

The second leading approach of the federal government is to subsidize low-income public housing. This program is administered by the Public Housing Administration through local housing authorities. To determine eligibility for admission, the criteria of maximum rather than minimum income levels are applied. In contrast to the FHA and VA programs, most public housing projects have been constructed in the central cities rather than in the suburbs. Commenting on the impact of the two kinds of programs, Eunice and George Grier declared: "The differences between the two programs thus reinforce each other in their effects upon patterns of residence. While the FHA and VA have helped promote white dominance in the suburbs, public housing has helped enhance Negro dominance in the cities."[9]

The third major federal program is urban renewal. This program was established by the Housing Act of 1949. Its leading objective is to combat physical decay in the central cities. While the program shifts its emphasis from time to time, its chief effect over the years has been to clear blighted sections and—so far as housing is concerned—replace them with middle-to-upper income housing units.[10]

To arrive at a fair assessment of these federal housing policies is not any easy matter. On the negative side, these policies have been subjected to three major criticisms.[11] It is charged that the programs have favored those who are better-off and, therefore, worked against the best interests of the poor. It is also alleged that the policies destroy urbanism, a term presumably synonymous in this context with "civilized life." Finally, it is maintained that the federal programs fail to create "a valid form of community expansion and community building."[12] By this is meant that American community expansion has tended to be haphazard, unplanned, and unaesthetic.

Clearly, there is some truth to all of these criticisms. The FHA and VA programs, while not directed toward the "better-off," were aimed at the median family. In providing new housing for millions of families, both programs have been notably successful. At the same time, the poor have fared badly. The major effort on behalf of the poor has been public housing, and Congress has consistently starved this endeavor. Nor have the poor benefitted proportionately from urban renewal. On this point, one expert, Nathan Glazer, has asserted: "Urban renewal has unquestionably reduced the quantity of low-cost housing and raised rents for the poor."[13]

It is the third criticism—the charge that American community expansion has been largely unplanned and uncoordinated—that carries the most weight, however. In comparison with other countries, the United States' policies appear extravagantly shortsighted and wasteful. It is not by chance that England and France have managed to avoid most of the "urban sprawl" that has come to characterize vast stretches of the United States.

In addition to the foregoing standard criticisms of federal housing programs, a new and very serious charge has recently been added to the list. This is the charge that federal policies have helped to create the present segregated housing patterns, and the charge is largely valid. It is true that this was not the avowed objective of government action, and that the impact of the action was slow in being appreciated. It is also true that there were many other factors responsible for creating the present situation, discrimination, for example, by the mortgage, real-estate, and housebuilding industries. But the judgment of the Griers is worth recording: "Combined with rapid population growth in the metropolitan areas, the interacting effects of federal policies and practices in the postwar era did much to produce the present segregated patterns."[14]

REPLACING THE SLUMS

Even people who believe in housing segregation on the basis of income or race are likely to feel that government should do something about improving life in the slums. Despite the general condemnation of slums as such, some investigators have found merit in particular slums. Herbert J. Gans, for example, examined an Italian working-class neighborhood in Boston, which had been condemned and cleared for urban redevelopment. He concluded that the area was not really a slum, but rather a tightly-knit community of hard-working, low-income, decent people.[15] But, as Lawrence M. Friedman observed in his excellent study of slum housing, no serious scholars have argued that *all* slums have positive qualities.[16]

Given the present high degree of consensus that something positive should be done, it may seem remarkable that America was so late in embarking upon any large-scale program of public housing. No doubt the once prevalent feeling that governmental action was in theory undesirable, or should in any event be undertaken only as a last and desperate resort, was largely responsible for this lag. But even after federal financing became relatively abundant, the give-and-take of ordinary municipal politics often retarded action.

Chicago furnishes a splendid illustration of this phenomenon.[17] In the late 1940's and early 1950's a majority of the city's board of aldermen were in favor of public housing in principle. But—and here is the rub—they did not want such housing in their own wards. "They did not want low-income neighbors, and they wanted no Negroes of any kind."[18] Consequently, this resistance nearly crippled public housing in Chicago. When construction finally did get underway it was located on sites not considered particularly satisfactory by the Chicago Housing Authority.

Public housing in many countries is not necessarily aimed at the poor, but in the United States this is the direction that has been taken. More and more, this type of housing has been consigned to the dependent poor. With hindsight, as Friedman notes, it is possible to read this tendency into the original Housing Act of 1937. Initially, this was not, however, the stated purpose of the program. Rather, the objective was to house the submerged and potential urban middle class. The program began with great promise and enthusiasm, so that by February, 1938, funds had been authorized for work in 50 cities in 19 states.[19] New York State, in 1939, voted authorization for state-financed housing as well.

World War II stopped the drive for public, low-rent housing by diverting funds into defense and temporary war housing. Revived after the termination of the war, the public housing program continued, but it never regained its earlier momentum. Politically speaking, it had lost its glamour to the newer programs of urban redevelopment and urban renewal. When the limitations of public housing in slum clearance were realized, general interest turned to urban redevelopment and urban renewal as new plans for demolishing the slums. In both cases the guiding concept was to treat the problem on a metropolitan as opposed to a purely neighborhood basis.

Urban redevelopment on a meaningful scale began with the Housing Act of 1949. Title I of this statute offered federal funds to subsidize the buying, assembling, and clearing of land for redevelopment. Under the procedure which was established, the federal government could make grants of up to two-thirds of "net project cost." In summary, the procedure ran as follows: Local authorities were authorized to draw up plans, buy land, clear it, and then sell it to a private developer. The developer would buy the land at its market value, which would be less than the local authority had paid. Prior to the clearing of the land it was usually occupied by rooming houses, tenements, and commercial structures. The authority acquired these properties on the theory that they were income-producing. The authority, of course, then proceeded to demolish the properties, which added an additional cost. What the developer paid was the "fair value" of the raw land.

The federal government entered into the transaction by paying two-thirds of the difference between what the developer had paid and the net cost to the local agency. The remaining third was paid by the local community, but this did not have to be in cash. It could be, for example, in the form of parks or public buildings.

As a program, urban redevelopment was designed to appeal to many interests: the developers, the planners, the business interests, the ordinary citizen who was troubled by his city's blighted areas. Under the 1949 act urban redevelopment projects were limited to areas which, before redevelopment, were "predominantly residential" or which were developed or redeveloped "for predominantly residential uses." This meant that federal money could be spent only under two conditions: one, that the area to be redeveloped had been a slum or, two, that the developer would convert a blighted commercial area into a residential area after having cleared the land.

Under the terms of the statute, it was perfectly possible to pull down a slum and erect nonresidential projects.[20] This appealed, of course, to city planners who hoped to create new municipal buildings, civic centers, parking lots, and open spaces. At the same time the legislation did not require the construction of low-cost housing.

Since the emphasis of the act was on the slum, not on the urban poor, it seemed perfectly reasonable to replace the slum buildings with high-rent apartments for the well-to-do. It was assumed that the local authority would find other quarters for the poor who were dispossessed.

Once in operation, the program produced some startling results —startling, in any event, to persons concerned with the housing of the urban poor. Taking a broad interpretation of the language of the statute, New York City allowed Robert Moses to build his coliseum at Columbus Circle. This is a good example of what Friedman termed the "construction-minded" predilection of the program.[21] The other major predilection—"clearance-minded"—was illustrated in Nashville, which used redevelopment funds to eliminate nasty slums which had surrounded the state capitol.[22] This action eliminated a condition "which had been difficult to explain to visitors."

Prior to 1960, only a very small amount of public, low-cost housing was built on urban renewal locations. The emphasis, rather, was on middle-income and even luxury apartments.[23] Recent programs have increased the number of low-cost projects, but the number of units created has been miniscule in relation to the potential number of clients. In destroying thousands of homes, redevelopment obviously displaced thousands of persons. Urban redevelopment succeeded in rebuilding downtown areas of many of the nation's cities, but it did not and does not help the urban poor.

Dissatisfaction with redevelopment—especially, with its bull-dozer features—contributed to the development of the more selective program of urban renewal. In the Housing Act of 1954 it was provided that federal help would henceforth be available for a variety of projects. Using conservation, rehabilitation, and code enforcement as tools, the new program tightened the links between urban renewal and general urban planning. To qualify for urban renewal funds, a city had to present a "workable program" to "utilize appropriate private and public resources to eliminate, and prevent the development or spread of, slums and urban blight, to encourage needed urban rehabilitation, [and] to provide for the redevelopment of blighted, deteriorated, or slum areas."[24]

Despite the continuous raising of federal requirements—housing codes, for example, were at first only encouraged, but are now mandatory—the renewal program rests firmly in local hands. Local governing bodies retain their veto power, and local control is evident in several ways. In the first place, the local renewal body has the power to propose projects. Secondly, the local "governing body" plays a major role. And lastly, it is required by law that there be citizen participation.[25] Essentially, the federal government performs two functions: It reviews local renewal plans to see that they comply with the legal requirements, and it acquires and clears the land. The Department of Housing and Urban Development "plans and builds nothing."[26]

To determine the political impact of urban renewal would require a comparative examination of local studies which do not yet exist. What is evident, in a general way, is that many urban groups have reacted with unfeigned enthusiasm to the injection of federal renewal funds into their municipalities. Downtown business interests, for example, look with favor on renewal plans which will enhance the value and attractiveness of the central commercial districts. Middle-class citizens may view renewal as a way of stopping the spread of urban blight and of stabilizing neighborhoods. In some instances, renewal may bring about, in particular sections of a city, the same type of segregation by income and race which can be practiced through zoning and related ordinances in small towns. The most sizeable group which appears on balance to lose rather than to gain is the urban poor, even though the renewal program may claim to be for their benefit.[27]

Lacking political leverage, there is not much the poor can accomplish through traditional means. Nor have they proved to be —despite some attempts at organization—an effective interest group. They stand more or less outside the traditional arena of brokerage politics. There is, however, one thing they can do to get attention, and sometimes results, as well. This is simply to misbehave. As Friedman appositely observes: ". . . the way is open to the poor to achieve some goals by raising the price of good behavior. The poor have the power to harass, to annoy, to riot, and to picket."[28]

SOME FACTORS LIMITING URBAN RENEWAL

If urban renewal benefits nearly every group except the urban poor, what are the principal factors which work against really large-scale reconstruction of blighted urban sections?

To begin with, there is the economic factor. Americans have not to this point shown themselves willing to assign urban reconstruction the same economic priority they have accorded to, say, the Vietnam war, or the automobile, or the exploration of space. As a result, the expenditures for urban redevelopment and renewal have been inadequate to accomplish their stated objectives.

A second factor, often overlooked, is governmental and constitutional. In urban reconstruction, the most clear-cut relationship has been between the municipality and the federal government. This fact has obscured the constitutional reality that the cities are creatures of the state and that they are severely limited in what they can do on their own initiative. Even if the cities themselves had ample funds for reconstruction—and they do not—they would still require state authorization in order to proceed. Such authorization is far from automatically accorded by state legislatures, which love to delve deeply into municipal affairs. Two authorities on metropolitan affairs—Scott Greer and David W. Minar—have questioned whether urban development is possible unless it is accompanied by substantial "political redevelopment." Governmental fragmentation appears to them a strong barrier against action.[29] Besides the economic and constitutional limitations, there is a third set of factors which are attitudinal in character. This outlook is revealed in such frequently heard expressions as "the quality of urban life continues to deteriorate" or "cities are no longer pleasant places in which to live."

It is difficult to pinpoint the causes of this "urban unease," as James Q. Wilson has termed it.[30] In an attempt to explore the problem Wilson and a colleague polled a thousand Boston homeowners to find out what they thought was the biggest problem facing the city. To the surprise of the investigators, only 18 percent of those questioned mentioned the conventional problems such as housing, transportation, pollution, urban renewal and the like. A mere 9 percent referred to jobs and employment. The chief concern of the respondents was stated in various ways—crime, violence, rebellious youth, racial tension, public immorality, delinquency. But, Wilson wrote: "However stated, the common theme seemed to be a concern for improper behavior in public places."[31]

After analyzing the responses to the Boston survey, Wilson concluded that what constitutes the "urban problem" for a large percentage of urban citizens is "a sense of the failure of community."[32] By concern for community, he meant "a desire for the observance of standards of right and seemly conduct in the public places in which one lives and moves, those standards to be consistent with—and supportive of—the values and life styles of the particular individual."[33] It is by no means clear what, if anything, government can do about this vaguely defined but apparently very real problem.

TWO CASE STUDIES
OF URBAN RENEWAL

In the late 1950's a group of University of Chicago sociologists headed by Peter H. Rossi and Robert A. Dentler undertook to study what citizens actually did to contribute to the urban renewal planning operation in a Chicago community.[34] Both federal and state laws require that renewal planning come in part from community-wide citizen participation and endorsement. Because of this requirement, any program, to be successful, must depend in part on the active involvement of the citizens. This means that there must be open communication between officials and citizens.

The community chosen for investigation is known as Hyde Park-Kenwood, a mixed area which includes the University of Chicago. The area had been relatively stable racially prior to World War II. After 1950, Black in-migration rapidly accelerated, with the result that the Black population climbed from 6 percent in 1950 to 36 percent in 1956.[35] During the same period a substantial number of whites moved out of the area.

The University of Chicago was the largest local employer in the Hyde Park-Kenwood area. At the time of the study some 1,200 persons were employed at the professional level, in addition to a substantial number of nonacademic employees.[36] In contrast to many other university faculties, the University of Chicago faculty members remained remarkably stable in their preference for Hyde Park-Kenwood as a residential area. This attachment persisted despite some apprehension over neighborhood changes that occurred after 1950.[37] These changes were not only demographic in character, but included physical deterioration in buildings and the threat that the urban blight that covered much of the city would in time engulf Hyde Park-Kenwood.

To arrest the deterioration and to restore the community to its once favored position became the aim of numerous civic organizations. The strategy finally agreed upon by the community leaders was urban renewal, under terms of the 1954 Housing Act. As it turned out, urban renewal was the "key" which held together a set of interlocking programs which made possible an attack on a variety of sectors at the same time.[38] For example, it made it

244 / Urban Politics

possible for the University of Chicago, which had a mammoth stake in the success of the program, to encourage private investments in the area by banks and mortgage houses.

The interest of the University of Chicago in maintaining and improving the neighborhood—the investigators tell us—was clearly "unequivocal."[39] After some false starts, the University gave substantial backing to the urban renewal planning efforts. It did this primarily by pursuing the "downtown" road to renewal, that is, it concentrated on the power centers in municipal government.[40] But at many points the University's goals were, in fact, modified as a "direct result of citizen participation through local organizations."[41] Overall, the University program "underlay and buttressed" the entire range of renewal efforts in Hyde Park-Kenwood.[42]

In creating plans to conserve and to renew the area in which they lived, the citizens had two roles to fulfill. The first was simply to refuse to move out of the neighborhood. By staying put, they could visibly demonstrate their confidence in the future of Hyde Park-Kenwood. The second main role of the citizens was to "provide mass support and understanding for the renewal plan itself."[43] Without such support it seemed unlikely that public officials would approve of any projected plans.

The Hyde Park-Kenwood Community Conference, founded in 1949, played an important part in bridging the gap between planners and city officials on the one hand and the citizenry on the other. In doing so, the Conference did more than simply act as a transmission belt. At many points, ". . . it not only mediated but influenced the conservation planning process."[44] The Conference did not always achieve the level of consensus it was seeking—in particular, there was considerable opposition to the renewal proposals in the Black press. Thus, while in the southwest sector the Conference failed to mediate effectively between the planners and the residents, in northwest Hyde Park the Conference "scored a notable success."[45]

When, in the winter of 1957–58, the Final Plan was ready for submission to City Council, it appeared that quick approval would be forthcoming. Unexpectedly, two sources of dissent began to be heard. The first was a Tenants and Home Owners Association, which claimed to speak for lower-income residents. Objection from this source was quickly overshadowed, however, by a demand from the Cardinal's Committee on Conservation and Urban Renewal— an agency of the Roman Catholic Church—for reconsideration of the entire plan. After failing to receive mass support from Catholic clergy and laymen, the Committee softpedaled its criticisms and the Plan once again moved forward. Finally, by a vote of forty-four to nothing, following an endorsement by Mayor Daley, the Council approved the Plan on November 7, 1958.[46]

It is not entirely certain what the implications of the Hyde Park-Kenwood experience in urban renewal planning are for other university neighborhoods. In Morningside Heights, which contains Columbia University, citizen resistance to any planning or expansion on the part of the university has been considerable. Similarly, community groups have long opposed plans sponsored by Temple University for changes in the North Philadelphia neighborhood which encloses the campus. Whether the conditions which existed in the Chicago situation are replicable remains a moot point.

Rossi and Dentler had no doubts as to the importance of a strong community organization per se in the total planning process. "It seems likely," they concluded, "that successful urban renewal in large cities—successful in the sense of widely accepted both within and without the neighborhoods under renewal—will come primarily either in neighborhoods that have an indigenous successful community organization or in neighborhoods in which some outside agency manages to create one."[47]

A second major study of urban renewal was undertaken by Harold Kaplan, who was both a student and a practitioner of the subject.[48] In a case study of Newark, New Jersey, the Kaplan investigation centered on the role of the Newark Housing Authority (NHA). They concentrated in particular on how it launched nine clearance projects during its first ten years under Title I of the 1949 Federal Housing Act. The effort in Newark is described as "successful," presumably because it resulted in the planned spending of a good deal of money and in the completion of projects. It is also said to be "atypical" in that it was successful.[49]

Even though some cities dawdled for years in taking advantage of federal renewal money, Newark did not. It was the first city in New Jersey—and among the earliest in the country—to embark upon an urban renewal program. From the passage of the 1949 Housing Act to the announcement of Newark's first slum clearance project was a period of only eighteen months.[50] The reason for this comparative speed was the readiness of NHA to act. In this respect, Newark was almost unique.

So far as the Newark "politicos"—the elected officials at City Hall were concerned—public projects deserved municipal support. This belief was based on firmly held political convictions. "The politicos favored public projects in their neighborhoods, since projects were low-rise, garden-apartment structures built on vacant sites and occupied by people of the vicinity."[51] Furthermore, "Each commissioner viewed a project in his home area as an important source of support; the tenants of a public housing project usually turned out in record pluralities for their sponsor."[52]

According to Kaplan's informants, the approved projects were rotated among the city's commissioners in order to accommodate the city's major ethnic groups. "In 1948," Kaplan reports, "there were two Irish, one Negro, two Italian, and two Jewish projects."[53] This was brokerage politics at its classical best.

Newark's business and professional groups became alienated from the city's political life earlier and more completely than in most other northern cities. As they moved to the suburbs in the post-World War II period, leaders of these groups dropped or reduced their support for civic improvement associations.[54] During the first decade of public housing in Newark, the business, real-estate, and civic improvement groups "staunchly opposed every step" in the Newark Housing Authority's program.[55] But the ineffectiveness of such opposition paralleled the movement of its leadership to residential areas outside the city limits. In any case, the city commissioners paid little attention to the negative advice proferred by civic and business interests on the subject of public housing.

When it came to downtown economic redevelopment, the outlook of the civic (as opposed to the political) leaders was entirely different. They were, in time, to become enthusiastic supporters of plans to rebuild the downtown areas of Newark. Some of the plans were fulfilled in relatively spectacular fashion, partly because of cooperation between the civic leaders and the Central Planning Board.

In one very important respect, the Newark experience in redevelopment contrasts sharply with that in Hyde Park-Kenwood. In Chicago, grass roots efforts were able to affect the Final Plan in important ways; in Newark, grass roots opposition was inconsequential. "Not once between 1949 and 1960," Kaplan reported, "did a neighborhood committee succeed in altering or delaying NHA's plans for an area."[56] Continuing, he noted: "The opposition of site residents, small businesses, and neighborhood associations may present a serious threat to some redevelopment agencies; to NHA such opposition is a minor irritant."[57]

There were two aspects to the question of grass roots opposition. Seldom did any organized or sustained opposition appear. But when, on a few occasions, it did appear, it was ineffectual. This was often because the grass roots leaders lacked access to key public officials and were unable to "penetrate the network of regular renewal participants."[58] In short, they were effectively excluded from the decision-making process.

Kaplan gives an illustration of how this was done. From time-to-time Black leaders within the Central Ward approached NHA and suggested that they hold discussions on a regular basis with top members of the housing authority's staff. But NHA—under the strong leadership of its executive director, Louis Danzig—steadfastly refused. To NHA, the role of the Black leaders was clear—they should see to it that proposed projects gained local acceptance. When the same leaders demanded that NHA consult them before embarking on a project, NHA consistently declined to accede to their requests. Naturally, the Black leaders felt hurt and outraged, although there was usually little they could do about the situation.

In explaining these refusals to confer in advance, NHA officials fell back on the argument that the Black leaders had to be treated in the same way as other parties. "The staff repeated the answer," wrote Kaplan, "it had given other local interests: if those affected by clearance were consulted at every stage of planning and the plans tailored to meet their demands, renewal projects would never get off the ground."[59]

During the period covered in the Newark study, NHA got into serious trouble with the Council on one occasion. The source of the difficulty was racial. It was believed by some councilmen that large-scale integrated public housing projects were instrumental in influencing many rural southern Blacks to migrate to Newark. It was also charged that NHA's renewal program was dispersing Blacks throughout the city, whereas some councilmen preferred to concentrate Blacks in specific areas. However, NHA rode out that particular storm.[60]

THE MODEL CITIES PROGRAM

In 1966 Congress passed an omnibus housing law which contained a section establishing a model cities program intended to pump additional funds into needy cities.[61] An important part of President Johnson's Great Society plan, the model cities program (known at the time of enactment as "demonstration cities") authorized federal grants to urban areas for a coordinated attack on urban blight.[62]

Congress intended this bill to confront social as well as purely physical problems. Participating cities were to receive federal grants equal to as much as 80 percent of the financial contribution they were required to make (under existing law) as their share of federally assisted programs included in a model cities plan.

When enacting the statute, Congress had envisaged a restructuring of the total environment of model city neighborhoods.[63] In the selected locations, federal funds could be used for such purposes as education and antipoverty and related social programs, as well as for the more traditional programs aimed at physical decay. A major objective of the program was to demonstrate how a coordination of federal and local programs could eliminate blight in the chosen cities. It was thought that cities not included in the program would benefit from constructive demonstrations. Officials in Housing and Urban Development regarded the newly authorized coordination as a vital innovation in the rehabilitation campaign.

Despite its apparent enthusiasm for the model cities program, Congress in the initial three-year period did not fund the project at anywhere near the authorized level of $1.2 billion; nevertheless the program got underway. On Nov. 16, 1967, the Department of Housing and Urban Development was able to announce that 63 cities—large and small—had been chosen to draw up plans for the model cities program. New York City was among them.[64]

A year later New York was allocated $65 million from Housing and Urban Development for the city's three most poverty-stricken areas.[65] The recipient communities were Harlem, Central Brooklyn, and South Bronx. In August, 1970, a review of the program in Central Brooklyn indicated the kinds of projects which were approved and how many were actually in operation. At that time Central Brooklyn with an allocation of $29 million had 38 programs which had been approved, of which 18 were operational. Those which were under way included emergency repair services, a bookmobile, an ambulance service and methadone maintenance for drug addicts. In South Bronx, whose allocation amounted to $21.5 million, the listing was roughly similar, with the addition of sanitation services and family day-care centers.

For Harlem—the third New York City area—the allocation came to $14.5 million. Of the three operational programs, only the one in Harlem was in serious difficulty, and the reasons for this situation are instructive.

Of the 46 projects approved by the federal government for Harlem, only four permanent projects were functioning as of the summer of 1970. And of these, only one—an emergency household repair unit—was reported as delivering "direct services to the community residents."[66] This was not because of a lack of money, for millions of dollars were in fact available to put into operation the approved projects. Why then, did the Model Cities program in Harlem find it so hard to spend money?

According to top officials in the program and close observers, four principal elements were responsible for the lag in the Harlem program behind the others in New York City.[67] These were as follows:

1) There was a struggle for control of the program between the central office which had over-all responsibility and the neighborhood office in Harlem.

2) Personal animosity existed between Joseph B. Williams, the central administrator, and John Edmonds, the neighborhood director. Williams was said to subscribe to the doctrine of strong central control, while Edmonds was considered a vigorous proponent of complete decentralization.

3) Disagreement on employment policy occurred between the two offices. While the central office supported strict enforcement of civil service standards, the neighborhood office felt that such enforcement would exclude from jobs the very people the Model Cities program was designed to serve.

4) Conflicts took place at the neighborhood level between Blacks and Puerto Ricans. Feeling was so intense that the Puerto Rican staff director established a separate office.

As the Model Cities program was set up, proposals suggested by the communities involved (through a locally elected policy committee and a neighborhood office) must first be approved by the Model Cities central office, then the city's Board of Estimate, and finally by the Department of Housing and Urban Development in Washington.

It was this hierarchical arrangement—in effect placing Model Cities under city hall—to which Edmonds objected. To Edmonds, formerly the deputy administrator of the city's top antipoverty agency, the practice followed by the Office of Economic Opportunity antipoverty program was much more desirable. Under that program, the OEO allocated money directly to community groups, which had considerable latitude as to how to spend the funds. If this plan were to be applied to Model Cities, funds would go directly from Housing and Urban Development to the neighborhood office for deposit in local banks, thereby bypassing completely the central office and the city government. To Williams, the central administrator of all of the city's Model Cities programs, such an arrangement was both politically and legally out of the question.

Beneath the obvious struggle for control over programs, personnel and funds, existed another disagreement that was only infrequently made explicit by proponents of each camp. This was the question as to the role of the community resident in the actual decision-making process. The philosophy which guided the OEO tended to view the citizens' role in terms of community control. But the Model Cities program was built on an entirely different concept. In that view, the community residents' function was one of citizen participation. The two concepts frequently are—and in the Harlem case they actually were—at opposite poles.

PLANNING, PARTICIPATION, AND POLITICS

Up to the present time, nearly all federal programs intended to improve housing in the cities have had mixed, and often unintended, results. This is puzzling, because a good deal of imaginative planning and hard work—as well as cash—have gone into the efforts of the last two decades. Are there any general explanations for the relative failure of the public housing, urban renewal, and Model Cities programs to live up to expectations?

One expert, Charles Abrams, believed that the cause of the trouble is an incorrect objective on the part of the federal government. "From President Hoover to President Johnson," he wrote, "federal objectives in housing have stemmed primarily from an interest in home ownership or in the building industry rather than from a concern for cities."[68] To change this orientation, he proposed that the emphasis of the public housing programs be shifted from slum clearance to increasing the housing inventory for low-income families."[69]

In the analysis of another leading authority, Norton E. Long, the programs—urban renewal, in particular—rested on unexpressed economic assumptions, many of which were invalid.[70] Long referred with approval to the reservations expressed by Senator Robert Taft: "The late Senator Taft feared that the urban renewal program would mean that instead of subsidizing the housing of those who could not afford it we would end up by subsidizing housing for those who could. In this he has proved prophetic."[71]

Reviewing the record after a period of 14 years, a third leading analyst of urban problems, James Q. Wilson, agreed with other assessments that the accomplishments of urban renewal had been "relatively slight."[72] After examining the commonly cited reasons for this condition—red tape, difficulty in finding developers, and so on—Wilson asserted: "But the most important reason for controversy and slow progress is the mounting disagreement over the methods and even the objectives of urban renewal.[73] The coalition of liberals, planners, mayors, businessmen, and real estate interests ". . . which originally made renewal politically so irresistible has begun to fall apart."[74] With the collapse of this once united front, it became more and more difficult for planners to muster adequate support for renewal programs. The programs had lost much of their political appeal to those who appropriated and allocated funds.

Another factor noted by Wilson and others is the growing resistance of neighborhoods to all clearance and urban renewal programs.[75] The phenomenon is nation-wide, as witnessed by the "community" opposition to institutional expansion in the cases, among others, of the University of California at Berkeley and Drexel University in Philadelphia. Where citizen participation is sought on a city-wide basis, it is not difficult to obtain support. Yet when the citizens of a neighborhood are asked to condone a renewal project, that is, to agree that their homes should be torn down, the results are usually entirely different. In this respect, the history of citizen participation in the planning for the Hyde Park-Kenwood renewal project was atypical and perhaps misleading. After reviewing what he considered more typical cases, Wilson concluded: "The higher the level of indigenous organization in a lower-class neighborhood, the poorer the prospects for renewal in that area."[76]

In determining whether to go along with the demands for improvements, the mayor is often in the middle. If he pushes city-wide improvements, he will need the support of neighborhood associations. But he will get support from these associations only if in the past he has worked for their specific demands. In short, the planning process is deeply political, as we are about to see.

THE POLITICAL ENVIRONMENT
OF URBAN REHABILITATION

Housing and urban renewal are highly technical activities which are concerned with the *what* aspects of urban rehabilitation. But these activities occur within a framework composed of law, administration, and politics. It is within this larger area that the policy questions of *how, where,* and *for whom* are propounded and answered.[77]

At one time the policy process seemed remarkably clear and simple. The planners, armed with technology, eminent domain, and money, did what they thought best for the city and its individual neighborhoods. Opposition, if any, was undercut by the generally shared belief that any rehabilitation was in the long run for the greatest good of the greatest number. If, in the course of renewal, some persons were diplaced, lost their homes, or were otherwise inconvenienced, this was only the price one had to expect for progress.

In the last two decades this comfortable outlook has been shattered by two principal developments. The first is the rising demand that the affected neighborhoods participate in the decision-making process of urban renewal. Community involvement formerly meant mere acquiescence in the decisions of the planners. Today community involvement means community participation. The shift has been from a passive to an aggressive, even militant, stance on the part of the community. Whether a community comes out for or against particular proposals, the emphasis is on community action, community demands, and community needs. More often than not, such "participatory democracy" slows urban rehabilitation to a turtle's pace. Infrequently, whole projects are killed through atrophy. But the local community is now a force to be reckoned with.

The second important development has been the rise of a politics of race. When the politics of housing and the politics of race overlap—as they usually do in the large cities—an entirely new dimension is added to public housing and urban renewal. It is not merely race which complicates the picture, but also social class, for the politics of race is also in part one of social class. To untangle the resulting skein and redesign it according to a rational plan of urban renewal is often beyond the abilities of the actors involved in the "game." The social forces are too strong for the players to control.

In consequence of these developments, the arena in which the politics of urban rehabilitation is performed has been substantially enlarged. As we have seen in our discussion of urban education, the level of intensity of the action has also been sharply increased. There is a larger stage, there are more actors, and there is more activity.

Added together, these new factors mean that urban rehabilitation is becoming more and more politically shaped and determined. What was once a relatively isolated process is now seen to be integral to urban politics generally. And the prospect is for an increasing politicization of housing and urban renewal in the foreseeable future.

CHAPTER
NOTES

1. National Commission on Urban Problems, *Building the American City* (Washington: Government Printing Office, no date). Published as House Document No. 91–34, 91st Congress, 1st Session.

2. *Ibid.*, p. 7.

3. *Ibid.*, p. 7.

4. *Ibid.*, p. 7.

5. *Ibid.*, p. 13.

6. *Ibid.*, p. 16.

7. Charles Abrams, *The City Is The Frontier* (New York: Harper & Row, Colophon edition, 1967), p. 4.

8. For a survey of the programs, see Eunice and George Grier, "Equality and Beyond: Housing Segregation in the Great Society," pp. 300–324 in H. R. Mahood and Edward I. Angus, eds., *Urban Politics and Problems* (New York: Charles Scribner's Sons, 1969).

9. *Ibid.*, p. 307.

10. *Ibid.*, p. 307.

11. See Nathan Glazer, "Housing Problems and Housing Policies," in Mahood and Angus, *op. cit.*, pp. 270–299.

12. *Ibid.*, p. 281.

13. *Ibid.*, p. 296.

14. Eunice and George Grier, *op. cit.*, p. 308.

15. Herbert J. Gans, *The Urban Villagers: Group and Class in the Life of Italian-Americans* (Glencoe, Ill.: Free Press, 1962).

16. Lawrence M. Friedman, *Government and Slum Housing* (Chicago: Rand McNally, 1968), p. 17.

17. This account is taken from Friedman, *op. cit.*, p. 17.

18. *Ibid.*, p. 17.

19. *Ibid.*, p. 116.

20. *Ibid.*, p. 150.

21. *Ibid.*, p. 155.

22. *Ibid.*, p. 155.

23. *Ibid.*, p. 160.

24. 68 Stat. 623, 624 (1954); cited in Friedman, *op. cit.*, p. 162.

25. Friedman, *op. cit.*, p. 164.

26. Friedman, *op. cit.*, p. 165, quoting a top official of HUD, Dorn McGrath.

27. *Ibid.*, p. 166.

28. *Ibid.*, p. 194.

29. Scott Greer and David W. Minar, "The Political Side of Urban Development." Vol. 352, *The Annals* (March, 1964), pp. 62–73.

30. See James Q. Wilson, "The Urban Unease: Community versus City," No. 12, Vol. II *The Public Interest* (Summer, 1968), pp. 25–39.

31. *Ibid.*, p. 26.

32. *Ibid.*, p. 27.

33. *Ibid.*, p. 27.

34. Peter H. Rossi and Robert A. Dentler, *The Politics of Urban Renewal* (Glencoe, Ill.: Free Press, 1961).

35. *Ibid.*, p. 40.

36. *Ibid.*, p. 33.

37. *Ibid.*, p. 34.

38. *Ibid.*, p. 62.

39. *Ibid.*, p. 67.

40. *Ibid.*, p. 99.

41. *Ibid.*, p. 99.

42. *Ibid.*, p. 100.

43. *Ibid.*, p. 102.

44. *Ibid.*, p. 103. For a history of the Conference, see Julia Abrahamson, *A Neighborhood Finds Itself* (New York: Harper & Brothers, 1959).

45. Rossi and Dentler, *op. cit.*, p. 191.

46. *Ibid.*, p. 226.

47. *Ibid.,* p. 292.

48. Harold Kaplan, *Urban Renewal Politics* (New York: Columbia University Press, 1963).

49. *Ibid.,* p. 2.

50. *Ibid.,* p. 10.

51. *Ibid.,* p. 39.

52. *Ibid.,* p. 40.

53. *Ibid.,* p. 40.

54. *Ibid.,* p. 61.

55. *Ibid.,* p. 63.

56. *Ibid.,* p. 135.

57. *Ibid.,* p. 135.

58. *Ibid.,* p. 135.

59. *Ibid.,* p. 155.

60. *Ibid.,* p. 155.

61. The statute was The Demonstration Cities and Metropolitan Development Act of 1966—Public Law 89–754. Title II established the Model Cities program.

62. For the legislative history of the statute and of related statutes, see *Congress and the Nation,* Vol. II, 1965–1968, pp. 185–209 (Washington: Congressional Quarterly Service, 1969).

63. *Ibid.,* p. 184.

64. *Ibid.,* p. 212.

65. See the feature article by Charlayne Hunter, "Friction Slows Harlem Model Cities Program," *New York Times,* August 22, 1970, pp. 1 and 13.

66. *Ibid.*

67. *Ibid.*

68. Abrams, *op. cit.,* p. 254.

69. *Ibid.,* p. 266.

70. Norton E. Long, "Local Government and Renewal Policies," in James Q. Wilson, ed., *Urban Renewal: The Record and the Controversy* (Cambridge, Mass.: The M.I.T. Press, paperback edit., 1967), pp. 422–434.

71. Long, *op. cit.,* p. 426.

72. James Q. Wilson, "Planning and Politics: Citizenship Participation in Urban Renewal," in Wilson, ed., *Urban Renewal, op. cit.,* pp. 407–421.

73. *Ibid.,* p. 408.

74. *Ibid.*, p. 408.

75. *Ibid.*, p. 409.

76. *Ibid.*, p. 417.

77. An excellent collection of readings related to this section of the chapter is contained in Jewel Bellush and Murray Hausknecht, *Urban Renewal: People, Politics, and Planning* (Garden City, N.Y.: Doubleday, 1967).

11

The Politics

of Law

and Order

For the average citizen, the most conspicuous and omnipresent symbol of governmental authority is the ordinary policeman. Whether the officer is assigned to patrol or to traffic duty, what distinguishes him from other governmental agents is his very high visibility. Less in the public view than the uniformed patrolman—but much more glamorized and publicized —is his colleague, the detective. In addition, the police force of a large metropolitan city will contain a substantial number of specialists, headquarters personnel, and supervisors who rarely if ever appear on the public stage. At the top of the hierarchy is the police commissioner, responsible to the mayor and city council for the performance of his department.

Like the patrolman on the beat, the commissioner is constantly on public display. What he says and does is likely to make the evening headlines and television newscasts. The commissioner, of course, has more authority and commands a much higher salary than the men who work under him. Another noteworthy discrepancy is not his decision-making *per se*—the lowliest patrolman is constantly making quick decisions—but the fact that the commissioner's decisions almost always take place in a highly charged political atmosphere. This statement tends to hold true even though most commissioners would publicly deny its validity.

To insulate the police from the political process would be difficult even if it were desirable. For one thing, there are a great many police and police departments in the country. At present, the nation's local police forces number more than 300,000 men and women, who are organized into 40,000 separate agencies.[1] More than 200,000 police are in the 39,695 agencies serving county and smaller local units, and 110,000 are in the large departments of cities with a population in excess of 250,000. The largest force, numbering 32,000, is found in New York City.

It is a perfectly safe prediction that these local police forces will continue to grow. In this respect, police work may be said to be something of a growth industry. This is made apparent by Figure 11.1, prepared by the Federal Bureau of Investigation, which shows in graphic form the relative increases in both crime and population for the period 1960–1969. While specialists may dispute the precise percentages of the crime rise in the United States, there is no disagreement on the fact that the increase has been substantial and is continuing.

FIGURE 11.1
CRIME AND POPULATION
1960–1969
PERCENT CHANGE OVER 1960

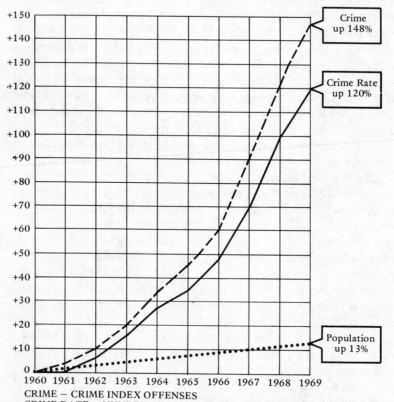

CRIME – CRIME INDEX OFFENSES
CRIME RATE – NUMBER OF OFFENSES PER 1,000,000 POPULATION

SOURCE: *Uniform Crime Reports for the United States, 1969* (Washington, D.C.: Government Printing Office, 1970), Chart I, p. 2.

As crime has grown, so have public expenditures to contain it. The *U.S. News & World Report* calculated that the "crime burden" in the fall of 1970 was running at an annual rate of $51 billion, or more than five percent of the gross national product. In the same survey, it was found that "law-enforcement costs" amounted to $8.6 billion per year, broken down as follows: police (federal, state, local)—$5.0 billion; penal system—$1.8 billion; court system—$1.8 billion.[2] Even by hyperbolic American standards, these figures are impressive.

THE POLICE: AN OVERVIEW

As one would expect, the literature dealing with police work—especially with police administration—is vast. But it has only been within the last few years that political scientists have studied police forces with the same intensity as their analyses of, for example, veterans' or farmers' groups; the police are rapidly losing their former status of *terra incognita*.[3]

What has emerged from the studies of political and other social scientists is a much more complicated picture than was at one time perceived. Indeed, the work of the police is remarkably complex, and the relationships surrounding the police are both varied and delicate. As Richard C. Donnelly has observed, "Law enforcement requires a sensitive and wise discretion in police decisions whether or not to invoke the criminal process when law violators are uncovered."[4]

The general situation is further complicated by the tenet of democratic theory which holds that the police must be subordinate to popular control. Yet the tendency for any skilled professional group—in this case, the police—is to seek autonomy on the ground that the experts know best. What results is the typical dilemma that has always plagued professing democrats—how do elected amateurs responsibly control career professionals?[5]

Though the police perform many functions, their primary objectives are to maintain order and to enforce the law. To some extent, these objectives are more antithetical than complementary. While the police like to publicize their law enforcement role, it is a role which is widely shared with other agencies—the correctional, judicial, and penal systems. In addition, only a small fraction of the working time of the ordinary patrolman is spent on law enforcement. On the other hand, maintaining order takes the lion's share of the average policeman's time and energy, and it is in this area that the police role is paramount.

The problem of standards or criteria further complicates an assessment of the importance of the two principal police objectives. Generally, police administrators are not in agreement as to what constitutes a satisfactory performance of the order maintenance function. When it comes to the other main function—law enforcement—there is more agreement on the objective: the law is to be enforced and crime is to be eliminated. However, there is no agreement on the strategy to be employed to achieve this agreed-on objective. Because of their inability to agree on these questions, police administrators differ markedly in their approach to and their handling of concrete situations.[6]

Yet James Q. Wilson, in a pioneering study—*Varieties of Police Behavior, The Management of Law and Order in Eight Communities*—found certain patterns in the styles of police administration.[7] Wilson examined how the uniformed officer in these eight communities dealt with such common offenses as assault, theft, drunkenness, vice, traffic, and disorderly conduct. Of the communities, six are in New York State: Albany, Amsterdam, Brighton, Nassau County, Newburgh, and Syracuse. The remaining two are Highland Park, Illinois, and Oakland, California.

The study found that there were three different styles or strategies which formed the operating codes of the municipalities under investigation. The first—the watchman style—emphasizes the order maintenance role of the police. Law is used to maintain order, not to regulate conduct. In this style, the requirements of order are judged differentially, depending on the character of the group in which the infraction takes place. For example, in Newburgh, Blacks were left alone by the police except for very serious matters. In the watchman category were listed, in addition to Newburgh, the cities of Albany and Amsterdam.[8]

Under the second or "legalistic" style, the law enforcement view is stressed. The police administrator ". . . uses such control as he has over the patrolmen's behavior to induce them to handle commonplace situations as if they were matters of law enforcement rather than order maintenance."[9] What this means in practice is that the police will act on the assumption that there is a single standard of community conduct—that prescribed by the law—which applies to all groups. For example, the same rather than different standards will be applied to juveniles, Negroes, traffic violators, and drunks. The legalistic style was found in Oakland and in Highland Park and, to a growing extent, in Syracuse.[10]

Lastly, there is the service style. This means that the police take seriously all requests for either law enforcement or order maintenance. "The police intervene frequently but not formally."[11] This style was found to prevail in Brighton and in Nassau County.

When communities with an identical police style were compared, it was found that they had certain similarities. Thus, cities with the watchman police style had these characteristics in common: working class and lower-middle class populations; a high degree of ethnic identification; a system of exchanges of favors in local politics; low tax rates; a low level of municipal services.[12]

Where the legalistic style prevailed, the most obvious similarity was that Oakland and Highland Park both had a city-manager form. Syracuse, which did not have a manager, was also tending toward the legalistic group. In the three cities, the principal effect of the political culture on the police ". . . has been to make possible the appointment of chiefs strongly committed to the doctrine of 'police professionalism' " and to insulate the departments from community pressures seeking changes in police policies.[13]

The communities with a service style also had certain similarities. In all such localities a great deal more was expected of government than merely sweeping the streets. The voters were thought to have high standards of public life, and the official conduct tended to reflect this belief.[14] In social terms, the communities with the service style were homogeneous, middle-class suburbs.[15]

What the tripartite classification of police styles strongly implies is that the police forces of the eight communities operate under the influence of a political culture. But to grant this assumption still leaves unanswered the very important question as to the influence of explicit community decisions in shaping the prevailing police style. On the basis of the evidence available to him, Wilson judged that community decisions were relatively unimportant. In the eight localities which were examined, it was the police themselves who made the decisions (whom to arrest, whom to ignore, when or when not to intervene) which determined the style which would predominate. Simply understanding the political life of a community will not in and of itself, Wilson concluded, ". . . provide a sufficient explanation of the police policies in effect."[16]

Sometimes police policies are affected by forces outside the community over which an individual police department has practically no influence; for instance one of the most important of these environmental factors consists of the attitudes of Americans toward the police. In recent years there has developed a strong degree of antagonism toward the police, especially on the part of Blacks.[17] On occasion this critical attitude may be transformed into overt hostile behavior, as in random killings of police officers—the most publicized of which tend to be blamed on the Black Panthers and other militant groups.[18]

To recognize that the police have an "image problem" is not difficult. To improve or change the popular image (or images) is an extraordinarily intricate matter. It is now evident that the traditional kind of police involvement in community affairs—sponsorship, for example, of a Police Athletic League—is not much more effective than one man's effort to hold back the sea. Nor do the usual public relations gimmicks appear to be very useful in changing the attitudes of minority groups and ghetto residents toward the police.

What may be needed is a drastic shift in the understanding both of the police and of the public as to the nature of police work. In a careful consideration of this problem, Bruce J. Terris wrote: "The image of police officers must be radically changed to consider them as a part of the broad category of occupations which deal with people who are sometimes difficult to handle."[19] Other groups which would fall into the same general classification would include teachers, gang workers, recreation workers, and parole, probation, and correctional officials. It is Terris's opinion that such a change in the conception of police activity would be especially useful in improving the relations between the police and minority groups.

In any overall consideration of crime, the distribution of criminal acts is both of practical importance and also of public interest. The incidence of serious crime in the big cities differs markedly. ("Serious crime" includes murder, rape, robbery, aggravated assault, burglary, larceny of $50 and over, and auto theft.) When the cities with more than 250,000 population were ranked according to the number of serious crimes per 1,000 inhabitants for the year 1969, Oakland stood at the top of the list of 50 localities with a figure of 78.0. At the bottom of the list was Philadelphia with a figure of 18.2, making it, theoretically, the most crime-free big city in the country.[20]

Following Oakland as the top ranking city in proportion of crimes came Washington, Newark, San Francisco, Detroit, St. Louis, Baltimore, Denver, Cleveland, and Boston. In ascending order, Jersey City was somewhat less crime-prone than Philadelphia. Other cities, ranked from lower to higher criminal rates, were El Paso, Austin, Milwaukee, Toledo, Cincinnati, Oklahoma City, San Diego, and—to round out the safest ten—San Jose.

When all serious crimes are lumped together, there is, of course, a very great possibility that the results will be distorted. A more precise index—which again reveals the extent and seriousness of major crime in urban America—is shown in Table 11.1.

Close observers of police work have drawn attention to three leading developments which are currently affecting urban police forces. Of particular interest is the emphasis on professionalization. In concrete terms, professionalization involves careful selection and training of officers, an adequate career service, and the deployment and utilization of officers according to best management practices. Beyond this, professionalization implies—or at least often implies—that the police ought not to be directly controlled by civilians. In other words, professionalization has overtones of a self-regulating guild, although there is the probable consequence of relative insulation of the police force from civilian control.[21]

Closely related to professionalization is the trend toward greater centralization of the police. Basically, the argument is that the police must be rigidly and efficiently organized in order to combat disciplined opponents, for example, the Mafia or the Black Panthers. In this development there is clearly an analogy with military organizations. Though the analogy is only partial and is in many respects downright misleading, the comparison of the police with the military is attractive to many police officials.

Lastly, there has been an emphasis on the relationship between the police and the communities in which they function. Banton, in his sociological study of police in Britain and in the United States, declared that it is ". . . the policemen's participation in the society which most affects the way he exercises his powers."[22] For example, a policeman who participates extensively in community affairs when off-duty is likely to have a very different view of his police role than one who stands aloof and distant or does not live in the community. Partly as a result of Banton's insight, police officials and police institutes are now giving a great deal of attention to the inter-relation between the policeman's occupational and his private role.

POLITICAL ACTION

"Everybody else can indulge in politics—every black group, every political party group, every church group," says Carl Parsell, president of the 3,500-member Detroit Police Officers Association (DPOA). "Why are police officers so different?"
(Quoted in article by Art Glickman, *Wall Street Journal*, Oct. 30, 1969.)[23]

It tends to be the current conventional American belief that politics and the police should be insulated from each other. This belief rests on the assumption that

TABLE 11.1
Number of Offenses Known to the Police, 1969, Cities Over 250,000 in Population

City	Total Crime Index	Criminal Homicide		Forcible rape	Robbery	Aggravated assault	Burglary—breaking or entering	Larceny—theft		Auto theft
		Murder and non-negligent manslaughter	Manslaughter by negligence					$50 and over	Under $50	
Akron, Ohio	12,750	23	12	91	747	433	3,943	4,286	4,545	3,227
Albuquerque, N. Mex.	13,248	11	26	98	402	849	5,427	4,710	6,639	1,751
Atlanta, Ga.	21,254	175	71	173	1,107	1,192	8,740	5,859	10,841	4,008
Austin, Tex.	6,523	27	17	44	233	744	3,091	1,373	7,073	1,011
Baltimore, Md.	61,355	236	98	675	8,864	9,023	19,367	12,829	17,291	10,361
Birmingham, Ala.	11,843	92	35	87	305	1,500	3,724	4,230	3,800	1,905
Boston, Mass.	35,397	91	31	253	2,984	1,529	9,002	6,348	4,385	15,190
Buffalo, N.Y.	16,783	44	—	140	1,057	780	5,622	5,310	5,393	3,830
Charlotte, N.C.	11,256	56	22	67	422	2,083	4,392	3,148	3,416	1,088
Chicago, Ill.	128,426	715	320	1,334	21,476	12,767	36,465	19,641	70,859	36,028
Cincinnati, Ohio	13,154	66	32	179	860	700	5,068	4,449	7,654	1,832
Cleveland, Ohio	49,623	266	48	303	5,638	2,073	11,867	7,197	11,055	22,279
Columbus, Ohio	21,865	52	34	270	1,384	769	8,124	6,928	8,187	4,338
Dallas, Tex.	42,446	232	108	431	2,531	3,666	19,848	8,037	29,550	7,701

City										
Dayton, Ohio	12,368	58	25	83	1,017	784	5,068	3,077	5,919	2,281
Denver, Colo.	30,594	68	56	330	1,702	1,522	11,415	8,993	9,595	6,564
Detroit, Mich.	109,638	439	43	913	17,414	4,934	41,264	22,236	25,970	22,438
El Paso, Tex.	8,429	15	39	41	223	397	4,054	2,006	7,727	1,693
Fort Worth, Tex.	13,949	87	10	92	965	611	6,571	2,194	12,266	3,429
Honolulu, Hawaii	14,428	17	10	56	230	118	6,194	4,646	7,064	3,167
Houston, Tex.	57,887	281	72	405	5,395	2,753	24,684	11,796	16,530	12,573
Indianapolis, Ind.	21,265	65	50	165	1,651	859	8,926	4,666	11,069	4,933
Jacksonville, Fla.	20,782	71	—	214	1,145	1,948	9,059	5,709	7,573	2,636
Jersey City, N.J.	6,318	33	8	41	579	231	1,455	282	651	3,697
Kansas City, Mo.	31,946	105	50	375	2,679	1,995	12,269	7,507	10,238	6,926
Long Beach, Calif.	14,767	29	4	189	903	516	5,834	4,433	6,109	2,863
Los Angeles, Calif.	169,742	377	206	2,115	11,909	14,798	64,515	43,879	47,014	32,149
Louisville, Ky.	19,869	76	66	96	1,443	694	5,166	6,592	4,404	5,802
Memphis, Tenn.	18,556	88	44	108	1,175	688	8,507	5,494	5,539	2,496
Miami, Fla.	20,723	72	35	89	2,749	2,548	7,094	5,092	6,366	3,079
Milwaukee, Wis.	19,219	43	28	78	643	688	4,381	8,350	8,640	5,036
Minneapolis, Minn.	23,179	30	9	174	1,646	582	9,382	5,766	8,455	5,599
Nashville, Tenn.	16,619	73	53	132	837	1,305	6,295	4,590	3,775	3,387
Newark, N.J.	30,491	101	43	234	3,888	2,213	10,884	5,826	5,749	7,345
New Orleans, La.	28,383	76	48	323	2,539	2,283	8,459	8,181	7,426	6,522
New York, N.Y.	478,357	1,043	73	2,120	59,152	29,717	171,393	129,136	61,404	85,796
Norfolk, Va.	12,418	36	19	82	917	1,043	4,206	4,224	4,139	1,910
Oakland, Calif.	30,900	74	28	197	2,572	1,118	14,182	6,488	13,702	6,269
Oklahoma City, Okla.	10,540	44	60	95	534	783	5,565	1,339	7,032	2,180
Omaha, Nebr.	11,096	28	15	51	648	983	3,398	2,850	6,423	3,138

City	Total Crime Index	Criminal Homicide		Forcible rape	Robbery	Aggravated assault	Burglary—breaking or entering	Larceny—Theft		Auto theft
		Murder and non-negligent manslaughter	Manslaughter by negligence					$50 and over	Under $50	
Philadelphia, Pa.	37,060	271	98	505	4,859	3,617	14,063	3,377	17,376	10,368
Phoenix, Ariz.	25,980	46	60	166	1,167	1,969	11,659	6,798	16,846	4,175
Pittsburgh, Pa.	32,113	46	20	249	2,841	1,739	10,125	7,867	4,689	9,246
Portland, Oreg.	20,260	30	39	118	1,292	793	7,752	7,221	8,546	3,054
Rochester, N.Y.	9,850	35	7	59	360	508	3,391	4,309	7,321	1,188
Sacramento, Calif.	11,195	21	15	47	589	385	4,245	3,607	7,047	2,301
St. Louis, Mo.	47,164	254	43	604	4,957	3,493	19,073	4,349	29,387	14,434
St. Paul, Minn.	15,718	16	14	88	984	590	6,015	3,978	4,992	4,047
San Antonio, Tex.	26,989	95	96	215	895	2,057	11,533	7,058	16,060	5,136
San Diego, Calif.	19,498	36	63	155	763	789	5,002	9,286	13,069	3,467
San Francisco, Calif.	53,781	127	69	598	6,502	2,966	18,637	7,418	25,555	17,533
San Jose, Calif.	12,697	13	14	161	369	547	6,274	2,263	16,549	3,070
Seattle, Wash.	35,186	58	13	248	2,559	1,096	14,820	10,514	13,392	5,891
Tampa, Fla.	12,297	29	33	64	760	986	5,508	3,632	6,441	1,318
Toledo, Ohio	10,178	19	17	75	819	422	3,743	3,633	7,889	1,467
Tulsa, Okla.	11,431	18	21	79	362	522	3,817	4,707	4,470	1,236
Washington, D.C.	62,229	287	28	336	12,366	3,609	22,933	11,508	20,402	11,190
Wichita, Kans.	8,553	12	7	46	285	371	3,310	3,265	8,887	1,264

Source: *Uniform Crime Reports for the United States, 1969*, Table 58, pp. 169–170.

any combination of the two factors will result in the corruption of the police by the politicians. That the police might corrupt the politicians is a sentiment that is rarely voiced, and would not be believed if it were. Like oil and water the two elements are held to make a poor mixture. As Mark H. Furstenberg has put it, "That politics and the police are incompatible is an unquestioned article of the professional policeman's faith."[24]

In the official manuals used to indoctrinate police recruits in their duties a good deal of emphasis is placed on the obligation of the police to be nonpartisan. This ideal is further reinforced by the academic literature relating to police administration. For example, the leading text by O. W. Wilson, a noted police commissioner as well as professor, fails to list either "politics" or "political parties" in its index.[25]

So far as recruitment of police is concerned, it is now axiomatic —even if the axiom is not always observed—that tests of partisanship should not be applied to candidates. Yet, in the first third of this century, it was common for police to be chosen on the basis of political party or of religion. Once on the force, the officers were expected to perform chores for the organization in power. Eventually, a popular reaction to these practices set in, and civil service procedures were established as part of a broad municipal reform movement. Under the new provisions political activities were prohibited or severely restricted.

The campaign to apply civil service methods and standards to urban police forces was part of the more general effort to bring about municipal reform. In this process, the reformers and the police administrators frequently found themselves on different sides of the fence. Though disagreement between the two groups could be found in large cities across the country, the situation in Chicago was especially acute, and its case is therefore particularly instructive.

Civic Reformers and Police Leadership: Chicago

The relationship of the police to the reigning political organization is colored by many factors. Among the most important of them is the character and effectiveness of any civic reform movement. Where such a movement is short-lived, it is hard to arrive at any worthwhile generalized conclusions. But where a movement has a considerable history, it is possible for scholars both to create a typology of the police-reform movement relationship and also to suggest findings that may be true in more than one city. Of all American municipal police forces, Chicago's has been the most intensively examined over the years. Drawing on previous investigations as well as his own original research, historian Mark H. Haller has examined police reform in Chicago for the period 1905–1935. The following comments are based on his study.[26]

In the first third of the century Chicago's civic reformers concentrated on campaigns to reform the police force. These campaigns were led by prominent citizens who had high social prestige and were often wealthy. Their values were generally shared by the editors and publishers of the city's leading newspapers. Yet, on balance, ". . . these civic leaders had only a limited impact upon the administration and operation of the police department."[27] The central question is, of course, why?

In reviewing the reform movement, Haller was struck by the social differences between the civic reformers and the police—social differences which were also mirrored in political distinctions. By and large, the civic reformers were apolitical; they stood outside the usual factional quarrels. On the other hand, the police were intimately involved in such political factions, and they were largely recruited from the ethnic neighborhoods. In 1930, for example, some 76 percent of the police captains in Chicago were of Irish background.[28]

A particular constraint on the police was the close tie between some criminal activities—prostitution, gambling, and, in the 1920's, bootlegging—and politics. For political reasons, certain criminals could not be arrested by the police. As a consequence, the police "acted more to regulate than to eliminate professional criminal activity."[29] There was also an extensive system of pay-offs and shakedowns which bound the criminals and the police to each other. Naturally, the reformers were shocked by this situation, which they held would be corrected if only the police would enforce existing laws.

Yet it was at this point that a second general weakness in the reformers' position became evident. The reformers, it turned out, were far from united with regard to priorities. A high level of agreement upon common values was insufficient to bring about a common plan of action. As Haller reconstructed the picture, one group—the moral reformers—was concerned with "the moral quality of neighborhood life in the city."[30] This group therefore advocated that police resources be mobilized against prostitution, gambling, and liquor law violations—activities that were presumed to victimize the poor. While elaborate campaigns were launched and achieved some success—brothels, for example were eventually closed down—the price of such crusades was continual warfare within the police department itself. Though the moral reformers were quite willing to search for "corruption" in the ranks of the police, the force itself viewed such an enterprise with understandable restraint. It was, and remains, too much to expect that a police department will voluntarily indict itself.

For the second group of reformers—the business and commercial elite—the general objective of police reform was not moral uplift—but an improvement in public safety. This section of the civic elite contended that the police should primarily concern themselves with crimes against persons and property: assault, robbery, and similar offenses.[31] In order to achieve this objective, the business reformers urged the police department to improve its administration and the calibre of its personnel. Clearly, the demands of this group were much more compatible with the traditional police perspective than those of the moral reformers. After all, it usually takes additional funds to improve governmental services. With respect to their willingness to accept new appropriations, the police are no different from other municipal agencies. In any case, between 1929 and 1932, the civic leaders, through the famous Citizens' Police Committee, ". . . completed a major reform of the administrative structure of the Chicago police department."[32]

There were, then, two models of police reform in Chicago during the 1905–1935 period. Under one model, the goal of the reformers was to improve the operational and technological capabilities of the police. Police resources were to be used to combat crimes against persons and property. Under the second model, the objective was to end gambling, prostitution, and liquor violations, and to eliminate any corruption of the police force which stemmed from such illegal activities. In Chicago, as elsewhere, movements for police reform involved some aspects of each model.[33] It is also likely that the tension between police officials and civic reformers —so evident in Chicago—existed in other major urban centers.

The New Activism of the Police

If the early municipal reformers were upset by what they considered laxity or corruption on the part of urban police forces, they would be totally appalled by the police activism of the last few years, for this activism has involved the police in political and social areas that have usually in the past been considered outside the interests or the competence of the police. At the same time that the area of police concerns has been enlarged, there has been a dramatic increase in police militancy generally.

The evolution of police militancy—as shown, for example, in demonstrations and even strikes—has been traced in some detail by Jerome H. Skolnick, Director of the Task Force on Violent Aspects of Protest and Confrontation of the National Commission on the Causes and Prevention of Violence.[34] He noted that political involvement of the police is not new; they have cooperated often in the past with local political organizations. But they generally played very minor roles in active partisan politics.[35]

In addition, the police have often acted as an active arm of the status quo. For example, they were formerly very important in labor disputes. Today, they are prominent in the handling of anti-war protests and other public demonstrations.[36]

Yet these types of political involvement, though important, were considered by Skolnick to be less significant than the more recent trend toward the "politicization" of the police. As evidence, he cited illegal police strikes, lobbying, and political organizing. What Skolnick underscored was the transformation of police guild, fraternal, and social organizations into effective interest groups which lobby and propagandize on behalf of what the police consider their proper concerns. One of these groups—the Fraternal Order of Police—claims a membership of 130,000. This means that militancy and politicization have been able to build upon an organizational framework already in existence.[37]

Indeed, the concerns of the national Fraternal Order of Police and of similar local organizations have proved to be remarkably broad. As one would expect, there has been substantial activism on behalf of material benefits: higher wages, shorter hours, and working conditions. In these areas, police organizations have acted in the same manner as trade unions or guilds.

But it is police activism in the area of social policy that has raised the most serious questions. The Skolnick Report drew attention to several examples of this trend. The famous confrontation between the police and demonstrators at the 1968 Democratic National Convention in Chicago was termed "police violence" by some observers.[38] There was also considerable evidence, the Report maintained, of police revolts against higher authority. A prime illustration was said to be the widespread police opposition to Cleveland's Mayor Carl Stokes following the July 23, 1968, shootout between police and Black militants.[39] Other examples of police involvement in matters of broad social policy came from efforts to defeat proposals for civilian police review boards, lobbying activities to raise salaries, and attempts to have state legislatures revise criminal procedures and criminal statutes.

Taken together, the combination of the new and the traditional interest group activities of police associations has produced a nation-wide police militancy that is unprecedented. There is, as the Skolnick Report put it, a ". . . growing tendency of the police to see themselves as an independent, militant minority asserting itself in the political arena."[40]

Nowhere is the new police activism more apparent than in election campaigns themselves. In many cities, police have shed their nonpartisan role and have engaged in direct political activity. The municipal elections of 1969, particularly, furnish some splendid examples of the new interventionist attitude of police forces.[41]

In the Los Angeles mayoralty election, held in the spring of the year, white police officers campaigned for the re-election of Mayor Sam Yorty. White officers also were active on behalf of Charles Stenvig, a detective, who was running as a mayoralty candidate in Minneapolis.

Very extensive police participation took place in the fall contest to choose a mayor of Detroit. In the campaign—which pitted Wayne County Sheriff Roman S. Gribbs (white) against Wayne County Auditor Richard H. Austin (Black), the police did the following things:

1) The Detroit Police Officers Association (DPOA) endorsed Gribbs and eight other whites standing for the city's Common Council.
2) Off-duty patrolmen registered voters.
3) On November 4, off-duty patrolmen helped voters to get to the polls.
4) In addition to the activities of the DPOA, the 525-member Detroit Police Lieutenants and Sergeants Association and the 500-member Detroit Police Detectives Association also contributed men and money to the Gribbs campaign.

In the same fall 1969 municipal elections, the police were also active in a number of other cities. In Seattle, the Seattle Police Officers Guild played an electoral role. In Hartford, where the state law prohibits policemen from political activity, policemen's wives worked unsuccessfully to elect George Kinsella to the post of mayor. In Houston, though Texas law prohibits political activity, some officers were reported to be campaigning for Mayor Louie Welch for re-election.

A final illustration comes from Cleveland. There, the usually non-political Fraternal Order of Police took out a full-page newspaper advertisement listing the alleged shortcomings in police administration and calling on Mayor Carl Stokes, a Black, for improvement. The general suspicion was that the ad had been run to help Stokes' challenger, Ralph J. Perk.

Besides being evident in campaigns for election to office, "blue power" has also been employed in other political contexts. In Los Angeles and in Cleveland, police went ". . . directly to the ballot for pay raises or retirement benefits refused by the city fathers."[42] In 1968, police lobbied successfully in the New York State legislature for repeal of a law which more closely defined justifiable homicides. A similar bill was killed in committee in California in 1967.[43]

For a dramatic attempt at seizing power, it woud be hard to top the struggle in New York City between the Patrolmen's Benevolent Association (PBA) and the Lindsay administration. The contest was generally viewed as an effort by the PBA, under its president, John Cassese, to "usurp" the authority of Police Commissioner Howard Leary. The showdown came in the summer of 1968 over the question of who would issue guidelines to the police—Cassese or Leary. Cassese eventually backed down, but not before he had demonstrated that the PBA had become a "major political power" in New York City politics.[44] (Leary, a policeman who had formerly been Police Commissioner in Philadelphia, resigned unexpectedly and without explanation in the fall of 1970—to the dismay and embarrassment of Mayor Lindsay.)

Commenting on the developments in New York City and elsewhere, political analyst Ed Cray declared: "Law Enforcement is testing its political muscle, emboldened by the easily sensed mood of a public demanding domestic tranquillity at any price."[45]

The Police and the Protesters

Throughout the latter half of the 1960's, the police were faced with the job of maintaining public order in the face of an ever mounting number of street demonstrations. Normally simply outdoor exercises in free speech and assembly, increasingly the demonstrations ended in violent confrontations between the police and the demonstrators. This denouement occurred with disheartening frequency when the protesters were anti-war students or Black militants.

This escalation of violence between police and demonstrators was a cause of concern for Americans committed both to the doctrine of free speech and of public order. It was often noted—the Skolnick Report is a case in point—that there had been a steady escalation in violence, the causes of which became a matter of considerable controversy.

The Skolnick Report maintained that official violence on the part of the police was a major cause of the escalated conflict. In rebutting this charge, spokesmen for law enforcement agencies blamed the increase directly on the actions of certain organized agitators and indirectly on "permissiveness" and other conditions alleged to be widespread in American society. Basing their arguments on entirely different premises, the opponents came, understandably, to entirely different conclusions. What to the critics was "police brutality"—i.e., illegal violence—was to the police simply prudent action in the public interest.

Though there has been some criticism of "police violence," there is also very strong public support for the police when they use extra-legal methods against some kinds of public dissenters. For example, the "roughing up" of long-haired but peaceful anti-war protesters. William A. Gamson and James McEvoy, in their study of the question, concluded: "Extra-legal police actions directed against unpopular targets are unlikely to draw censure or even disapproval from those substantial segments of the American public for whom the police are the 'good guys.' "[46] This finding confirms the conclusion of an earlier study of what respondents thought about police action at the Democratic convention at Chicago in 1968. Overwhelmingly, they approved. The evidence indicates that the police may expect to find a good deal of popular support when they use extra-legal means to suppress certain kinds of public dissenters.[47]

CIVILIAN REVIEW BOARDS

Nowhere in city government has the demand for citizens' grievance machinery been more insistent than in connection with police administration. The mechanism most advocated in recent years has been a non-judicial 'review board' apart from the police authorities.

Walter Gellhorn[48]

The principle that acts of an individual policeman should be subject to review by higher authority has long been accepted in the United States. But application of the principle is anything but simple and self-executing. For most police forces, an internal review board has been the device most commonly relied on to hear citizens' complaints against individual officers. Under this procedure the board is composed of police officials, that is, high ranking colleagues of the officer against whom the complaint has been lodged. The review board and the defendant officer are thus "insiders," while the complainant is an "outsider." The system is open to the obvious criticism that the interests of justice and of police morale may be in conflict—to the possible detriment of the complainant.

So long as the average complainant was poor or an habitual criminal, that is, without power, the internal review board procedure attracted little attention except from civil liberties lawyers. But once the ranks of complainants began to include civil-rights-conscious minority persons and middle-class demonstrators, that is, people with a capacity for attracting public attention, the established system came under increasing attack. No longer was it possible to keep the hearings themselves secret or quasi-secret, nor was it possible easily to keep their findings and judgments from the press.

As a result of such pressures, police departments developed a high degree of sensitivity to the problem of review boards. The International Association of Police Chiefs, which acts as a national spokesman, went on record in 1964 as favoring internal boards only.[49] Taking this as their lead, other police associations adopted a similar position, as did individual police departments. Quite quickly, a line was drawn on this issue between police agencies and their critics. In the camp opposing the police stood assorted civil rights and minority groups. To them the solution to the problem was to establish external review boards which were not under the control of the police authorities. Only under such a procedure, they contended, could citizen complainants be assured of an impartial hearing which could result in affirmative action against an offending officer. It is against this general background that the dramatic events associated with the November 8, 1966 referendum over civilian review took place in New York City.

The November 8, 1966, Referendum in New York City

The issue of civilian review of the police created an intensity of public attention and controversy seldom equalled in New York's political history. The crucial factors of public safety, crime, and race relations lay beneath the question of whether or not to set up a review board.[50]

As an issue, civilian review was not new. For some years civil rights and Black groups had proposed that civilians be added to the existing internal review board (called the Police Department's Civilian Complaint Review Board—"civilian" referring to the source of complaints, not the membership of the Board). This proposal was vigorously opposed by all the police, but the center of opposition was the Patrolmen's Benevolent Association. This organization had a membership of 25,000 out of a total of 28,000 policemen.

In the 1965 mayoralty campaign, John V. Lindsay, the Republican candidate, had suggested adding four civilians to the Police Department's board which, at that time, consisted of three deputy police commissioners. This proposal represented a halfway step toward the completely independent board demanded by civil rights groups and Blacks.

After his inauguration, Lindsay took steps to implement his proposal. As an initial measure, the new mayor did not reappoint Police Commissioner Vincent L. Broderick, who was opposed to a civilian board. Instead, on February 15, 1966, Lindsay appointed Howard R. Leary who, though opposed to the civilian board principle, had indicated he would cooperate with the mayor if a civilian board were established. At this point, the president of the PBA, John J. Cassese, announced that his organization was prepared to spend its whole treasury to combat the board idea.

True to his word, Mayor Lindsay and his new police commissioner jointly announced on May 2 the creation, by executive order, of a civilian-controlled review board. The board was to consist of four civilians from outside the municipal government and three police members. On July 11, Lindsay appointed one Black, one Puerto Rican, one Irish Catholic (active in interracial work), and, as chairman of the board, Algernon D. Black, a leader of the New York Society for Ethical Culture. Of the three police members, one was Black.

Instead of calming passions, the creation of the new board inflamed them. While Black organizations criticized the agency for its alleged inadequacies, the PBA challenged its very existence. The PBA, through Cassese, announced it would continue to oppose the board unless it were approved by the voters in a referendum. The PBA then began to collect signatures on a petition for a referendum. Its plan was to place before the electorate for a referendum vote an amendment to the city charter which would in effect make illegal the civilian-expanded board of Mayor Lindsay.

Acting through legal channels, the mayor attempted to keep the civilian review question off the ballot. The courts, however, upheld the validity of the PBA petition. Meanwhile, the Conservative party, which had filed its own petition against a civilian review board, revoked its action in order to avoid splitting the anti-review board ranks.

The opposing forces during the campaign were formidable. Rallying to support the PBA in the drive against a review board were the Conservative party, American Legion posts, parents' and taxpayers' groups, the Brooklyn Bar Association, and certain right-wing organizations. The New York City Civil Liberties Union took the leadership in building up support for the board. Included in the pro-board coalition—Federated Associations for Impartial Review (FAIR)—were various labor, civil rights, civic, and religious organizations.

As the campaign proceeded, an impressive number of important political figures became involved. Both of New York's senators—Jacob K. Javits (Republican) and Robert F. Kennedy (Democrat)—came out on behalf of Mayor Lindsay's plan. Governor Nelson A. Rockefeller (Republican) and New York City Council President Frank D. O'Connor (Democrat) said they supported the board but did not campaign for it. Lesser figures also became involved because their constituencies were deeply concerned over the outcome of the referendum.

On the face of it, the issues before the electorate seemed simple enough. The PBA maintained that the board would impair police efficiency and would lower morale on the force. In contrast, the pro-board coalition maintained that the institution of a civilian review agency would help "restore" public confidence in the police.

But underneath the surface of official statements was one issue which dominated all the others—race. Because it was generally regarded by the public and the press as a means to satisfy Black and Puerto Rican demands, a civilian review board became identified as a civil rights issue. The result of this identification was to make the referendum a measure of the degree of "white backlash," that is, resentment by white voters against Blacks and rights for Blacks.[51]

In addition, the referendum became in part an indication of approval or of disapproval of Mayor Lindsay's first year in office. Taking into account the time and energy Lindsay threw into the campaign brought about by the referendum, this position was comprehensible.

The verdict of the voters, on November 8, 1966, constituted a monumental defeat for the civilian review board. The vote was 1,313,161 (63 percent) "yes" (to abolish civilian review) to 765,468 "no" (to retain civilian review). In those areas heavily populated by Black and Puerto Ricans the vote was in favor of the board. Most of these districts were in Manhattan, the only borough to give a majority in favor of the board. Elsewhere throughout the city, with a few scattered exceptions, the board proposal went down in a sea of adverse votes.

In her study of the 1966 elections, Lucy S. Dawidowicz analyzed the referendum vote in New York City.[52] She found that German, Irish, and Italian voters voted heavily to abolish the civilian review board. But Jewish voters split, and they did so along economic and class lines. There was also a high correlation between voting to abolish the board and supporting the Conservative party. Finally, major party affiliation had no particular bearing on how people voted in the referendum.[53]

A second study by David W. Abbott, Louis H. Gold, and Edward T. Rogowsky also throws light on the complexities involved in the referendum. Immediately after the election, a random sample of 374 white voters throughout Brooklyn was interviewed in an effort to probe public attitudes.[54] The results, which are consistent with those obtained by Dawidowicz, are, in general terms, as follows: 1) In relation to other referenda, the participation was very high. 2) The division ran along religious lines, with Catholic voters overwhelmingly opposed to the review board, and Jews more evenly divided. 3) So far as the major parties were concerned, partisan affiliation was not a factor. But Conservatives mostly opposed the board. 4) The fear of lawlessness was very high, and the PBA was able to capitalize on this fear. 5) Whites tended to view the police quite favorably, and were not impressed by charges of police brutality. 6) There was considerable disillusionment with the civil rights movement. 7) There was little evidence that the Brooklyn respondents were expressing attitudes of blatant racial bigotry.

As to the overall importance of the referendum vote, the investigators concluded: "The CRB referendum proved to be a rout for the civil-rights forces. For the first time in years, New York's liberal electorate rejected a civil-rights position."[55]

The Ombudsman as an Alternative to Review Boards

In retrospect, the experience in New York City appears to have dampened much of the earlier enthusiasm for civilian review boards. To be sure, the cry for such agencies is still heard from civil rights and Black groups, but the public as a whole seems to have lost interest in the matter.

According to law professor Walter Gellhorn, both internal and external review boards have a common vice which cannot be overcome: they rapidly degenerate into adversary proceedings between a citizen complainant and a police defendant. In his opinion, "Adversariness has yielded few positive results."[56] The typical dispute, he argued, is not really between two individuals. What the complainant actually desires is a method for bringing certain police actions to the attention of the superior police administrators. In this view, the emphasis is on improvement of police services, not on the punishment of an individual police officer.

One frequently suggested method for handling complaints against the police without undergoing the deficiencies inherent in the review board approach is to establish a municipal ombudsman. Unlike the civilian review board—which focuses entirely on complaints against the police—the municipal ombudsman would hear complaints against all city agencies, including the police department. The ombudsman, at the conclusion of his investigation, would make suggestions to the appropriate agency. It is extremely unlikely that he would be given the authority to issue commands. To give him such powers would be construed as undercutting the capacity of the executive—whether mayor or city manager—to fulfill assigned functions. In addition, councilmen—and other politicians—would be resentful of binding "interference" by an ombudsman into what they consider one of their own areas of expertise, that is, the handling of citizens' complaints against the municipal agencies.

Despite the fact that an ombudsman's authority would in all probability be suggestive rather than mandatory, the concept of a municipal ombudsman has its attractive features. At its minimum, the very existence of an office of ombudsman could be expected to make all the city agencies—including the police—sensitive in their dealings with citizens.[57]

THE POLICE AND
THE COMMUNITY

The need for reinforcement and change in police work has become more urgent than ever in the last decade because of rising rates of crime, increased resort to violence, and rising tension, in many communities, between disaffected or angry groups and the police.

McGeorge Bundy[58]

In the summer of 1967 large-scale disorders occurred in a substantial number of American cities. These outbursts prompted President Lyndon B. Johnson to appoint a National Advisory Commission on Civil Disorders. The President instructed the commission to look into the causes of the recent riots and to suggest remedies. In particular, the President asked the commission to find out (1) what had happened; (2) why it had happened; and (3) what could be done to prevent it from happening again.

Otto Kerner, Governor of Illinois was named chairman of the commission. Vice chairman was John V. Lindsay, Mayor of New York City. The Kerner Commission, as it came to be called, issued its report in 1968. It was the Introduction to the Summary of the *Report* which contained these words which soon became famous:

This is our basic conclusion: Our Nation is moving toward two societies, one black, one white—separate and unequal.[59]

The Commission noted that the riots had exacerbated the existing abrasive relationships between the police and Blacks and other minority groups. But basically, the problem was found to go beyond mere hostility toward the police. For the policeman in the ghetto was found to be the symbol not only of law but of the whole political and social system.[60]

As the commission viewed the entire situation, they cited the following five "basic problem areas":

The need for change in police operations in the ghetto, to insure proper conduct by individual officers and to eliminate abrasive practices.

The need for more adequate police protection of ghetto residents, to eliminate the present high sense of insecurity to person and property.

The need for effective mechanisms for resolving citizen grievances against the police.

The need for policy guidelines to assist police in areas where police conduct can create tension.

The need to develop community support for law enforcement.[61]

To gain community support for law enforcement the Commission recommended several concrete steps. First on the list was the proposal to step up the recruitment, assignment and promotion of Black officers. The ratio of nonwhite to all policemen—as of the time of the commission's *Report*—is shown in Table 11.2.

TABLE 11.2
Nonwhite Personnel in Selected Police Departments

Name of department	Number[5] police officers	Number[5] Nonwhite police officers	Number sergeants[5]		Number lieutenants[5]		Number captains[5]		Number above captain[5]	
			Non-white	White	Non-white	White	Non-white	White	Non-white	White
Atlanta, Ga.	968	98	2	12	3	56	0	15	0	6
Baltimore, Md.	3,046	208	7	389	3	105	1	17	1	21
Boston, Mass.	2,508	49	1	228	0	80	0	20	0	12
Buffalo, N.Y.	1,375	37	1	60	1	93	0	24	0	32
Chicago, Ill.	11,091	1,842	87	1,067	2	266	1	73	6	66
Cincinnati, Ohio	891	54	2	68	2	34	0	13	0	7
Cleveland, Ohio	2,216	165	6	155	0	78	0	26	0	17
Dayton, Ohio	417	16	1	58	0	13	0	6	0	4
Detroit, Mich.	4,326	227	9	339	2	156	0	0	1	62
Hartford, Conn.	342	38	0	32	1	16	0	9	0	2
Kansas City, Mo.	927	51	7	158	0	36	0	11	1	14

Louisville, Ky	562	35	1	42	1	29	0	10	1	7
Memphis, Tenn.	869	46	0	0	4	192	0	45	0	44
Michigan State Police	1,502	1	0	135	0	24	0	19	0	3
New Haven, Conn.	446	31	0	20	0	16	0	12	0	6
New Orleans, La.	1,308	54	7	107	1	51	0	27	0	10
New York, N.Y.	27,610	1,485	65	1,785	20	925	2	273	3	157
New Jersey State Police	1,224	5	0	187	0	43	0	17	0	4
Newark, N.J.	1,869	184	5	97	3	95	1	22	0	0
Oakland, Calif.	658	27	1	95	0	25	1	10	0	3
Oklahoma City, Okla.	438	16	0	32	1	19	0	11	0	6
Philadelphia, Pa.	6,890	1,377	26	314	8	139	3	46	0	23
Phoenix, Ariz.	707	7	0	88	1	22	0	10	0	4
Pittsburgh, Pa.	1,558	109	3	137	3	47	0	4	1	6
St. Louis, Mo.	2,042	224	21	201	3	46	4	17	0	11
San Francisco, Calif.	1,754	102	0	217	0	66	0	15	0	10
Tampa, Fla.	511	17	0	50	0	12	0	13	0	8
Washington, D.C.	2,721	559	19	216	3	107	3	37	0	31
Total	80,621	7,046	271	6,289	62	2,791	16	802	14	576

281

Name of department	Percent nonwhite population	Percent nonwhite police officers	Ratio: Sergeants to officers		Ratio: Lieutenants to officers		Ratio: Captains to officers		Ratio: Above captain to officers	
			Nonwhite	White	Nonwhite	White	Nonwhite	White	Nonwhite	White
Atlanta, Ga.	[1]38	10	1:49	1:73	1:33	1:16	0:98	1:58	0:98	1:14
Baltimore, Md.	[1]41	7	1:30	1:7	1:69	1:27	1:208	1:167	1:208	1:135
Boston, Mass.	[1]11	2	1:49	1:11	0:49	1:31	0:49	1:123	0:49	1:205
Buffalo, N.Y.	[1]18	3	1:37	1:22	1:37	1:14	0:37	1:56	0:37	1:42
Chicago, Ill.	[1]27	17	1:21	1:9	1:921	1:35	1:1842	1:127	1:307	1:140
Cincinnati, Ohio	[1]28	6	1:27	1:12	1:27	1:25	0:54	1:64	0:54	1:120
Cleveland, Ohio	[1]34	7	1:28	1:13	0:165	1:26	0:165	1:79	0:165	1:121
Dayton, Ohio	[1]26	4	1:16	1:7	0:16	1:30	0:16	1:67	0:16	1:100
Detroit, Mich.	[2]39	5	1:25	1:12	1:114	1:26	No such rank		1:227	1:66
Hartford, Conn.	[2]20	11	0:38	1:10	1:38	1:20	0:38	1:34	0:38	1:152
Kansas City, Mo.	[1]20	6	1:7	1:6	0:51	1:24	0:51	1:80	1:51	1:63
Louisville, Ky.	[1]21	6	1:35	1:13	1:35	1:18	0:35	1:53	1:35	1:75
Memphis, Tenn.	[1]38	(4) 5	No such rank		1:12	1:4	0:46	1:18	0:46	1:19
Michigan State Police	[3]9		0:1	1:11	0:1	1:63	0:1	1:79	0:1	1:500
New Haven, Conn.	[2]19	7	0:31	1:21	0:31	1:26	0:31	1:35	0:31	1:69

New Orleans, La.	[1] 41	4	1:8	1:12	1:54	1:25	0:54	1:46	0:54	1:125
New York, N.Y.	[1] 16	5	1:23	1:15	1:74	1:28	1:743	1:96	1:495	1:166
New Jersey State Police..	[3] 9	(4)	0:5	1:7	0:5	1:28	0:5	1:72	0:5	1:305
Newark, N.J.	[1] 40	10	1:37	1:17	1:61	1:18	1:184	1:77	None listed	1:210
Oakland, Calif.	[1] 31	4	1:27	1:7	0:27	1:25	1:27	1:63	0:27	1:70
Oklahoma City, Okla. ..	[1] 15	4	0:16	1:13	1:16	1:22	0:16	1:38	0:16	1:240
Philadelphia, Pa.	[1] 29	20	1:53	1:18	1:172	1:40	1:459	1:120	0:1377	1:175
Phoenix, Ariz.	[1] 8	1	0:7	1:8	1:7	1:32	0:7	1:70	0:7	1:175
Pittsburgh, Pa.	[1] 19	7	1:36	1:11	1:36	1:31	0:109	1:362	1:109	1:242
St. Louis, Mo.	[1] 37	11	1:11	1:9	1:75	1:40	1:56	1:107	0:224	1:165
San Francisco, Calif.	[1] 14	6	0:102	1:8	0:102	1:25	0:102	1:110	0:102	1:165
Tampa, Fla.	[1] 17	3	0:17	1:10	0:17	1:41	0:17	1:38	0:17	1:62
Washington, D.C.	[1] 63	21	1:29	1:10	1:186	1:20	1:186	1:58	0:559	1:70

[1] Percent Negro population figures, 1965 estimates by the Center for Research in Marketing, Cong. Quarterly, Weekly Report, No. 36, Sept. 8, 1967.

[2] Percent Negro population figures, 1966 estimates, Office of Economic Opportunity.

[3] Percent Negro population figures for States of Michigan and New Jersey, 1960 Census figures.

[4] Less than 1/2 of 1 percent.

[5] All police data from a survey conducted for the Commission by the International Association of Chiefs of Police in October 1967.

SOURCE: Report of National Advisory Commission on Civil Disorders, Table A, p. 169.

As its second recommendation, the commission advised the police to stress their community service functions. Finally, the commission urged the police to establish community relations programs. Where the programs have been merely public relations efforts, the commission noted, they have often failed. But some more fundamental programs have been very successful. One instance was the Crime Prevention Bureau in Atlanta, which had ". . . within 2 years established a good relationship with the community, particularly with young people."[62] Equally successful programs were reported in Baltimore and in Winston-Salem.[63]

Indeed, there is much support for the contention that the police should expand their functions into traditionally nonpolice areas. Herman Goldstein, for example, rejects the view that the police should engage only in crime-control activities.[64] If the police really wish to gain community acceptance and to reduce citizen hostility toward them, they should—in Goldstein's opinion—be prepared to broaden considerably their own conception of their job functions. An example of such an expanded view comes from the experimental Family Crisis Intervention Project in New York City. Under this plan, specially trained officers respond quickly and expertly to situations involving domestic disturbances.

In some cases the initiative in altering the traditional police-community relationships has come from citizens' groups. The Dayton View Citizens Action Team is an illustration. Dayton View is a racially mixed neighborhood in the southern Ohio city of Dayton. For some time the citizens had been troubled by crime which the police were often unable to control. In response to this situation, a citizen surveillance group was organized for the purpose of patrolling the streets of Dayton View at night. Using nine patrol cars, the Team followed the technique of radioing information to the police when there was suspicion of crime. As of the spring of 1970, there were seven such surveillance groups operating in Dayton alone.[65]

The activities of the Dayton citizens' surveillance groups have been duplicated in other cities. In some cities the police have been dubious about the efforts of well-meaning but possibly over-zealous volunteer helpers. In other cities, the police have been apprehensive about Black groups, some of whom are armed, who have taken it upon themselves to purge neighborhoods of drug pushers and other criminals. The police in New York City have discouraged most attempts to form neighborhood patrol groups. Instead, they have promoted the formation of an Auxiliary Police

Force. This organization in 1970 consisted of 3,000 members who had received special police training and special uniforms—but no firearms.[66]

While the groups just cited were formed on the assumption that the police were not active enough, other groups have been organized on the premise that the police have been too active—on a selective basis. For instance, in Philadelphia a group of citizens organized a Council of Organizations on Philadelphia Police Accountability and Responsibility (COPPAR). A typical operation occurred during the great anti-war demonstration held in Philadelphia in early May, 1970. While the police kept some 12,000 demonstrators under surveillance, the police themselves were under the surveillance of COPPAR. The citizens' group—some twenty observers—stood at the edge of the crowd as nonparticipants and recorded police behavior in their notebooks and on film. In this case, no improper behavior by the police was reported.[67]

In a position paper endorsed by the twenty-two organizations which formed the Philadelphia police observers' group, it was stated that ". . . there is an acceleration of serious friction between the police and the community—black, Spanish-speaking, and white." The statement continued: "While various civic and community organizations share concern over the lack of meaningful police accountability, it has now become apparent that there is need for a citywide organization whose concern will be police conduct."[68] What appears to have given impetus to the formation of the surveillance group was the abolition of Philadelphia's Police Advisory Board, which was made up of civilians. The board was held to be illegal by the lower courts. Subsequently, the State Supreme Court overturned the earlier ruling, but Mayor James Tate refused to reconstitute the board.

Where a similar situation exists elsewhere, it seems reasonable to suppose that pressures also exist for the creation of some kind of police observers' group. In any case, the type of organization that was formed in Philadelphia has sprung up in many other large cities. And everywhere the relations between the police and these citizen observers have ranged from chilly to frigid.

Hostility between the police and a particular community reaches its peak when the division between the two groups is—or is viewed as being—basically racial in character. It is often as though two rival powers were vying for territorial control. Indeed, this is the military analogy drawn by novelist James Baldwin, who lived in Harlem during the early period of his life. Harlem, he wrote in

1966, ". . . is policed like occupied territory."[69] With the Black population of northern cities in mind, he continued: "And the police are simply the hired enemies of this population. They are present to keep the Negro in his place and to protect white business interests, and they have no other function."[70] Therefore, he concluded on this point: "To respect the law, in the context in which the American Negro finds himself, is simply to surrender his self-respect."[71]

Baldwin's bitterly made point was buttressed by the report of the Kerner Commission and other studies dealing with race relations and civil rights. In any case, the implication is clear in Baldwin's comments that Blacks can obtain protection and justice only through local control of the police forces in their communities. By the end of the 1960–70 decade, the demand for community control over police forces in the large cities enjoyed considerable Black support.

The Case for Community Control

In presenting the case for community control of the police, a good deal of reliance will be placed on the argument advanced by Arthur I. Waskow, a social critic who is prominent in the ranks of those who would re-structure American society by decentralizing it. When it comes to presenting the case against community control, the chief witness will be James Q. Wilson, who has been referred to previously in other connections.

In his brief for community control, Waskow begins with this assumption: "In almost every American metropolis, the police no longer are under civilian control—that is to say, democratic public control."[72] The reason is that they are said to have developed a high degree of autonomy. There are two ways in which this autonomy has been gained: 1) by constructing "a police subculture of lifelong policemen—defining their own norms, rewards, etc."; and 2) by organizing "quasi unions with considerable political power" to "negotiate" practical autonomy.[73]

Waskow maintains that there are three possible directions in which to achieve democratic control over the police. The first is "Formal restructuring of metropolitan police departments into federations of neighborhood police forces, with control of each neighborhood force in the hands of neighborhood people through election of commissions."[74]

The second is "Creation of countervailing organizations (in effect, 'trade unions' of those policed) responsible to a real political base, able to hear grievances and force change."[75]

The third possible direction is "Transformation of the police 'profession' and role so as to end the isolation of policemen from the rest of the community, and thus to establish de facto community control by chiefly informal means."[76]

Under the first approach—the commission plan—there would be agreement on the ideal size of a community. Waskow mentions a population of 100,000. Any community inside the city with about that population would be entitled to its own police force. In Black communities, this would result in a Black police force controlled by Black commissioners, and so on. The two leading objections to this plan are the difficulties of resolving the jurisdictional or territorial problem involving the different police forces inside the city and the property problem. While the first type of problem is obvious, the second is not. What Waskow has in mind is the fact that different community police forces might take differing views toward the protection of property. Would a Black force, for example, be especially vigorous in protecting white-owned shops and stores against vandalism committed by unemployed Black teen-agers? Would this, in short, rank very high on the list of priorities of a Black-controlled police force?

As to the second approach—that of countervailing power— there are in existence two actual models. The emergence of local surveillance groups in Watts and elsewhere (sometimes called Community Alert Patrols—or CAPs) has already been noted. These groups tag along with the police, keep them under surveillance, and report any police excesses to non-police organizations. Then there is also a second actual model, of which the Community Review Board created by the Mexican-American community in Denver is an illustration. This chicano organization investigates charges of illegitimate or unjust police behavior and then uses political pressure to support demands for remedial or corrective action by the police. The major advantage of this approach, in Waskow's view, is that it can be instituted without the agreement of those in power.

At the heart of the third possible direction is the idea of cracking or breaking up the police subculture. The peace-keeping function now performed by a city's police would be turned over to unarmed, non-career men drawn from the local community. At the same time, the role of the "downtown" police would accordingly be redefined and delimited.

What have been the actual demands put forth by community groups for neighborhood control of the police? So far as Model I—the commission model—is concerned, the only sustained demand that Waskow could find has come from the Black United Front in Washington, D.C. Model II—that built on countervailing power—has been supported by certain Black and Spanish-speaking communities, but it has received only "momentary support from the federal government or foundations."[77] Model III—which calls for cracking the police subculture and for radically deprofessionalizing some of the present police roles—has attracted little political or community interest.

For Waskow, the goal of community control of the police could best be achieved by some combination of Models I and III. To further that objective, the most promising immediate strategy, he asserts, would be to work for the realization of Model II—countervailing power.

That this would not be an easy or simple path to follow is plain to Waskow. "It must be clear," he concludes, "that such a community union to police the police would be a focus of intense political conflict, including great hostility and possibly physical danger from the police."[78]

The Case against
Community Control

As noted earlier, James Q. Wilson is very dubious about the value of community control of the police in a large, heterogeneous city. What the proponents of community control propose, he says, is that each neighborhood be allowed to determine its own style of law enforcement.[79] The model for this plan is, of course, the suburb. But, and this is one of Wilson's main points, the suburbs are different from the central cities.

The most obvious difference—that of size—is not the most important in this context. Of much greater importance is the differentiation in class structure between the central city and the residential suburbs. To improve police-community relations, Wilson argues, requires the outlook and behavior patterns of a middle-class suburb.[80] In short, there can be no significant improvement until the cities become middle-class.

In Wilson's analysis, the relationship between Blacks and the police in the large cities is fundamentally a class, not a racial, problem. On this point, he writes: "If the fundamental problem is one of class (admittedly greatly complicated by the problem of race), what can a police administrator do in the short run while he waits for society somehow to solve the class problem? If the point of view presented here is correct, not a great deal."[81]

On the other hand, Wilson favors certain administrative changes which would keep concentrated the authority which governs the police but which would decentralize the functions of the police. Specifically, he would give the precinct commander greater freedom of action and more control over his patrolmen. But he does not want the precinct commander—as in a "dispersed department" —to surrender control to whatever political forces may be in control of the neighborhood.[82] He would have the police stress order maintenance as their central function. Such law enforcement as the police engage in would be performed under centralized command. For Wilson, the goal would be "a decentralized, neighborhood-oriented, order maintenance patrol force."[83] Such an arrangement, he believes, would be a distinct improvement over the present departmental organization found in the large cities. At the same time, he feels that his suggestions are both practically and theoretically superior to the plans advanced under the banners of community control.

SUMMARY

Whether community control of police forces is desirable or not depends largely on one's objectives and on their priority. While Waskow and Wilson both, presumably, think that the police operations should have something to do with "justice," they differ on what concretely is involved in achieving this objective. In the case of Waskow, substantial urban minorities, especially Blacks, can achieve justice only if they have community control over police forces. But Wilson refuses to break up the central cities in the manner of suburbs because he still sees considerable social as well as technical advantages in a unified system of police operations. Justice, he implies, is more likely to be achieved under this plan than under one of extreme decentralization. For Wilson, urban social reform in the long run will come from a general upgrading of "lower" into middle classes in the urban areas. The police can do practically nothing about the social situation in which slum communities find themselves. Therefore, it is pointless to consider the police as though they were an instrumentality for social reform.

Stated in this manner, it is evident that the positions of the pro- and the anti-community control adherents are—at least for the foreseeable future—antithetical. There would be little merit in expecting that a consensus could be achieved by the usual bureaucratic device of appointing commissions, holding conferences, and publishing position papers. The differences are too basic for such a glib reconciliation.

To say this is not to imply that the question of community control over the police is unimportant and will wither away. On the contrary, the evidence points clearly in the other direction. It seems as certain as one can be in these matters that the issue will receive increasing public attention, that it will be the focus of continuing controversy, and that it will be with us for many years to come. Consequently, the police are likely to be increasingly swept into the vortex of community politics.

When the experience of the police with the community is added to the other components of this chapter—direct political action and civilian review boards—the message is clear. The police have increasingly entered into the political process of the cities they patrol. The area of their involvement has considerably expanded. At the same time, the intensity of police involvement has obviously increased. In this sense, then, it may be said that the politicization of the police has substantially advanced during the last decade or so. This trend will in all probability continue, perhaps at an accelerating rate.

CONCLUSION TO PART FIVE— "POLICY POLITICS"

Perhaps it would be helpful here to briefly review the basic components of our analysis of Part Five. It was stated in the introductory paragraphs to Part Five that one of the purposes of the three chapters that compose this part was to test one of the two elements—the community/state dichotomy—of the pluralistic model against the real world. We also noted that this dichotomy has two deductions: first, that the area of political activity is both confined and clearly delineated; and, secondly, that the level of political activity is low.

In measuring our model against the actual political behavior, the community/state dichotomy was used as an analytical tool in examining three important areas of urban politics: education, housing and urban renewal, and law and order. Our objective was to examine whether the political activity in these three areas had increased, and, if so, whether the model was still relevant. On the basis of the evidence presented in this part, it is apparent that in education, housing and urban renewal, and law and order, the area of political activity has expanded. Furthermore, the intensity of political conflict has risen in each of the three arenas.

It seems safe to conclude from our analysis then that the community/state dichotomy—essential to the functioning of the pluralistic model—is largely invalid when applied to the urban world of today. Since we have previously determined that the first component of the same model—the group theory ingredient—is also largely invalid in the present-day urban situation, there is only one overall conclusion which can be entertained—that the official pluralistic urban model—so cherished and praised by social scientists and political figures—is itself now obsolete.

CHAPTER
NOTES

1. The Ford Foundation, *A More Effective Arm: A Report on a Police Development Fund, Newly Established by the Ford Foundation* (New York: Ford Foundation, 1970), p. 5.

2. *U.S. News & World Report*, Oct. 26, 1970, pp. 30–34.

3. On the development of a political science literature relating to the police, see Jameson W. Doig, "Police Problems, Proposals, and Strategies for Change," Vol. XXVIII, No. 5, *Public Administration Review* (Sept./Oct., 1968), pp. 393–406.

4. Richard C. Donnelly, "Police Authority and Practices," Vol. 339, *The Annals* (Jan., 1962), pp. 90–110, citation at p. 90.

5. On the sheer complexity of modern police work, see the article by Bruce J. Terris, "The Role of the Police," Vol. 374, *The Annals* (Nov., 1967), pp. 58–69. A prominent Washington attorney, Terris was Assistant to the Solicitor General from 1958 to 1965.

6. On the problems facing police officials generally, see James Q. Wilson, "Dilemmas of Police Administration," Vol. XXVIII, No. 5, *Public Administration Review* (Sept./Oct., 1968), pp. 407–417.

7. James Q. Wilson, *Varieties of Police Behavior, The Management of Law and Order in Eight Communities* (Cambridge, Mass.: Harvard University Press, 1968).

8. *Ibid.,* p. 141.

9. *Ibid.,* p. 173.

10. *Ibid.,* p. 172.

11. *Ibid.,* p. 200.

12. *Ibid.,* p. 236.

13. *Ibid.,* p. 259.

14. *Ibid.,* p. 250.

15. *Ibid.,* p. 200.

16. *Ibid.,* p. 232.

17. For detailed documentation of public hostility toward the police, see President's Commission on Law Enforcement and Administration of Justice, *Task Force Report: The Police* (Washington, D.C.: Government Printing Office, 1967), pp. 145–149.

18. For an account of police reactions to anti-police hostility, see Herman Goldstein, "Police Response to Urban Crisis," Vol. XXVIII, No. 5, *Public Administration Review* (Sept./Oct., 1968), pp. 417–423.

19. Bruce J. Terris, *op. cit.,* p. 68.

20. *U.S. News & World Report, op. cit.,* p. 33.

21. On the trend toward professionalization, see Terris, *op. cit.*

22. Michael Banton, *The Policeman in the Community* (New York: Basic Books, 1964), p. 267.

23. Art Glickman, "Blue Power," a feature story in *Wall Street Journal,* Oct. 30, 1969, pp. 1 and 29.

24. Mark H. Furstenberg, "Police and Politics," Vol. XXV, No. 8, *The Police Chief* (August, 1968), p. 12.

25. O. W. Wilson, *Police Administration* (New York: McGraw-Hill, 1950).

26. Mark H. Haller, "Police Reform in Chicago, 1905–1935," reprint from *American Behavioral Scientist,* Vol. XIII, Nos. 5 & 6, May, June, July and August, 1970, Sage Publications, Inc., 1970. Professor Haller is completing a book on crime and justice in Chicago for the years 1900–1935.

27. *Ibid.,* p. 649.

28. *Ibid.,* p. 650.

29. *Ibid.,* p. 650.

30. *Ibid.,* p. 652.

31. *Ibid.,* p. 652.

32. *Ibid.,* p. 662. For a survey of the work of the Citizens' Police Committee, see Haller, pp. 658–662.

33. *Ibid.*, p. 663.

34. The Skolnick Report was not a report of the National Commission on the Causes and Prevention of Violence but of the Director of the Task Force on Violent Aspects of Protest and Confrontation. For the complete report, see Jerome H. Skolnick, *The Politics of Protest* (New York: Ballantine Books, 1969).

35. *Ibid.*, p. 268.

36. *Ibid.*, p. 269.

37. *Ibid.*, p. 271.

38. *Ibid.*, p. 274.

39. *Ibid.*, pp. 244, 276.

40. *Ibid.*, p. 278.

41. Glickman, *op. cit.*

42. Ed Cray, "The Politics of Blue Power," Vol. 208, *The Nation* (April 21, 1969), pp. 493–496, citation at p. 496.

43. *Ibid.*, p. 496.

44. *Ibid.*, p. 495.

45. *Ibid.*, p. 496.

46. William A. Gamson and James McEvoy, "Police Violence and Its Public Support," Vol. 391, *The Annals* (Sept., 1970), pp. 97–110. Citation at p. 110.

47. See, John P. Robinson, "Public Reaction to Political Protest: Chicago, 1968," *Public Opinion Quarterly* (Spring, 1970), pp. 1–9. See, also, the general discussion in the pamphlet by Irvin Block, *Violence in America* (New York: Public Affairs Committee, Inc., July, 1970. Public Affairs Pamphlet No. 450).

48. Walter Gellhorn, "Police Review Boards: Hoax or Hope?," Vol. IX, No. 3, *Columbia University Forum* (Summer, 1966), pp. 5–10, citation at p. 5.

49. For the official police attitude toward review boards, see the February, 1964 issue of *The Police Chief* (Vol. XXI, No. 2). This issue reprinted a long "note" from the January, 1964 *Harvard Law Review* on the subject, and then gave an "IACP Critique of the Study." The exchange of views was both thorough and dispassionate.

50. This account is taken, generally, from David W. Abbott, Louis H. Gold, and Edward T. Rogowsky, *Police, Politics and Race* (New York: The American Jewish Committee, 1969).

51. *Ibid.*, p. 8.

52. Lucy S. Dawidowicz, *The 1966 Elections: A Political Patchwork* (New York: The American Jewish Committee, April, 1967).

53. *Ibid.*, p. 19.

54. Abbott, Gold, and Rogowsky, *op. cit.*

55. *Ibid.*, p. 44.

56. Gellhorn, *op. cit.*, p. 9.

57. For a discussion of possible police department reforms in New York City, see Paul Chevigny, *Police Power, Police Abuses in New York City* (New York: Pantheon Books, 1969). For a general analysis of the arguments for and against the office of ombudsman in American society, see Stanley V. Anderson, ed., *Ombudsmen for American Government?* (Englewood Cliffs, N.J.: Prentice-Hall, 1968). William H. Angus and Milton Kaplan, in chapter 4—"The Ombudsman and Local Government"—touch directly on how an ombudsman would relate to the police.

58. The Ford Foundation, *A More Effective Arm, op. cit.*, p. 1. In June, 1970, McGeorge Bundy, president of the Ford Foundation, announced the establishment of the Police Development Fund. The purpose was ". . . to assist a limited number of police departments in experiments and demonstrations aimed at improving operations and to support special education and training projects." The Fund was to receive $30 million and was conceived primarily as a grant-making agency—making funds directly available to local police departments.

59. National Advisory Commission on Civil Disorders, *Report* (Washington, D.C.: Government Printing Office, 1968), p. 1.

60. *Ibid.*, p. 157.

61. *Ibid.*, p. 158.

62. *Ibid.*, p. 167.

63. *Ibid.*, p. 167.

64. Goldstein, *op. cit.*

65. See the article by Seth S. King, "In Many Cities, That Man on the Beat in a Crime-Ridden Area May Be a Neighbor Assisting the Police," *New York Times*, May 3, 1970, p. 72.

66. *Ibid.*

67. See the piece by Kitsi Burkhart, in the Philadelphia *Bulletin* of May 10, 1970, p. 1.

68. *Ibid.*

69. James Baldwin, "To Whom It May Concern: A Report from Occupied Territory," Vol. 203, *The Nation* (July 11, 1966), pp. 39–43, citation at p. 40.

70. *Ibid.*, p. 41.

71. *Ibid.*, p. 41.

72. Arthur I. Waskow, "Comment: Community Control of the Police," Vol. 7, No. 2, *Trans-action* (Dec., 1969), pp. 4–7. Citation at p. 4.

73. *Ibid.*, p. 4.

74. *Ibid.*, p. 4.

75. *Ibid.*, p. 4.

76. *Ibid.*, p. 4.

77. *Ibid.*, p. 7.

78. *Ibid.*, p. 7.

79. See Wilson, *Varieties of Police Behavior, op. cit.*, pp. 285–295, for his discussion of problems inherent in community control.

80. Wilson, "Dilemmas of Police Administration," *op. cit.*, p. 411.

81. *Ibid.*, p. 412.

82. Wilson, *Varieties of Police Behavior, op. cit.*, p. 290.

83. *Ibid.*, p. 293.

12

Toward

a New

Style

Politics

Our analysis has continued to point out that traditional brokerage politics has become outmoded in dealing with present-day realities of the urban political situation. In particular, we have noted how the group theory and community/state dichotomy of the pluralistic model are incapable of leading to sound political decisions such as are needed for our contemporary cities to survive.

Under the circumstances, it is natural to look for a more satisfactory explanation of urban politics than that which is offered by the now discredited official doctrine. A new model of urban politics —one which is in harmony with the present urban world—seems to be developing. An analysis of such developments as are emerging from the real world of metropolitan and city politics should reveal at least some of the principal elements which will go into a new and more relevant model. To put the matter somewhat differently, if we could identify the leading elements in the developing New Style politics, we should be able to make considerable progress in building a new model to replace the pluralistic one which we have found to be no longer functional.

NEW DEVELOPMENTS AND CHANGING RELATIONSHIPS

Racial and Ethnic Realignments

Race and ethnicity—along with income and religion—have long provided fairly reliable indicators as to how given sections of the electorate would vote. This has always been understood by brokerage style politicians. During the last thirty years the relative impact of the different factors on voting behavior has been intensively studied by social scientists. There is nothing at all novel, then, in pointing to the existence of racial and ethnic voting patterns in urban areas.

What *is* different is the suggestion that large racial and ethnic groups should turn from the role of party-supporter to that of interest group-manipulator. It involves a shift from the idea, for example, that New York City Blacks should automatically support the Democrats to the belief that Blacks should back any party which offers the most to the Blacks. This might mean throwing the bulk of Black strength to the Republicans one year, the Liberals or the Conservatives another year, and perhaps eventually back to the Democrats. This would be based on the conviction that the politics of interest groups offers a more substantial payoff than the politics of the traditional parties.

It is an extension of this bloc concept which certain Black leaders have in mind when they lovingly contemplate the exact date at which Philadelphia or Chicago may be expected to have an absolute Black majority. They dream of larger Garys and Newarks with Black mayors. To the extent that this new politics of race is successful in large cities, it will involve the formation of new types of intra-state coalitions. This will be so because Black-controlled urban parties will—for many reasons—have to come to understandings and arrangements with the white-dominated parties of the suburbs and of the states at large.

In any new urban politics built on blackness as the rallying point, there will still be room for the small, agitational type of interest group represented, for example, by the Black Panthers. Their role—and that of similar groups—should be seen as prodding the Black party leaders to discuss or react to particular problems and issues which party leaders would normally just as soon not discuss. In this respect, such groups would perform the same function that scores of propaganda-minded (as against election-oriented) socialist associations have often done in the past.[1]

But Blacks are not the only unassimilated racial group that seeks social objectives through political action. A new militancy on the part of Mexican-Americans is emerging, and its urban manifestations are particularly evident in Los Angeles, San Antonio, and Denver. In the person of Cesar Chavez, the organizer of agricultural workers, the *chicanos* have found a leader of national stature. There are 5.6 million Mexican-Americans in the United

States, and many of them live in rural areas. Yet where they have heavy urban concentrations, they may be expected increasingly to play a more active political role—both inside the parties and as an interest group. Like "Black Power," "Brown Power" may take varying political forms. New alignments and new coalitions will undoubtedly be forged in many cities of California and of the southwest.[2]

Yet the newest rallying cry in urban politics relates not to Black or brown groups but to white ethnic groups. As Prof. Paul Mundy, a Loyola University sociologist put it: "The third generation remembers what the second generation would like to forget—its ethnic identity."[3]

"Ethnic Power" comes from first- and second-generation "hyphenated" white Americans, most of whose members live in 58 major industrial cities, and who are said to number approximately 40 million persons.[4] The roots of this large group lie in Central and Southern Europe. Its members are primarily in the working class. The "ethnic American" experienced throughout the 1960's a growing degree of frustration, dissatisfaction, and alienation.

In analyzing the reasons for this large-scale disaffection, Barbara Mikulski, a spokesman for the Polish community in Baltimore, singled out several factors.[5] These included unfavorable treatment of ethnic Americans in the mass media, neglect by all levels of government, inferior housing and educational facilities, and scorn from limousine-liberals. But the most important reason for complaint was economic. As members of the working class, ethnic Americans for the most part fell within the $5,000–$10,000 yearly brackets. This meant that they were too "rich" for their children to receive scholarship aid and too "poor" to buy a house of their own. Generally, they were losing ground economically and they felt that no one noticed or cared. From their point of view, most government programs were tailored to help the Blacks, or the suburban middle class, or the rich—never the 40 million ethnics.

Under these circumstances, city-dwelling ethnic Americans began to turn in on themselves.[6] In northern cities, communities of such citizens began to attach a new importance to a cultural identity which had earlier faded when confronted with the "American dream."

In striving to make themselves heard, ethnic groups deliberately adopted the same tactics which had been used by Black civil rights activists. In Cleveland, for example, such groups demanded a voice on municipal boards and commissions. They also insisted on their right to examine school textbooks "to be sure an ethnic identity could be found in the history books our children study."[7] In Pittsburgh, the Pan Slavic Alliance, inactive for many years, was revived and began to agitate for government-sponsored research centers. Italian-Americans organized in order to be able to expose misrepresentations of their group in the mass media.

It took some time for national religious leaders to take seriously the complaints which were arising from ethnic neighborhoods. In Chicago, many of these complaints were related to resistance to the efforts of the Rev. Martin Luther King, Jr., and other Black leaders to desegregate all-white residential areas. The white ethnic communities were mostly Roman Catholic or Jewish. In looking for assistance, they turned to their national religious leaders. But the response—from the point of view of the ethnic groups—was inadequate and unhelpful.[8]

Eventually, when the national leadership began to understand the seriousness of the problem, in Chicago and elsewhere, steps were taken to cope with the overall situation. The American Jewish Committee organized the first national "Consultation on Ethnic Americans" at Fordham University, New York City, in June, 1968. A short while afterwards the National Conference of Catholic Bishops established a Task Force on Urban Problems. Monsignor Geno C. Baroni, its director of program development, served as chief strategist of a nascent ethnic movement with local alliances in ten cities.[9]

Whether Monsignor Baroni or any one else can unite the Poles, Italians, Slavs, Hungarians, Greeks, and others who constitute ethnic America into a cohesive electoral bloc would seem to be most unlikely. Yet in particular cities at particular times, local electoral alliances of the ethnics could prove to be pivotal.

Cities and Suburbs

As we have noted, the 1970 Census confirmed what some had suspected for the preceding five years —the population of the suburbs had become larger than that of the central cities. Looking into the political future, does this mean that the politics of metropolitan areas will increasingly be dominated by the politics of the suburbs? Will this result in the "suburbanization" of politics within the large metropolitan areas? Will the political systems of the suburbs become the dominant systems in urban politics?

There are reasons for believing that the response to these questions is "no." In the first place, America's suburbs vary economically, ethnically, and racially, and their political interests are not identical. Even though the suburban political systems are becoming increasingly autonomous in relation to the systems of the central cities, the suburban systems are not as alike as peas in a pod. They compete with each other, as well as with the central cities. It is also a mistake to separate too sharply the governmental concerns of the suburbs from those of the central cities. Education, policing, and public housing may be locally managed, but transportation, air and water pollution, sewage disposal and water supply—even welfare—and many aspects of land use and planning are usually considered to require regional management.

To put the matter in this way is not to deny that there are more often than not substantial partisan differences in the politics of the central cities and those of the suburbs. As was noted previously, in the northern half of the country, the central city is now generally Democratic and is surrounded by Republican suburbs. There is the possibility that conflict over race in the central cities may drive a wedge in the Democratic party coalition between Blacks and low income white ethnics. Or, substantial groups of working class ethnics might, given increasing affluence, move to the suburbs in response to what they regard as Black aggression. In commenting on this situation, Thomas R. Dye has asserted: "These party differences suggest that for many years to come it will be difficult, if not impossible, to achieve the consolidation of metropolitan governments."[10]

Though he did not stress the political aspects of consolidating governments in metropolitan regions, Charles E. Gilbert arrived at the same conclusion as Dye. Gilbert was dubious that regionalism, metropolitan government, or structural changes could bring about a rationalized public policy for large urban areas.[11] He came to this conclusion after studying the counties in Pennsylvania which surround Philadelphia. He favored a revitalization of county government as the most hopeful means of dealing with the needs of the metropolitan area. Admitting that some might find this position "seemingly conservative," Gilbert nonetheless added: "On the other hand, neither administrative, political, nor social analysis leads one to thoroughgoing regional consolidation."[12] Known under various titles, but most frequently that of "metropolitan government," is a proposal which calls for the consolidation of the various units of government inside the particular metropolitan region. The objectives have usually been stated in economic terms, for example, greater operating efficiency, enlarged financial resources, and more adequate public services. Taxpayers' organizations and economy leagues—self-appointed watchdogs over the public treasuries—were at one time in the front ranks of organizations advocating metropolitan government.

In the last decade the initial glow of enthusiasm for this plan has faded. One reason, developed in Robert C. Wood's excellent study of the New York metropolitan region, is that only the planners like the scheme.[13] Wood and his associates engaged in an intensive examination of the "political economy" of the 22-county region which includes parts of three states. They found that the obstacles to regional government were formidable.

There were very few political figures who were desirous of any form of governmental consolidation.[14] When it came to business leaders, little favorable interest was forthcoming. Nor was there any evidence that the electorates in the 1400 governments which constituted the metropolitan region were anxious for regional government. Quite to the contrary, according to Wood: "If the Region's leadership shows little inclination to take giant strides, it is not likely to be pushed by the electorate."[15] In short, by and large, it could be inferred that the people were sufficiently satisfied with the existing situation so as not to demand drastic changes.[16]

Aside from public indifference to regional government, there also developed in some areas a mood of positive public hostility. An example comes from the Hartford region in central Connecticut. In the early 1960's metropolitan government was widely acclaimed as the device which would bring about a more equitable and efficient administration of services common to all units of the region. This belief was based in part on the success of the metropolitan water district. If consolidation worked in this area, why not, it was asked, would it not operate equally well in others?

To the city planners in Hartford, metropolitan government at first looked like an easy solution to some of the city's problems. The well-to-do suburbs could share their financial and intellectual resources with the central city, presumably for the common benefit of all. As the financial implications of such brotherliness became apparent, hostility toward consolidation became vocal in West Hartford, in Simsbury, in Farmington, in East Hartford, in Glastonbury, in Wethersfield, and in Rocky Hill.

But there developed another type of hostility which no one had foreseen. The supposed beneficiaries of metropolitan government —especially the Blacks and Puerto Ricans in the North End of Hartford—began to reassess the demographic realities of metropolitan government. Under the existing system, they had a growing voice in the politics and government of the city, particularly in the public school system. Under the consolidation plan, the city population of 160,000 would have been swamped in the total regional population of half a million. By the end of the 1960–70 decade, leaders of substantial minority groups in Hartford were understandably extremely chilly toward metropolitan government. Their reservations on this subject were widely shared throughout the city.

Urban Areas and the State

One of the basic principles of the traditional American system of government is that cities and other urban areas possess only those powers which have been delegated to them by the states. There is, in short, no inherent right to "home rule," and even where the term is used, it tends to imply more self-determination than really exists. This is because the states have ordinarily regarded the cities as potential if not actual rivals and have hedged delegations of power with numerous and often irritating restrictions. Nonetheless, the states do bear a primary responsibility for the welfare of their urban citizens.

How well has this responsibility been met? In the opinion of experts in the field of state government—not very well. Daniel J. Elazar, for instance, a staunch supporter of federalism and of the power of state governments in general, has conceded that the states have fallen short of the mark in this area. He wrote: ". . . there remains one major unsolved problem, whose importance cannot be over-emphasized: that of the metropolitan areas. By and large, the states have been unwilling or unable to do enough to meet metropolitan problems."[17] The future role of the states, he added, will be determined by what they do or fail to do in dealing with this problem.[18]

Whether the states will or will not take adequate action to help meet metropolitan needs is therefore of great importance. But specialists in state government are not optimistic in their assessments of the capacity of the states to help. In fact, many of the experts are downright pessimistic regarding the future effectiveness of state governments in any of their historic roles.[19]

Alan K. Campbell declared that students of governmental affairs agree that the states, of all parts of the federal system, have performed "least well."[20] He saw no signs of a "breakthrough" in state urban action.[21] He believed that the states ". . . are particularly responsible for the kinds of problems created by the contemporary urban crisis."[22] Yet he did not expect that the states would in fact seriously attempt to find solutions to the problems of metropolitanism. "Before this occurs," he stated, "new life and vigor must be injected into state government."[23]

As a result of this situation, the cities find themselves in a dilemma. On the one hand, they can wait for the solution to their problems until the states enjoy a newfound prosperity, presumably with federal funds under a revenue-sharing plan. Or, on the other hand, refusing to sit tight until the Day of Awakening finally arrives, the cities can take their case directly to the federal government. Blocked by the states in their efforts to make progress in an over-the-center power play, the cities can attempt to bypass the states by an around-end manoeuvre. This strategy has suggested itself to many mayors, and they have begun to employ it both before federal agencies and Congressional committees.

Understandably, politicians and scholars who view the states as the keystone of the American governmental structure have been alarmed by this development. They see the tendency to create direct federal-city relationships as a challenge to "state integrity," and cite the Office of Economic Opportunity grants to communities as frightening examples of what they have in mind.[24] There is, however, little evidence that the mayors of the largest cities, increasingly more desperate for funds, have been impressed by this line of reasoning.

The "New Federalism"

In seeking to distinguish their Administrations from those of their predecessors, incoming Presidents find it useful to produce a new definition of federalism. In recent years, the country has witnessed the birth of "cooperative federalism" and of "creative federalism." In the case of President Nixon, the official designation became the "new federalism."

President Nixon announced his New Federalism concept in an address on domestic policy delivered on August 8, 1969. At that time he indicated his support for three specific proposals which would implement the newly announced policy. These were a Family Assistance program, revenue-sharing with the states, and a comprehensive manpower plan. Together, these programs constituted the heart of Mr. Nixon's approach to domestic reform.[25]

So far as the states were concerned, Mr. Nixon's proposals that the federal government assume a large proportion of welfare costs and that it share some of its revenues with the states could not have come at a more welcome time. State governments were in the midst of an increasingly severe financial squeeze, aggravated by inflation and increased welfare roles. Some, such as New York, had virtually exhausted new sources of revenue. Others, such as Connecticut, New Jersey, and Pennsylvania were considering resorting to adoption of a politically repugnant progressive personal income tax. Pennsylvania adopted an ungraduated income tax in 1971.

Everywhere the increasing relative inability of the states to raise funds to meet the demands of their citizens was paralleled by a financial crisis in the large cities. Arthur Naftalin, former mayor of Minneapolis, on Dec. 8, 1970 advised the 47th Congress of the National League of Cities that the cities should ". . . throw themselves upon the mercy of their adversaries."[26] Mayor John V. Lindsay of New York City told the same gathering that ". . . the first priority of this country must be a new system of federal revenue sharing" with the states and cities. Both Naftalin and Lindsay called for "massive" federal aid to the cities, and the New York mayor suggested that Congress appropriate $10 billion for the first year of the program in 1971.

In their general approach, the nation's mayors were consistent with the position taken in October, 1969 by the 36th American Assembly. The *Final Report* of the Assembly included this recommendation:

Congress should enact a revenue sharing plan with state and local governments, including: (a) allocations related to state and local tax effort; (b) a mandatory 'pass-through' to local governments above a minimum population, based on current state-local divisions of fiscal responsibility; (c) demonstration of state intention and ability to deal with local governmental and urban problems.[27]

What the states and cities were saying as clearly and loudly as they knew how was that they needed a massive and continuing inflow of federal funds in order to meet the requirements of their citizens. Otherwise, as a *New York Times* editorial put it, ". . . the federal system, already severely strained, may break down altogether with practically every problem being managed directly by the national government."[28]

Whether there would be any substantial revenue sharing, and the conditions under which it would occur, would eventually be determined not by the pleas and lamentations of the states and cities but by the actions of the White House and Congress. For any real breakthrough, it appeared likely that the states and urban

America would have to embark on an intensive and continuing lobbying campaign to persuade Congress that the crisis required the dramatic federal action which the President had recommended.

This action was placed in considerable jeopardy during the latter half of 1971 because of the serious financial deterioration in the position of the federal government. With an extraordinarily high federal budgetary deficit in view, Representative Wilbur D. Mills of Arkansas, chairman of the powerful House Ways and Means Committee, glumly observed: "The Federal Government simply has no revenue to share!" Nonetheless, efforts may be expected to continue to arrive at some form of revenue-sharing in order to alleviate the current situation facing the states and cities.

Contribution of the
McCarthy Movement

The campaign waged by Senator Eugene J. McCarthy in the spring of 1968 in various Democratic presidential preference primaries had all the earmarks of a movement. As an immediate goal, the objective was to deny renomination to President Lyndon B. Johnson. The longer-range goal was to end American participation in the Indochina war. In this "crusade"—as the mass media termed the Senator's efforts—McCarthy relied largely upon volunteer amateur politicians as his shock troops. In particular, he enlisted under his banners large numbers of young, middle-class professionals who normally did not participate actively in politics. He also received substantial support from students, many of whom took off time from their regular studies to campaign extensively on the Senator's behalf.

To discuss the eventual collapse of the McCarthy campaign and the dissolution of the movement would transcend the purposes of the present analysis. In any event, the history of 1968 is well-known and has been amply recorded. From our point of view, a significant question is this: Was there any important spill-off from the 1968 McCarthy movement to the urban elections of 1969?

Admittedly, the evidence is fragmentary and impressionistic, but it is clear that in at least one case—the re-election of John V. Lindsay as mayor of New York City—the *style* of the McCarthy campaign was duplicated. Mayor Lindsay relied heavily on students and on middle-class volunteers for canvassing and also for raising money at campaign tables in the streets.

Without relating the 1969 municipal elections directly to the national elections of a year earlier, Samuel Lubell saw those municipal contests as reflecting a "revolt" of the voters.[29] Generally, he saw a weakening of party identification and an erosion of party loyalties. The McCarthy movement may well have contributed to this widespread disenchantment with the prevailing party patterns.

The McCarthy movement probably contributed to the fading away of the Old Style politics, but it did not of itself usher in a new style. It helped to set the stage for the emerging style both by establishing a new mood and by challenging various aspects of the established political organization. But we must look elsewhere to find the main elements in the emerging pattern.

ELEMENTS OF THE
NEW STYLE POLITICS

What can be said regarding the New Style which is in the process of replacing Old Style politics? In response to this query, we are now in a position to identify those principal elements which we may expect to be included within the new and developing system.

The new system will have to be able to set up and to enforce priorities to get things done. It is not yet clear how this may be achieved, but it is certain that some kinds of persuasion or coercion not currently employed under the present system will have to be utilized. There will have to be recognition of the idea that not every group and interest can advance at a rate decided on by itself. Public authority will have to be just that—authority. Also, some new forms will have to evolve under the New Style politics.

To begin with, let us consider several forms that do not seem to have any particular future. Participatory democracy, often praised these days, does not appear very promising as an element in the evolving New Style of politics. If it means anything, participatory democracy means that a person will have a direct voice in decisions affecting his own life. This sounds simple, but it is not. From a political point of view, participatory democracy—if taken literally —spells the end of representative government.

Recent experience with participatory democracy, notably involving community action agency boards, has not been encouraging. Voter turn-out to elect representatives of "the poor" has almost universally been ludicrously low—perhaps because the real control over the War on Poverty funds remained in Washington, and that this condition undercut local interest. Nonetheless, the lack of participation by eligible residents in the selection process creates doubt as to the value of this procedure.[30]

Nor has the record been much better in the related area of "participative administration." Citizen participation in public administration was found by investigator Marvin Meade to be more wishful thinking than a tangible reality.[31]

Participatory democracy, in short, is not of much use because of its social and psychological limitations. For example, the doctrine requires that its practitioners reorganize their lives so that participation replaces other values in the hierarchy of values. This probably means that one's life would be spent in a never-ending series of meetings. In other words, one would have totally to reorganize his conception of entertainment, of leisure, of work, of social life. In fact, these would probably be destroyed, or, at a minimum, would become unimportant.

Very little need be said about a second form—one which was at one time called the "New Left." Though it showed an initial possibility of developing into something of permanence, it has rapidly evaporated without leaving much of a trace on the political environment. It never solved its organizational problems. Intellectually, it has fallen into bankruptcy.

A third recent form—the so-called "students' movement"—also seems unlikely to become a harbinger of political developments in the new system. The movement probably hit its highest peak during the presidential primary campaign of Senator Eugene J. McCarthy in Wisconsin—at least, this is Theodore White's considered judgment.[32] During the 1970 Congressional elections, student participation for the most part followed traditional patterns. There was not much of a "movement" in sight anywhere. On the other hand, there is reason to believe that student participation through the existing political forms is on the increase. And the lowering of the voting age in state and local elections to 18 under the 26th Amendment guarantees further student involvement in urban politics. What seems unlikely in the immediate future is the development of an independent student movement.

It is sometimes said that a politics of "confrontation" may be expected to develop as an important form in the urban political process that is now unfolding. While such a political tactic may on occasion obtain satisfaction for immediate demands, this approach may well be negative and counter-productive in the long run, because confrontation politics inevitably isolates the group which espouses it from the rest of the body politic. A politics of confrontation in the long run is a politics of isolation. Since sustained movement toward political goals depends on the ability of groups to form and to maintain coalitions, confrontation politics appears to be of limited utility.

In contrast to these four approaches stands that of Common Cause. Headed by John W. Gardner, former secretary of Health, Education, and Welfare, this group—which thinks of itself as a citizens' lobby—has called for ". . . a renaissance of politics in this country."[33] It proposes to ". . . repair the outworn machinery of government and renew the system."[34] It conceives of itself as a "third force," not a third party, in American politics.

In explaining the long-range goals of Common Cause, Gardner and his associates speak in Olympian platitudes with which it would be hard for any reasonable person to disagree. When it comes to specifics, the group simply lists the great problems of our time and declares that solutions are in order. But one need not admire Gardner's high-minded and extremely vague prose in order to appreciate the truth of his pronouncements: the country is in trouble. The difficulty is that the cures which have so far been proposed by Common Cause are so fuzzy and generalized as to sound trivial, even, probably, irrelevant.

The so-called lobby—it is really simply a citizens' interest group —operates in the best tradition of the upper-class Reformers of sixty years ago. It may be considered to represent the Reform element within the Establishment. As such, it possesses a potential for stirring up political interest and action, but how much is impossible to say.

Much more likely to make an impact on the evolving New Style politics is the mass movement which is now being created in the ranks of America's Black citizenry. Though in its infancy, this movement already shows signs of developing considerable political clout as well as *savoir-faire*. At the same time, parallel movements are slowly emerging from the Puerto Rican and *chicano* populations. Such movements surely will play important roles in the new system of urban politics.

Indeed, it is possible that one of the great propelling forces of New Style politics will be the social movement which turns to politics for solutions to great issues. In addition to the Black, the Puerto Rican, and the *chicano* movements, two more movements must be considered to possess a political potential. These are a consumers' movement and a women's movement. Given sufficient organization and financing, they might develop into permanent and important factors in the urban political process.

Finally—but perhaps the most important of all the new forms— is the almost spontaneous drive in the great cities for community control over certain community activities. Some—but by no means all—of the elements of this drive have their origin in local groups sponsored by the anti-poverty program. Other sources include the desire for self-determination always nascent and now evident in many neighborhoods, and the generally current favorable attitude toward governmental decentralization at all levels.

An examination of the literature on community control shows that sentiment for such control is most marked in three areas: education, housing and urban renewal, and law and order. The examples from public education have been widely reported in the news media, for instance, the successful movement to acquire community control over the lower schools in New York City. While attracting less attention in the press, demands for local control over housing and urban renewal efforts have also been widespread. In most cities it is no longer possible for the authorities simply to announce, as they once did, the programs they intend to put into effect. Rather they must first obtain the consent of the community before any action at all may be undertaken. Increasingly, this consent has not been forthcoming, even after extensive negotiations.

In the third area where demands for community control are increasingly heard—the police—the situation is very complex. In many large cities sizeable groups are demanding the same type of local control over the police that exists in the suburbs. As an illustration, a city like Philadelphia might be divided up—for police purposes—into twenty or so communities of approximately 100,000 persons each. Each community would elect its own police commission, which would in turn select the chief of police. Under this plan, the police in the various communities in North Philadelphia would be Black, as would the commissioners and the chiefs. In Kensington, the police would be white, and the commissioners would mostly have Irish names. In South Philadelphia, several communities would, in the same manner, reflect their Italian ethnic base. In Oxford Circle, the police and the commissioners would be mostly Jewish. And so the procedure would be followed—with appropriate variations—throughout the city.

Now, some words of caution are in order regarding community control. It should be understood that the constitutional rights of all citizens must continue to take precedence over decisions by neighborhood groups. In the event that there is a clash between a consti-

310 / URBAN POLITICS

tutional right and a decision by a community organization, the latter must yield. Furthermore, it must be recognized that community control may on occasion exacerbate political controversy, and that this may in turn make it difficult to obtain adequate governmental financing for projects the community would like to develop. It is also argued by some critics that the comparison of city neighborhoods with the suburbs is unreal and misleading.

Yet, in spite of all reservations, the concept of community control over certain activities which take place within the community possesses a very strong psychological attraction. This is especially observable in the rapidly growing Black and Puerto Rican areas of the largest cities. The movement for community control has a very profound basis, and its roots go very deep. Beyond much doubt, the drive for greater community control will continue to gain momentum. It will be an important factor in the New Style politics.

Besides stressing new techniques for political activity and new forms for such activity, the new politics will also manifest some new features which distinguish it from the old politics. These characteristics may be summarized as follows:

1) There will be a rise of a new type of ethnic voting based on race. Class and racial voting will be highly correlated. Black solidarity will result in many Black-dominated city halls.
2) There will be an increasing demand for welfare-state type programs inside the cities. The disaffected do not have much use for the niceties and benefits of the free enterprise system.
3) It is possible that mass parties in the urban centers will replace the usual cadre parties which are the dominant American type. If this should happen, the United States may develop the European-style of membership party which Maurice Duverger considers the norm.[35]
4) Inside the cities, a kind of politics of federalism—based on the local communities—may develop.
5) The cities will attempt to forge a city-federal government axis, by-passing the states as much as possible.
6) The New Style politics will be marked by a increasing scope (or arena) of political activity and also by an increase in the intensity of that activity. Areas of life which were formerly not politicized will, in the process, become so.

Whatever develops specifically, it is quite certain as a general proposition that the New Style politics will be played under a different set of rules of the "game." Not only will the rules change, but there will also be new actors and new goals. In the process of developing the New Style politics, there will be important attitudinal changes on the part of the citizens. For example, the traditional attitude toward winning and losing elections is very likely to be altered—it may simply not be possible for some segments of the electorate to accept losing.

It is from these materials—means, forms, and characteristics—that the New Style politics is being fashioned. As this style continues its rapid development, some of its attributes will be able to be seen with more clarity. It will then be possible to gauge the relative importance of the particular attributes in relation to the total system. It will also be feasible to begin serious efforts to construct a new model of urban politics which will be useful in explaining and interpreting the New Style politics. For the new urban politics is a politics more attuned to conflict than to consensus. The emphasis has shifted from agreement to a stance of militancy, of no-compromise, and of non-cooperation. Political conflict tends to become a value in itself, rather than merely a means toward an end. The evidence of an increased militancy is visible in the activities of teachers, of police, and of other municipal employees. It is also evident in the activities of various community groups, especially those concerned with housing and land use. It is reflected in the tactics being used by organizations representing welfare recipients. The new politics likewise features a militancy on the part of urban Blacks which has hitherto been almost totally absent. In short, militancy is widespread, and there is every reason to suppose that it will increase. New, permanent, and influential actors have entered into the political arena.

The new urban politics revolves around policy, not around electoral considerations. The former narrow politics of the political party has given way to a broader politics of policy. To be sure, the urban political process continues to make use of the traditional network of elections, campaigns, and legislative divisions. But the framework within which the process operates has been enlarged. This has happened because the newer pressures generated by policy politics could not be contained within the previous rigid system. These pressures have subjected the political institutions of urban America to an unprecedented strain. Whether the responses of these institutions will prove to be adequate remains an open question.

CHAPTER
NOTES

1. The analogy between old-time socialist groups and certain of the new militant Black groups is appealing, although it may be stretched too far. The ten-point program of the Black Panthers, adopted in October 1966, calls for social objectives which can only come about through political action. Some of these objectives sound "revolutionary"; others are fairly prosaic. The program has been widely published in the daily press, for example, in the Philadelphia *Sunday Bulletin* of Sept. 6, 1970.

2. See the article "Tío Taco is Dead," *Newsweek,* June 29, 1970, pp. 22–28.

3. See the article by Bill Kovach, "Struggle for Identity: White Minorities Revive Heritage," *New York Times,* Nov. 27, 1970, p. 37.

4. See the article by Barbara Mikulski, "He Came in Search of Freedom and a Job But What Did He Find?," *New York Times,* Sept. 29, 1970, p. 43 c.

5. *Ibid.*

6. Kovach, *op. cit.*

7. Kovach, *op. cit.*

8. Kovach, *op. cit.*

9. See the article, "A Rising Cry: 'Ethnic Power'," *Newsweek,* Dec. 21, 1970, pp. 32–36.

10. Thomas R. Dye, *Politics in States and Communities* (Englewood Cliffs, N.J.: Prentice-Hall, 1969), p. 295.

11. See Charles E. Gilbert, *Governing the Suburbs* (Bloomington, Ind.: Indiana University Press, 1967).

12. *Ibid.,* p. 315.

13. Robert C. Wood, *1400 Governments, The Political Economy of the New York Metropolitan Region* (Cambridge, Mass.: Harvard University Press, 1961; Garden City, N.Y.: Doubleday Anchor Book edition, 1964).

14. *Ibid.,* Doubleday Anchor Book edition, p. 210.

15. *Ibid.,* p. 214.

16. *Ibid.,* p. 216.

17. Daniel J. Elazar, *American Federalism: A View from the States* (New York: Crowell, 1966), p. 199.

18. *Ibid.,* p. 200.

19. Alan K. Campbell, ed., *The States and the Urban Crisis* (Englewood Cliffs, N.J.: Prentice-Hall, 1970).

20. *Ibid.,* p. 24.

21. *Ibid.,* p. 202.

22. *Ibid.,* p. 209.

23. *Ibid.,* p. 209.

24. On these points, see Elazar, *op. cit.,* p. 210.

25. See the article by Richard P. Nathan, "Reforms of the New Federalism," *New York Times,* Oct. 10, 1970, p. 25. Nathan was Assistant Director of the President's Office of Management and Budget.

26. Associated Press dispatch, published in Philadelphia *Bulletin,* Dec. 8, 1970, p. 76.

27. *Final Report of the Thirty-Sixth American Assembly* (Harriman, N.Y.: American Assembly, no date), p. 7.

28. *New York Times,* Dec. 27, 1970.

29. Samuel Lubell, *The Hidden Crisis in American Politics* (New York: W. W. Norton, 1970). See especially Chapter Two, "Revolt of the Voters," pp. 39–68.

30. For a criticism of the whole program, including the role of the poor in choosing their local agency boards, see Daniel P. Moynihan, *Maximum Feasible Misunderstanding: Community Action in the War on Poverty* (New York: The Free Press, 1969).

31. Marvin Meade, " 'Participative Administration'—Emerging Reality or Wishful Thinking?," paper presented at the annual meeting of the American Political Science Association, New York City, Sept. 2–6, 1969.

32. Theodore H. White, *The Making of the President 1968* (New York: Pocket Book edition, 1970), p. 149.

33. John W. Gardner, "Sign In," *Signature,* Dec., 1970, p. 10.

34. *Ibid.,* p. 10.

35. See Maurice Duverger, *Political Parties* (New York: John Wiley & Sons, Inc., 1954). The original French edition appeared in 1951.

Index of Names

Index of Subjects